Beverley Callard

Unbroken

HODDER

First published in Great Britain in 2010 by Hodder & Stoughton
An Hachette UK company

First published in paperback in 2010

1

Copyright © Beverley Callard 2010

A CIP catalogue record for this title is available from the British Library.

ISBN 978 1 444 70529 4

Typeset in Sabon by Hewer Text UK Ltd, Edinburgh
Printed and bound by Clays Ltd, St Ives plc

Hodder & Stoughton policy is to use papers that are natural, renewable
and recyclable products and made from wood grown in sustainable
forests. The logging and manufacturing processes are expected to
conform to the environmental regulations of the country of origin.

Hodder & Stoughton Ltd
338 Euston Road
London NW1 3BH

www.hodder.co.uk

To my darling Jon, and your undying love for me.
You refused to let me stay in the black hole and
you kept the rope ladder there.

To my wonderful sister Steph, who has great strength and
love for mum and me – a woman with great courage.

To Guardsman Jonathan McEwan, you soldiered on for me.

To Rebecca and Joshua, my wonderful children.

Sonny and George, Grandma loves you.
X

CONTENTS

....

PROLOGUE

....

I was lying in a narrow bed in a small, whitewashed hospital room. I could feel sticky pads on my head and chest where the electrodes and monitors had just been placed. Next to me was a small machine with wires coming out of it and numbers flashing up in red neon lights. Any minute now I was going to have bursts of electricity from the machine pumped through my brain.

It sounds like something from a Frankenstein movie but electric shock treatment was the last resort in the doctor's attempts to find a cure for the depression that was paralysing me.

Huge quantities of all kinds of different drugs had failed to make me better and I'd spent weeks wishing I were dead. I had hidden my tablets in a bid to build up a stash big enough to overdose on, but that plan had been discovered. I'd also talked about smashing the lightbulb in my hospital room and using it to slit my wrists. I didn't care how I killed myself, I just wanted it all to be over. I didn't want to be alive any more. And so here I was.

It was spring 2009 and I was being treated amid tight security and secrecy at the Priory Clinic in Altrincham.

I'd spent weeks there just curled up on my bed in darkness in an almost comatose state, barely able to speak. I remember virtually nothing about this period at all and most of what I'm writing now has been told to me since that awful time by my partner, Jon, and by doctors at the Priory. My clinical depression was so extreme that my body had gone into almost total shutdown.

I was in a deep, dark hole and my doctor said I was one of the most extreme cases he'd ever had to treat.

If I got out of bed I could take only the tiniest steps and was hunched over like a woman of 100. I couldn't imagine things ever getting better, or even imagine them getting worse. I couldn't imagine any kind of future at all.

Now my family were desperately hoping that electric shock treatment − or electroconvulsive therapy (ECT) to give it its proper name − would jolt me out of my despair and return me to the woman they knew. But it was to be a long process and I would undergo twelve gruelling bouts of ECT in six weeks before my condition improved.

Anyone who had seen me in that tiny hospital room that day would have struggled to associate me with the bubbly Beverley Callard that people think they know from twenty years starring in *Coronation Street*. I was pale, thin and tired-looking, with my hair frizzy and matted around my face. But the reality of my life was by then a very long way from the image I liked to project of myself as a confident, carefree woman.

The viewers of *Coronation Street* would have had no idea that for about a year before my admission to hospital, beneath Liz McDonald's tarty outfits and heavy makeup I had been sinking into a dark pit of depression. Eventually, fans of the show were told that Liz had jetted off to Spain to look after her son, Andy, who'd hurt himself in an accident. In reality I'd had to be hurriedly written out after suffering a crippling breakdown and being rushed into the Priory.

I was overwhelmed with feelings of hopelessness. I felt useless at my job, rubbish as a partner, worthless as a mum and as a daughter.

It was my lowest time.

But it was a life-changing time too, because with a mixture of medication and ECT I did start to improve, my depression lifted and very, very slowly I began to feel better.

I'm still not a hundred per cent better, and have had many dips along the way where I've felt utterly flat and unable to face the world again. And I know that clinical depression will probably be something I have to battle for the rest of my life. But at the moment I am slowly moving along the road to recovery.

One of the biggest changes in my life that the breakdown has brought about is that for the first time I want to speak publicly about my struggle with depression. And that is why I've now chosen to look back over my life and write this book. I just hope the sections about my own depression help other people suffering in the same way to understand that they are not alone. And I desperately want to send out the message that depression is not a sign of being weak, it is a sign of trying to be too strong, for too long.

1
CHILDHOOD

....

Mum and I sat next to each other in the red fold-down seats at the Majestic Cinema in Leeds and waited for those huge velvet curtains to sweep back. It was the most exciting moment of my week – a Saturday-afternoon trip to the movies with Mum. Surrounded by the faded grandeur of the Majestic, we were transported from rain-lashed Yorkshire to another world, a world inhabited by tall, dark and handsome men and women whose lipstick never faded. When the Pearl & Dean advert music came on it made me feel as though I were part of show business myself.

Mum and I adored films. Seventeen times we saw *The Sound Of Music* at the cinema. Seventeen! I knew every single word of it and not just the songs – all the dialogue, too. Even then, aged just eight, I'd look at the screen and think, 'I'll do that one day.' It never occurred to me that I couldn't or wouldn't.

Mum loved Julie Andrews and was desperate for me to be just like her. She even tried styling my hair into a short bob like Maria's in the film but I had a mass of frizzy curls and by the time she had finished, it was all standing on end and I looked like I'd been electrocuted!

My mum, Mavis, had been a talented pianist when she was younger and had studied at Yorkshire College of Music under a teacher called Irene Ingram. There was a vocal coach at the college, Madame Lilian Stiles-Allen, who had taught Julie Andrews, so Mum liked to think she had a connection with the Hollywood star.

I guess my fascination with acting must have come from Mum and her interest in show business. She was twenty-seven when she had me, her first child, and by then she had given up playing the piano professionally but her love of music, theatre and cinema remained.

I was born Beverley Jane Moxon on 28 March 1957 at Hyde Terrace Hospital in Leeds. As my parents' first child, I was simply adored. My mum's parents were besotted with me, too. Grandad and Nans (as we called my grandma) totally ruined me and Grandad would call me the apple of his eye.

We saw Nans and Grandad all the time and they were massive influences on my life. Grandad's name was Pliny Brook and he had met Nans – who was called Ethel – when they were still at school. Like almost everyone else in their classes, they both went on to work in textile mills in their hometown of Morley, on the outskirts of Leeds.

Nans started as a weaver when she was fourteen and grew up to be a really strong woman, working two looms until she retired at sixty. Retirement didn't suit Nans though, and she missed her job so much that two years later she went back to work and carried on until she was seventy-two. Grandad worked in a nearby mill as a maintenance man.

In her youth, Nans was a real beauty, with long black hair that stretched down to her waist. I think she must have been good fun then, too. But when my mum was born, she became entirely focused on her daughter. From the beginning, Nans was determined that Mum wasn't going to work in the mill and would have a 'better life'. The family lived in a two-up two-down terraced house in Troy Road, Morley. It was one of the back-to-back terraces – if you lived in a through terrace in those days, you were dead posh. Everybody down the street worked in mills or factories but Nans was adamant that things would be different for her daughter.

After Mum was born, Nans apparently said, 'Never again!' and so Mum remained an only child. Later, Nans' much younger sister, Auntie Jean, came to live with the family when her own mother died. She was only a couple of years older than Mum and in a way they were like sisters, but I think she was treated very differently by Nans. Auntie Jean was made to go in the mill, whereas Mum was thought to be too good for that. It must have caused all sorts of resentment but when I was growing up it was just accepted as part of our family history.

On the one hand, Mum was totally spoilt as a little girl and given everything she ever wanted, but Nans was also very strict with her. When she was coming up for eleven, Mum was desperate for a piano and she nagged and nagged Nans and Grandad about having one. A piano would have cost a small fortune for them in those days, but slowly they saved up and bought one for the daughter they idolised. The thing was, once she had that piano, Nans insisted Mum practise it all the time. Mum would play for eight hours a day – and go to school as well!

Mum was still just eleven when she played in her first public concert, at Morley Town Hall. She loved it and must have had a natural ear for music, but she also succeeded because Nans was driving her very hard. She'd say, 'You asked for that piano, you've got it, now you've got to practise it.'

Sometimes, Mum would get so frustrated if she couldn't get a piece right that she'd get off the stool and kick the piano, but Nans would just say, 'Get back on that piano, you have to know this piece for when you see Miss Ingram.'

The pressure Nans put on Mum was tremendous and years later Mum confided in me that she thought she'd had some kind of nervous breakdown when she was about fifteen, because of the stress. She became incredibly nervous and shy and then she started wetting the bed and biting the skin around her fingers until they bled.

She did quite a lot of concerts around Yorkshire in her teens and early twenties. I think her dream was to play like Winifred Atwell, who was a really famous jazz pianist back then, but Nans insisted she stick to classical music. As a teenager she never went dancing or had boyfriends because she was always either studying or playing the piano. Even after she left school and went to Pitman Secretarial College to study shorthand and typing, she still had to practise her piano every evening.

Grandad was very different to Nans, though. He was the one who made Mum laugh, and he would get them both into trouble by doing things like sneaking off to buy her eleven ice creams and letting her eat them one after the other, just because they knew Nans wouldn't approve.

Mum first met my Dad, Clive Moxon, when she was eleven and he was twelve and they were both at Victoria Road School in Morley. There were separate boys' and girls' playgrounds and Dad would sneak up on Mum from behind the dividing wall and nick her hat. They only started going out once he returned to England from travelling round the world doing his national service. When Dad got back to Morley, the first thing he did was knock on Nans and Grandad's door and say, 'Hello, it's Clive Moxon here.'

Grandad took one look at him and in his broad Yorkshire accent said, 'By 'ell Clive Moxon, you're not a lad any more, you've turned into a man.'

Mum and Dad started courting and were married when she was twenty-three and Dad was twenty-four. Mum was a virgin on her wedding night and from the very beginning until the very end, they adored each other.

When she married, Mum stopped playing the piano, which I think was a massive relief to her. Nans thought differently though. For her, Mum should never have married and given up her hopes of a career. Grandad was simply broken-hearted that his little girl had left home and he could no longer hear her playing the music that he loved. But with Dad, Mum finally found peace away from all that pressure. She remained very, very shy and a bit nervy, but Dad made her laugh. When they were together she had an inner giggle.

At 5 feet 6 inches with a slim figure and immaculate clothes, Mum has always been very refined and ladylike – I've never even once heard her say a swear word. But my dad was a real man's man. He was about 5 feet 9 inches tall, handsome and looked like John Wayne – everybody said so! He'd boxed in the army and played football and cricket. He loved all sports. But Dad was quiet too, with a kind, inner strength that made everybody love him.

After his national service, Dad got a job in a baker's shop. He loved it and when I was six months old he and Mum bought their own baker's shop in Armley, Leeds, with a tiny flat above it that became our home. Mum and Dad worked like mad to make that shop a success. Dad was very artistic and would make amazing wedding cakes. Once he even made a tea service out of chocolate.

I was still just a toddler when Mum announced one day, 'That's it, I'm not living above a shop any more,' so with all the money they'd managed to save from the bakery, we moved to a tiny semi-detached in Armley.

Shortly afterwards, Mum gave birth to my little brother, Simon. I don't remember anything about it now but he only lived for a few hours. It was years later that Mum told us what had happened. The baby had been delivered in hospital and immediately afterwards, the nurses took him away. Mum was saying, 'Where's my baby? Where's my baby?' but all the nurses would say was, 'Don't worry, you be calm, don't worry.' And that was it, no one told her anything more.

Then, later that day, a nurse came to her bedside and said, 'We're terribly sorry Mrs Moxon, but we couldn't save him.' That was how she found out her child had died without her even being able to hold him.

I was too young to realise it then, but looking back I think maybe Mum started suffering from depression at that point. They didn't call it depression then, but she was put on the tranquiliser librium by her doctor.

Then, when I was six years old, my sister Stephanie was born and we were all ecstatic. I loved her from the very beginning. As a tiny baby she looked just like Alfred Hitchcock, with a bald head and chubby face, but when she got to the sitting-up stage she became really cute, with gorgeous ringlets, not fuzzy curls like mine. She was always more beautiful than me and grew up to be the clever one, too.

All my memories of that stage of growing up are happy ones. Mum and Dad loved each other so much. They would kiss and hug each other and they giggled all the time. Neither of them drank and Dad was never one of those men to go out with his mates after work. He and mum were homely people. All they ever needed was each other, their girls and the shops. That was their lives.

Dad worked so hard for his family. He'd leave the house in his baker's overalls at four o'clock in the morning to put the ovens on and wouldn't get home until after dark. He worked six and a half days a week and sometimes Steph and I wouldn't see him for days on end, but when he was at home he'd play and talk with us for hours. He used to dry out our hair with the towel after we'd had our baths and then brush it for ages, telling the most amazing stories that he'd made up in his head.

Our holidays were always fairly nearby, either in Scarborough or Filey or maybe in Bridlington, so that if there was an emergency with the ovens while we were away, Dad could get back. Mum would say, 'That bakehouse takes over everything!'

As Dad was at work so much, Mum did everything at home: all the cooking, cleaning, decorating and gardening. And she'd help out in the shop too, while Steph and I sat out the back, reading books or doing our homework.

When I was at junior school, we moved again to a bigger, four-bedroom semi in Pudsey, on the outskirts of Leeds. Dad's business was also growing and he worked up to having three shops and two bakehouses, where the bread and cakes were made. We were becoming quite well off – Mum was one of the first people round our way to have an automatic washing machine instead of a twin tub. We'd really arrived! And while we still went on holiday to Scarborough or Filey, by this time we were staying in nice hotels.

Mum and Dad weren't particularly strict with Steph and me but they were both very moral people. Mum used to say, 'It's nice to be nice.' They had definite ideas of right and wrong, and they were supportive and positive, too. From the very beginning, they made us feel we could achieve anything we wanted to do. For me, that was always going to be acting.

From as far back as I can remember, I loved performing. My big problem was applying myself to things I wasn't interested in. When I was still a toddler we went on holiday to Scarborough for a fortnight and Mum entered me into a beauty competition, thinking I might have a chance because of my white-blonde curly hair. The only thing the children had to do was toddle around a swimming pool in front of the judges.

I'll always remember Mum saying later, 'You were winning Beverley, you were winning. And then you decided you wanted no more of it so you sat down and wouldn't budge.' That's the story of my life!

Some of my earliest memories are of sitting at home on our bottle-green leather sofa (it may sound awful now but it was fashionable at the time!) watching black and white films on our huge, old-fashioned box television.

Mum introduced me to that whole word of glamour and excitement and I was soon hooked on acting. It was a shared passion. When she was a teenager she'd written off to all the Hollywood studios for photographs and autographs. She still has them now in an album, real legends like Olivia de Havilland and Tyrone Power, who she once even saw on stage in Leeds, as Zorro.

Mum's very favourite film was *Now, Voyager* with Bette Davis and Paul Hen-read (that's how we pronounced Henreid in Yorkshire). It became my favourite too, and now it's my daughter Rebecca's as well. It's got that famous scene where Paul Henreid lights two cigarettes and gives one to Bette Davis, and she says, 'Oh Jerry, don't let's ask for the moon, we have the stars.' Oh my God, how I loved that moment. Mum and I also adored Bette Davis in *What Ever Happened To Baby Jane?* and in *Dark Victory* where she played a woman going blind and dying. I loved them, loved them, loved them. I so desperately wanted to *be* Bette Davis or to be Barbra Streisand coming down that staircase in *Hello, Dolly!* Or to be Judy Garland or Liza Minnelli.

Hollywood seemed so glamorous and being an actress looked like having the world's biggest dressing-up box. I've always loved clothes and dressing up, and from the earliest age I would put on Mum's strappy sandals and jewels and then parade around the house at every opportunity.

Once we were in Schofields, a posh department store in Leeds, when Mum let go of my hand for a second and I wandered off. I was only three but when Mum found me I was following a lady's pair of red boots around. I wasn't looking at the woman, I was just transfixed by the boots. I'm still obsessed by shoes and boots now.

I was seven when I really became determined I wanted to act. I was at Waterloo Junior School in Pudsey and we were doing a play called *Darius the Page Boy*. We'd all auditioned for parts and a boy called Neil Stansfield got the role of Darius, while I was playing the lead woman. I was so excited that I learnt all the words for all the parts.

Then it turned out Neil Stansfield wasn't really very good, so Miss Jacobs, our drama and English teacher, said I could be Darius. I was delighted. Before the first performance I felt nervous, but as soon as I got on stage, I just completely relaxed and enjoyed myself. A couple of months earlier I'd been in a swimming gala doing breaststroke. I'd stood on the edge of the pool with my toes curled over the side, waiting for the whistle, and felt totally terrified. After the school play I told everyone, 'In the swimming gala I was so scared but with this I'm not at all. I just love it.' I knew then, for certain, that I wanted to act.

I became fascinated by accents and would imitate anyone that I met, loving the reaction if I could make people laugh with my impressions. When I was about nine, we went on holiday to Scarborough and stayed at a hotel called the Park Manor, where I met a couple called Bill and Jean and their daughter Patricia, from Edinburgh. I copied the way they spoke so well that until they met my mum and dad, they thought I was from Edinburgh, too!

My parents were always supportive about my dreams of becoming an actress, but although on the one hand Mum really wanted me to do it, on the other I think she told herself, 'People like us don't get to do things like that.' She was always keen that I should get good qualifications, in case my acting dreams didn't work out.

Plus, there was the fact that Mum had been pushed very hard by her own mother, so she never forced my sister or me to do things, even though she was ambitious for us. She would say, 'Don't just get married and have babies. You've got to have careers.' Mum was always telling me that she'd love me to be a 'lady doctor', although there wasn't much chance of that considering how little attention I paid in science at school. She had worked as a secretary at the Midland Bank before I was born and she would say, 'Why be a secretary when you could be the boss?' So she was quite a feminist in her own quiet way.

At school I loved English and drama, but I wasn't quite so enthusiastic about the other subjects. Every school report said the same: 'If Beverley likes something, she is good at it, if she doesn't, then she is just not interested.' Even at junior school I started being a bit naughty in lessons that didn't appeal to me. I loved being the class clown and making people laugh. I was the same at home, playing tricks on the others.

On Sundays, we'd go 'out for a run' in Dad's Vauxhall Victor Estate, as families used to do in those days. Dad would be driving, Mum would be in the front seat, Nans and Grandad were in the back and Steph and I were perched in the boot part of the estate.

I'd play terrible tricks on Nans, as she and I used to argue a lot (maybe I was more like her than the others). Once, I was sitting in the boot and I unpacked the picnic Nans had made, carefully separated the bread rolls she had buttered, then stuck them both on the back of her hat. Mum saw what I'd done and was hissing, 'Get those off, get those off.' Nans had no idea though and when we got where we were going, she was walking around with people looking at her, thinking, 'Look at that old lady with bread buns on her hat!' Grandad knew exactly what I'd done, but he loved that mischievousness.

Another time, we were travelling to Knaresborough for the day and I pinned Stephanie's badge collection on the back of Nans' coat. So when we arrived she got out of the car in her proper grandma anorak with a shoulder full of kids' badges. Dad would be saying, 'Bev-er-ley' in the tone he used whenever he was trying to tell me off. But I was always getting up to tricks like that.

We saw Nans and Grandad all the time. They'd either come to us or Steph and I would go to their terraced house in Morley, where Nans would cook us meat and potato pie, apple crumble and tinned sardines in tomato sauce – it was heaven.

Sometimes, Mum would take us to visit Nans where she worked at the mill. It was incredibly noisy with all the machinery clanking and whirring, but the women who worked there could all lip read and were still chatting away to each other. They were such strong women and there was an incredible camaraderie between them.

Dad was one of five children and his dad had died when he was still little. Grandma Moxon had brought her family up in the small Yorkshire village of Drighlington. I think maybe she thought Mum was a bit of a snob and so although we saw her sometimes, it wasn't as often as we saw Nans and Grandad.

During the long school summer holiday after leaving Waterloo Junior School, we moved house again to a village called Churwell, just outside Morley, and I prepared to begin the new term at Bruntcliffe Secondary Modern. This was a much bigger house again, on the left-hand side of the main road that ran through the village. The area was called Lane Side and it was where the mill owners had lived years ago, so it had been nicknamed 'Mill Owners Row', which then became 'Millionaires Row'. The people living there weren't real millionaires, of course, but they did have big, beautiful houses.

Ours had a huge front door with stained glass and mother-of-pearl inlaid in it. Mum's pride and joy was our front door, which had a stained-glass picture of the Roman goddess, Diana the huntress, which was hundreds of years old. It must have seemed worlds away from the back-to-back where she'd been brought up. We even had a grand piano in one of the bay windows, which Mum would sometimes play. She did try to get my sister and me interested in the piano but we never took to it.

Out the back there was a big garden where we girls played, as well as a rose garden, then beyond that there was nothing but fields. It was a fantastic home. Mum and Dad had got there through sheer hard work and, quite rightly, they were very proud of what they had achieved.

At secondary school I continued to love English and drama but in maths and science I was forever chatting or messing around. I loved entertaining everyone and playing tricks on teachers. I once hid the blackboard rubber in the piano so Mr Wright couldn't work out why it was making a funny noise. And I thought it would be hilarious, when our maths teacher, Mr Lockwood, was handing out textbooks, saying 'Pass them on', that I should pass them on straight out of the upstairs window where I was sitting into the pond below!

I got into real trouble for that one, but generally the teachers still liked me because I wasn't rude or nasty, just a bit cheeky. And in English and drama, the teachers loved me because I would volunteer to do all the readings at the carol service and be in the school plays. I was a member of the school drama club, took drama exams and even won my first public speaking contest at the Wharfedale Festival, reciting one poem called 'Last Leaves' and another entirely in Yorkshire dialect.

I was on the netball and hockey teams too, but my passion was acting. I was twelve when I wrote a comedy sketch for the school play with my best friend, Kathleen Partington, the vicar's daughter. She was so funny and together we were very naughty, skiving off lessons and mucking about in the classes that we did go to.

The sketch we wrote was about two old women working in a mill in Morley, so of course it was all based on Nans. The weekend before the performance I'd stayed at her house and pinched loads of clothes out of her wardrobe for Kathleen and me to wear in the show.

All the parents and grandparents turned out to watch the performance and Kathleen and I had hardly begun our sketch when Nans was heard to shout out from the audience in her strong Yorkshire accent, 'By gum she's got my best 'at on'!

I was quite terrible at that age. Everything for me was about having a laugh and making others laugh, too. I had no idea that something was about to happen that would end the laughter in our house for a very long time.

2
HAPPINESS SHATTERED

....

'I've killed someone. I've killed a man and I've got to hand myself in to the police,' Grandad said quietly to Nans, holding his head in his hands.

Nans looked at my grandad in total bewilderment. How could the man she had known since she was a child, who'd never been violent, never been in trouble and was always laughing and joking, have done such a thing? She decided Grandad must be going mad. Maybe his mind was getting confused in his old age. Why else would he be saying such ridiculous things? But as we soon found out, Grandad hadn't gone mad at all. He was telling the whole truth – and it was to change our family for ever.

The first I knew anything unusual was going on was when I came hurtling in the front door from school at around half past four one afternoon in 1970.

I'd just turned thirteen and was in the second year at Bruntcliffe Secondary Modern. I was becoming a proper self-obsessed teenager with my mind full of miniskirts, mascara and Marc Bolan. But even I was able to notice that things weren't right at home that day.

Mum was stood in the kitchen with Dad, which was pretty unusual in itself. Dad was never home from the bakehouse at half four on a weekday afternoon.

Nans was also there, along with her younger sister Auntie Jean and Jean's husband, Uncle Frank. Mum, Nans and Auntie Jean all had red eyes and blotchy faces and they'd obviously been crying.

I looked around the kitchen at each of them.

'Have you been crying?' I asked Mum.

'No, no,' she replied, in her very quiet, ladylike way. 'We've all got hay fever. Just take Stephanie into the dining room and you can both watch television.'

Now, it was weird having Dad home from work that early in the day, but being allowed to watch telly before we had done our homework was *really* strange. Something was obviously going on but it was clear that no one was going to tell me what it was. And, like most girls of that age, being fairly oblivious to the outside world, I didn't ask anything more.

What no one was telling me was what had happened the previous night, a Sunday. By that time, Mum and Dad had bought a caravan and the four of us would go away in it for weekends to the Yorkshire Dales and local beauty spots. That Sunday, we'd driven home with the caravan from Knaresborough and Mum and Dad had just put Steph and me to bed when Nans and Grandad turned up together.

Apparently, the four of them were sitting in the living room downstairs when Nans suddenly said to my parents, 'Your dad's flipped. He's gone completely mad. He keeps telling me he's killed someone.'

She told them how he'd been acting oddly for almost a

fortnight. 'He kept telling me he was in trouble but when I asked how, he'd just say, "Don't worry",' said Nans. 'And now today he's gone and told me he's killed someone. He's saying he's killed a foreign man. You've got to talk to him, Clive, I think he's gone doolally.'

Grandad sat there quietly all the while that Nans was talking before he finally said, 'I haven't gone mad. I have killed someone.'

Mum and Dad obviously thought the whole thing sounded ridiculous too and that Nans must be right. They looked at each other, wondering, 'Has his brain gone?'

Grandad was sixty-five and such a soft-natured man that everybody loved him. He might have got in trouble with Nans sometimes for stopping off in the pub on his way home from the mill rather than coming straight back for his tea, but he had never been in trouble with the police.

Grandad was insistent he had killed someone, though, and tried to explain what had happened. It turned out that he had started drinking regularly in a rough pub in Morley, after finishing work at the mill. He'd also been gambling and, basically, it emerged he'd developed a life that Nans knew nothing about. It had all begun when my mum got married, left home and stopped playing the piano. Grandad had always called Mum 'my Doy', which is Yorkshire dialect for 'my darling'. He'd say she was his 'one and only' and when she got married I suppose he didn't feel there was as much to go home for any more.

Nans was an amazing, strong woman but she was also very tough and very strict. She'd take Grandad's wages then give him pocket money. In many ways she could be a bit of a harridan. I don't think Grandad was very happy at home. So he'd started going to this pub and it was there that he met a Ukrainian man called Paul Suchar and some of his friends. Paul Suchar was trying to get a mortgage or loan to buy a house, but he was an illegal immigrant, so of course he couldn't. Grandad offered to get the mortgage in his name, then Paul Suchar would give him money for the monthly repayments.

Obviously, Grandad was already in the wrong for getting a loan for someone else, but then things got a whole lot worse. Paul Suchar was giving Grandad the money for the repayments, but instead of paying it into the bank, Grandad was using it to settle gambling debts. We discovered that he had become addicted to gambling and had previously been to my dad saying, 'You've got to help me out' because he was in trouble for owing money. Dad had given him the money, not knowing how serious my grandad's gambling had become, and had never told Mum or Nans anything about it.

By now Grandad's problems were even more serious. Letters were arriving at the house where Paul Suchar was living, saying that the mortgage hadn't been paid and people were knocking on the door demanding the missing money. So one evening, Paul Suchar went to the mill where Grandad worked, when there was no one else around, and confronted him. He was forty-two, more than twenty years younger than Grandad. He was also taller than him and known as a violent man who'd been in prison before and been arrested for stabbing someone.

The two men must have started rowing and then Paul Suchar attacked Grandad and beat him really badly. His shin was totally kicked in and he thought he was going to be killed. Grandad hit back and was really fighting for his life.

In the mill workshop there was a hammer lying on a bench and in desperation Grandad picked it up and hit Paul Suchar across the head with it. The younger man fell to the floor and when after a few seconds he didn't come round, Grandad realised he'd killed him. He had never been in a situation like this in his life and he didn't know what to do. He just panicked. In the end he pulled the body under a pile of coal next to the mill boiler and after a while he went home.

Grandad was guilt-stricken stricken by what he'd done and after almost two weeks he couldn't carry the secret any longer. That was when he confessed to Nans. We didn't think anyone had reported Paul Suchar missing; perhaps his friends just thought he'd done a disappearing act. As Paul Suchar was an illegal immigrant it was likely that no one was looking for him, so Grandad could probably have got away with never telling anyone, but he couldn't live with what he'd done. He wanted to confess everything to the police.

That Sunday night round at our house he asked my dad to go with him to the police station. Mum, Dad, Nans and Grandad sat up talking it through nearly all night.

In the end Dad said, 'It just doesn't make sense at all but he does appear to be talking sensibly so yes, we'll have to go to the police station.'

When they got to the station at Morley they were taken to a room by a Sergeant Billyard, who knew Grandad because he'd gone to school with him. Grandad went through the story again, about how he'd killed this man and his body was under a pile of coal at the mill. And again, Sergeant Billyard refused to believe him. For hours no one at the police station would accept the story because it seemed so far-fetched and out of character, but eventually, they took Grandad to Peel Street Mills to check the pile of coal, just in case he was telling the truth.

Inside the mill there was a huge boiler with a door the size of our front door and next to it was the pile of coal. 'He's in there,' Grandad told the police officers, pointing at the huge heap. A couple of officers began digging into it and sure enough, there was the body of Paul Suchar. He had been dead for thirteen days.

Grandad was taken back to the police station, arrested and interviewed for ages and ages and ages. It was that afternoon that Steph and I had come home from school to find all the adults shocked and crying.

For the next few days our house was filled with doom and gloom. Mum's inner giggle had gone and she was quiet and distracted. Really suddenly, all the laughter just disappeared from our lives. There seemed to be be whispered, private conversations going on everywhere and I was constantly being told to take Steph into another room while the adults talked.

Dad was at home a lot of the time and whereas before he was almost always in his baker's overalls apart from on Sunday afternoons, now he was wearing a suit and tie and Mum was in tailored suits for all these meetings they kept disappearing off to have. Steph and I didn't have a clue where they were going or what was happening. People were crying all the time and Nans moved in with us. I didn't know if Grandad had died or what was going on. All I knew was that everything was just totally weird.

Then one day Mum said Stephanie was going to school but I didn't have to, as they wanted to talk to me about something important. My first reaction was, 'Great, I don't have to go to school.' But it was scary too because I knew something bad was going on.

We went and sat in the front room. Mum and Dad were next to each other on the dark green leather Chesterfield sofa and I was in the matching armchair. There was a huge fireplace with antique rainbow tiles on it in the middle of the room and on the other side of that sat Nans, all dressed up smartly but unable to stop crying.

Dad explained to me gently that Grandad had got into a fight with a man and killed him but that it was all an accident and he was only sticking up for himself. He said Grandad had done the honourable thing and handed himself in at the police station but he'd been put in prison on remand while he was waiting to go on trial.

Then Mum and Dad told me the case had appeared before the magistrate's court so it was about to appear in the local newspapers and my friends would soon know all about it – they wanted to tell me before anyone else did. It turned out that, bizarrely, the magistrate who'd heard the case was my deputy headmaster, Leonard Peel.

As they were speaking, I just couldn't work it out. It was too much to take in.

I kept thinking about Grandad and what he was really like. He was the one who threw us up and down in the air while we laughed uncontrollably and he was the one who'd chase us around the garden until we all ran out of breath. In fact, it was him who made everyone laugh, with his silly stories and his broad Yorkshire dialect. Grandad had even made toys and rocking horses for all his neighbours' children. And now Mum was telling me he was in Armley Gaol! In Leeds, people don't call it Armley Prison, they call it Armley Gaol because it's like a proper old-fashioned gaol with huge, dark stone walls and foreboding thick wooden doors.

Mum and Dad said they thought it would be best for me to go and stay at my friend Carolyn Marshall's house for a while. They were really busy visiting Grandad and attending legal meetings in their smart clothes and I think they thought it would be better for me to be away from all the upset. So I went to Carolyn's for a few days but when I returned home the air of doom and gloom was still there. We were all devastated.

Grandad was held on remand in Armley Gaol for six months before his trial. Mum and Nans visited every day and we would all go on a Saturday and Sunday. We'd have to walk through the massive outer doors then through an inner door before reaching Grandad in a poky little room where he'd sit on one side of a desk and we'd sit on the other. There were bars at the windows and blank white tiles on the walls. I'd never been anywhere like that in my life before and it was scary.

The warders and even all the other inmates adored my grandad. The warders would say, 'He is an innocent man. We don't get many in here, but he is one.' I think he got special treatment in Armley because everyone thought he'd acted in self-defence. When we were waiting in the queue outside we'd get waved to the front and the warders often left us alone with Grandad at visiting time, rather than sitting in the corner of the room watching us. Then after a while Grandad was moved to the hospital wing of the prison, which was more comfortable for him. He was becoming poorly though, and needed treatment because septicaemia had set in on his shin where he had been injured during the fatal fight at the mill.

Grandad had always been artistic and he spent his days at Armley doing oil paintings. He painted scenes he remembered seeing when he'd been to Italy and Austria on Wallace Arnold coach trips with Nans. I've still got some of his pictures. He also did copperplate handwriting and calligraphy. And this was a man who'd had to borrow his sister's shoes for school, who'd had hardly any education and spent his adult life working in a mill. Once, he wrote out the words of the Elvis Presley song 'The Wonder Of You' in calligraphy for Mum on top of a picture he had painted of a stained-glass window. It looked as though light was shining on the words and it was truly beautiful.

Even during prison visiting times, Grandad could still make us laugh, but I was old enough then to know it was all an act to stop us from feeling scared and worried about him.

That period at school was a bit of a nightmare. I was a school librarian, which meant I had to keep the books in order and hand them out to the other pupils at lunchtimes. But of course in the library we got all the local newspapers and the week Grandad appeared in court, there was his story in black and white for everyone in the library to see.

I knew people were talking about my grandad, and some girls even avoided me. One girl told me I couldn't go round to her house for tea any more as had been planned.

'Oh. Why?' I asked.

'My mum and dad know about your grandad,' she replied.

I was really hurt but I wouldn't ever let it show. 'Well, I don't want to come for tea then,' I snapped back.

Mr Peel, my deputy head, who was the magistrate Grandad had appeared before, was very kind to me. He called me over to him and said I had to tell him immediately if I ever found myself getting upset.

It was such a strange time, like something from a film, and I couldn't ever quite believe it was happening to us. No one in our family had ever been in trouble before but now it felt like the police were always coming round. The officers who came to our house were lovely though, and one of them would always bring sweets for me and Steph and say, 'Don't worry, you'll have your grandad home soon.'

We were all convinced that once the trial was over, Grandad would be home. Everyone was telling us so. The police, lawyers, prison warders and governors were all saying it was self-defence and that Paul Suchar was known as a violent man. Mum told me and Steph over and over again, 'Your grandad fought for his life and you must hold your heads up high.' She'd say we should be proud of him because if he hadn't fought back he would have been a coward.

Mum had always been quiet and shy but inside she was strong. And Nans was a woman of iron. They both knew that every time they went to the shops or the post office in Morley, everyone was talking about them, but they never let it look as if it were getting to them.

When the murder trial started at Leeds Crown Court, Mum, Dad and Nans went every single day, sitting in the public gallery and listening to the evidence that was presented.

The prosecutor, Peter Taylor QC, who later became the Lord Chief Justice, was brilliant at his job and was determined to prove it was a premeditated attack. The judge was very cruel to my grandad. Mum told me afterwards that when Grandad spoke in his broad Yorkshire dialect, the judge said, 'If you can't speak properly, don't speak at all.'

It seemed everything was stacked against him. On the first day of the trial, his defence barrister didn't even turn up and sent an assistant instead. A pathologist's report, which said Paul Suchar's injuries were sustained in a way that tallied with my grandad's account of self-defence, wasn't even read out in court.

After only a week, Grandad was cleared of murder but found guilty of manslaughter. When it came to sentencing though, Judge Thesiger was very harsh and ordered him to serve six years. Afterwards even the prosecutor, Peter Taylor QC, stood up and said that seemed a long sentence for someone in his late sixties who had never been in trouble before.

Auntie Jean was looking after Steph and me at home when Mum, Dad and Nans got home that day. We'd been convinced Grandad would be walking back in the front door with them so when he wasn't there and the others came in looking all cried up, I just could not believe it. Everyone was crying and Nans was gasping for air. She had asthma and was using her inhaler but was still struggling to breathe. Mum told Steph and me what had happened in court and how Grandad had been given six years and sent to prison. We were all heartbroken.

His prison was a very different place to the hospital wing at Armley. Now, Grandad was in with really violent men who were serving long sentences. It was a very tough regime. Visitors were only allowed once a week, on Sunday afternoons.

One day we went to visit and Grandad looked freezing cold and poorly. He was wearing a pair of horrible hard slippers and no socks because prisoners weren't allowed them and his feet were blue with cold. Mum was usually so shy and quiet but she was furious about it. She called one of the warders over and said, 'My father's cold. How dare you leave him like this? Bring him a sweater.' And they did.

In just a few weeks in prison, Grandad turned into an old man. His face became grey and hollow and he got much thinner. In Armley he'd still been able to make us laugh and giggle when we visited. He'd still made us feel loved and he'd tell me 'You're the apple of my eye.' But now that spark had gone.

Mum and Dad were appealing against the sentence and began a campaign to get him moved somewhere closer to home. But the prison authorities said he couldn't be moved until after the appeal. Mum wouldn't give up though and she wrote to the Home Secretary, telling him Grandad was cold and not being properly looked after. It was a long fight but finally, through her sheer determination, she got him moved to a prison much closer to home and an open prison, so he could have his beloved oil paints again.

Grandad had always been an atheist but in prison he became really religious. We don't really know why, but he talked to the chaplain a lot there and made friends with a nun, Sister Lydia, who would also visit my mum and Nans. But the septicaemia in his leg was getting worse and he was becoming increasingly poorly.

Then one day while Steph and I were at school and Dad was at work, Mum was in the drive sweeping up leaves when Sister Lydia and the prison chaplain pulled up. They got out of the car and went up to mum. Their faces were grey and Mum knew it was bad news.

Grandad was dead. The septicaemia had caused a blood clot in his leg, which had travelled to his brain and killed him. He had died just a year after his conviction and before the appeal to clear his name had been heard. And it was horribly ironic that in the end he'd been killed by the injuries Paul Suchar inflicted on him in that terrible fight.

Mum stood in the driveway of our house and screamed.

The chaplain and Sister Lydia helped her inside and tried to calm her down, telling her Grandad had died peacefully in his sleep the previous night. But Mum was devastated; she and Grandad had been so close. It was after this loss that her depression really set in. The only thing that kept her going was continuing the fight for an appeal to clear his name.

By that time I was well into my rebellious teenage stage and the last Sunday before Grandad died, I hadn't been to visit him, choosing to get all dressed up in my maxi cardigan to see a band in Roundhay Park with my mates, instead. Oh, did I feel guilty about that afterwards. Mum was upset too. 'You didn't see him that last time,' she once said to me, tearfully. But I didn't need her to remind me of what I'd done. It was heartbreaking. Grandad had adored me and from my very first memory he'd made me feel special. For him to have died in a prison cell far away from his family seemed so cruel and unfair. I missed him terribly,

About three weeks after Grandad's funeral, Mum was at home alone again when the doorbell rang. It was Austin Mitchell, who later became an MP but at that time worked on the local TV news programme *Calendar*.

He said, 'Mrs Moxon, my name is Austin Mitchell, I need to speak to you about your father.' Mum invited him in and gave him a cup of tea. He explained that *Calendar* had been sent a letter, allegedly smuggled out of the prison, from seventy-eight inmates who said Grandad hadn't died peacefully in his sleep at all. The letter claimed Grandad had been in pain for a whole night but none of the warders had gone to him. They alleged that he'd been sick, then rolled into his own vomit and his oil paints before finally dying. The letter claimed the prison authorities had not wanted the details of my Grandad's death to be publicised.

Just as we had been desperately trying to put our lives back together, it all began again. For what felt like ages, every night on *Calendar* there would be a big black background come up and then Austin Mitchell or another presenter would say, 'And now we're bringing you up to date on the Pliny Brook case. This was an innocent man who acted in self-defence but was sent to prison and died there in terrible circumstances . . .' And so the reports would go on, night after night. They said they were going to clear his name but all the publicity just made everything that had happened seem more terrible than ever.

Sister Lydia and the chaplain from the prison were supporting my mum. They had truly believed what they'd told her about his death and they joined the campaign to clear Grandad's name. But Nans was completely destroyed. She wouldn't go out, even to the post office to collect her pension. She already knew he was gone for ever, but now to discover he'd apparently died in such pain was so awful for her. She'd coped with the trial but now everything was too much, and in the end Mum gave up on the appeal. She said, 'No matter what happened, we can't get him back. Now my girls just need to be able to grow up and have a normal life.'

After Grandad's death nothing in our family was ever really normal again. But I was certainly growing up – and fast.

3
REBELLIOUS TEEN
TO CHILD BRIDE

....

At home after Grandad died there was a sense of loss every-where I turned. Maybe it was partly to escape that terrible sadness that I threw myself wholeheartedly into my rebellious teenage years – before I'd even hit thirteen!

The biggest thing ever to hit our school was Miners makeup. Oh my God, that really was a revolution. Suddenly everyone had thick mascara, black eye liner and luscious-looking lips.

Everyone that is, apart from me.

Mum didn't wear any makeup at all. She was always nicely turned out with neat hair and great shoes but she thought makeup was too flashy and 'a bit common.' All my friends were wearing white lipstick or this deep, deep shade of burgundy called Black Cherry and I was desperate to be like them, but Mum wouldn't consider it. She wouldn't let me have my ears pierced either, because that was 'common' too! And my school uniform had to follow the very letter of the rules – there was nothing even remotely fashionable for me. It was a grey, box-pleat skirt, grey cardigan, white shirt, white socks, school tie and sensible black Tuf Go-Girl shoes. 'You'll thank me when you're older – you'll have lovely feet,' Mum would say whenever I moaned. 'Who cares about when I'm older,' I'd think. 'I want high heels now!'

There was a girl in my year called Pamela Hopkinson and she was so, so trendy. She was the sort whose school uniform was never quite what it was supposed to be – she had platform heels and a skirt with no pleats in it that was way shorter than everyone else's. All the frumps like me were frantically rolling their skirts up around the waistband to make them look shorter, like Pamela's, but all we really managed was make it look like we had massive spare tyres around our tummies. I started swapping my dinner tickets for the loan of trendier shoes during school hours. I'd do anything to look a little less square. I was no longer impressed by giggly, silly girls, I was impressed by cool girls and I desperately wanted to be one of them.

Jackie comic was the big influence in my life. I'd say, 'Mum, mum, I've seen this dress from Chelsea Girl in *Jackie* comic and I've absolutely GOT to have it.' Mum would agree to take me to Chelsea Girl and would look me up and down when I emerged from the changing rooms in some trendy little outfit, then say, 'But Beverley it's not made very well. Look at the hemming! Look at these seams, they're not overlocked.' And I'd be thinking, 'Who cares if they're overlocked? I want to look like the girls in *Jackie*!'

Jackie was like our bible but it gave a mega-false impression of real life. The stories in it would be about things like two girls who wore platform shoes and loads of makeup all the time, living in a flat and going next door to borrow something only to find a blond haired Adonis named Adam living there. It was total nonsense but I really thought my life was going to be like that.

In the meantime, though, I was using poster paints for makeup because Mum wouldn't let me have the real thing. On the school bus, I'd be applying black paint around my eyes. How ridiculous is that?

My hair was another major problem. It was very blonde and very curly and this was way before hair straighteners were around. I hated it, but Mum thought I should be proud of my curls and she'd spend ages brushing them until my whole head just exploded in a ball of frizz. Then she'd spray it with Silvikrin hairspray to keep the look.

As I got older, I was more and more desperate for my hair to be straight like everyone else's. I'd go to sleep with Sellotape wrapped around my head to flatten the curls. It hurt like hell when I ripped the tape out the next morning but who cared? I just wanted those curls gone. Sometimes I'd even lay my head on the ironing board, fan out my hair and then run the hot iron over it – it must have made it as dry as dust.

Every school photo day, minutes before I was due to have my picture taken, I would nip to the toilets and stick my head under the tap to flatten the curls. So in all my pictures my hair would be totally wet and flat except there would always be one bit that had dried and was sticking straight up. I looked like Wurzel Gummidge in every school photo for years.

One birthday I managed to nag Mum into buying me a poker-straight wig. I loved it! Soon afterwards, on a Sunday afternoon, we went 'out for the run' to Knaresborough in the Vauxhall Victor and met up with Mum and Dad's friends Joan and Gerry. They had three children including Geoffrey, who was about the same age as me, and who I was really keen on at the time. I'd decided to wear my wig to make a good impression on him but I probably just looked like a complete lunatic. It was all fine, though, until I started trying to impress him further by doing handstands. And at that point my wig fell off my head and landed on the ground. Geoffrey thought it was hilarious. I was utterly broken.

To really become cool, when I was fifteen, I started smoking. Cigarettes tasted foul at first but I wasn't going to let that get in the way of looking like a Hollywood movie star, was I? It was a fifteen-minute journey on the school bus from my house to Bruntcliffe Secondary Modern and my friends and I would smoke all the way there on the top deck.

Mum and Dad both smoked Senior Service, which were really strong with no filters, but for us kids the trendy cigarettes at the time were Player's No. 6 and Embassy. If you were really flash you'd have twenty Embassy, but most people just had packets of ten No. 6.

Dad used to sell cigarettes in his baker's shops – they were sold everywhere in those days. Then there was a break-in at one of the shops and the cigarettes were stolen, so Dad started bringing them home at night for safekeeping. Except that after he and Mum had gone to bed I'd nip downstairs and pinch two hundred No. 6 then dish them out on the school bus the next day. Everyone loved it.

I always got found out though. It must have been so obvious to my parents that all these fags were just disappearing. Plus, I was such a bad liar. One day, I hid my cigarettes on top of the old high-up toilet cistern at home. Later on I was stood on the toilet, reaching up, trying to get them down, when I sensed Dad behind me.

'Are these what you're looking for, Beverley?' he said slowly, holding up a packet of Player's No. 6.

'No,' I said. 'No, I wasn't looking for them.'

Like I said, I was a rubbish liar!

Stephanie was six years younger than me but she would often try to stick up for me when I was in trouble. Other times she knew how to blackmail me if she found out I'd been up to something that Mum and Dad wouldn't approve of. I even had to pay her off with Cadbury's Creme Eggs just to stop her hanging around when my friends came over!

When we moved to Churwell, I'd made some new friends, Carolyn Marshall and Susan Ianson, who were much cooler than me and whose clothes really were from Chelsea Girl. They looked more grown-up than me too, had bigger busts and even wore underwired bras, which my mum would never allow. I had to have Birley junior bras, which involved an excruciating trip to Schofields department store to be properly measured!

The centre point of our social life was the Methodist Chapel Youth Club, which met every Friday night. All week we'd look forward to going, planning what we were going to wear and discussing who might be there. It was Carolyn and Susan who invited me along to the youth club and I was beyond excited. That first Friday night, I was still very uncool. I wore a kilt in Black Watch green and black tartan (why it was that I have no idea) a pink nylon shirt, white socks and, of course, my sensible black Tuf Go-Girl shoes. I didn't have so much as a scrap of make up on.

I walked in the door of the church hall and looked at all the teenagers from the village sitting on low wooden gym forms around the edge of the room. Not one of the other girls was wearing socks, they all had tights or 'pantyhose' as we called them then. And everyone else had makeup on. I felt totally the odd one out.

I hadn't been there long when this girl came up to me, I'll call her Ellen. She was a couple of years older than me, really, really tough, and she chewed gum and everything. She was with her group of friends who were very hard, very fashionable and very scary.

Ellen started having a go at me, calling me old-fashioned and a snob. All her friends were laughing and I was absolutely terrified. I'd never met anyone like her before. My friends Carolyn and Susan were sticking up for me, but not too much because they were scared of Ellen, too. I was so frightened that when she finally walked off and left me alone, I started crying.

Then this guy came in. He had long hair and sideburns (most of the boys were too young to grow sideburns), massive bell-bottom jeans, quite high shoes, a royal-blue shiny shirt and a denim jacket with no sleeves. He was sooooo trendy. He and his two friends came over to where I was standing with Carolyn and Susan. 'Have you been crying?' he said to me.

'Yeah,' I replied, still a bit shaken up by Ellen.

'I know you,' he said. 'Your mum and dad own the baker's.' Then he walked off and went right up to Ellen.

'Don't you bully her again,' he said. 'I'm not having it.'

And I fell in love with him. Oh my God, at that moment, I fell completely and utterly in love with him.

Three years later, I married him.

Paul. He was three years older than me, so he was sixteen the night he took on Ellen. His best mates, who were also there that evening, were Dave Richardson (known as Richie) and Derek Horsfield (who was Ozzy). And if you went out with Akka, Richie or Ozzy, then everyone thought you were fantastic. All the girls fancied Akka and wanted to go out with him and actually, lots of them had been out with him; but never for long and he never took them anywhere nice like the cinema.

That first night I clapped eyes on Paul, I didn't think he'd give me a second look – not in my Black Watch tartan kilt! But slowly, as the weeks and months went on, I nagged Mum until she bought me some more trendy clothes. My favourite was a gold dress from Chelsea Girl, which was slinky and really short with a zip up the front. That took a lot of nagging but it was so worth it in the end. Then I got a Crombie coat and a maxi cardigan and a floppy hat. Nineteen-year-olds were all wearing those things at that stage and looked great but I was still fourteen or fifteen and just looked like I was trying a bit too hard!

I spent nearly every Friday night at the youth club. We'd all sit around chatting with our friends until the ladies who ran the session went off to pour out the orange squashes, at which point we'd off the lights and all dance to T-Rex. I loved Marc Bolan and had an entire bedroom wall devoted to pictures of him.

The worst thing that could happen in my world was to be banned from going to youth club by Mum and Dad. Usually it was for playing truant from school or messing about in classes. Sometimes I'd be able to persuade Mum to relent and let me go, and then I could get her to talk Dad round for me, too.

On Saturday nights there were parties at people's houses if their parents were going out. We'd take bottles of cider and if you were really cool you'd be snogging a boy in the corner.

I had a couple of boyfriends in my early teens, but nothing

serious, and I continued to adore Paul from afar, still convinced he'd never notice me. Sometimes, after school, Steph and I would have to go and sit in the back of Dad's shop while Mum helped out behind the counter. I'd spend the whole time desperately hoping Paul might get sent in by his boss to buy the snacks. He was an apprentice decorator and was often made to get the sandwiches and buns for his workmates. On the few occasions he did come in when I was there, I'd try to stand casually in the corner, too shy to say anything but smiling and hoping he might notice me.

Paul had a reputation in the village as a rebel. He came from a 'broken home' as they called it in those days and he lived with his grandma, who needed walking sticks to get around but who still had a big personality. Everyone knew he was always taking out different girls, but whenever he came in the shop Mum would say she knew he had a bad reputation but he had a 'bonny face' and she felt sorry for him because he seemed a nice lad inside. I don't think she thought that so much when I started going out with him, though!

By the time I hit fifteen, as well as dishing out fags on the school bus, I was becoming pretty wild at school. Not naughty like nowadays where being wild means drugs and promiscuity – then it was just messing around and bunking off lessons.

The senior mistress at our school was Mrs Mawson and I was in trouble with her every single day. We called her Old Ma Mawson and she was a proper old battleaxe with a huge bust, big hips, a big bottom and hair that was thinning but always looked as though it had been set in rollers but not combed out properly. She'd wear floral crimplene dresses and seemed to us to be about ninety, although she was probably only fifty.

Old Ma Mawson was constantly ringing Mum to report me

for smoking in the girls' toilets, skiving off to the park beyond the school playing fields or slipping round to someone's house whose mum worked during the day. One day we even rang up and sent the fire brigade round to Mrs Mawson's house just because we thought it would be funny. Another time we sent Kennedy's Caterers to her house with a delivery. The following morning in assembly she was demanding to know who had been playing these tricks on her. We thought it was hilarious!

In my fourth year, Monday afternoons were *treble* biology. Oh my God, there was nothing more boring in the whole world. So my friends and I would bunk off every single Monday afternoon and be in the toilets smoking, thinking that no one would notice.

One afternoon, four of us sat smoking inside the vaulting horse in the gymnasium. But of course we were discovered because there were clouds of smoke coming out of the sides of the horse. It was a bit of a giveaway really!

I always seemed to get found out and then Old Ma Mawson would be back on the phone to Mum. My mates would laugh because if Mum had received a call that day she would be standing at the end of our drive with her arms folded and a furious look on her face as the school bus pulled up. I'd be stumbling down the bus stairs and all my mates on the top deck would be cheering, 'Your mum's there, your mum's there – you're in trouble again!'

But Mum never shouted and screamed, she'd just get totally exasperated with me.

'What are you going to do with you life?' she'd say. 'You'll get no O-levels and what will you do then?'

I'd say, 'I will get my O-levels, I will. I'll be fine.'

Once, when I was caught truanting, Dad sat me down with

a copy of the *Yorkshire Evening Post* and a red Bic pen and told me to circle every job that required O-levels and see how many of them I fancied doing. I was there for two hours! Somehow, it didn't quite have the effect Mum and Dad had been hoping for, though. I wasn't really focussed on what I was going to do next, I was too busy enjoying being a teenager.

Mum and Dad were quite soft with me for a long time, but one day Old Ma Mawson rang Mum again and told her, 'You'll have to come up to the school. Beverley is completely out of control.' Mum was sick and tired of it all by then and just said, 'Well cane her then.' And Mrs Mawson did – one rap across my hand. It really hurt but I'd never have let her know it.

On Monday nights, all my friends started going to the Mecca nightclub in Leeds. There was no way Mum would let me go though – she said I was too young to be out so late on a school night. So I'd lie and say I was staying over at my friend Susan Ianson's house to do our homework together, then we'd nip off to the Mecca together. But if Mum and Dad found out what I'd done then I'd be in trouble for lying and grounded again.

Mum's life had been so sheltered as a teenager and she'd never been out with boys or gone dancing, so she found it hard to understand why I wanted to do these things.

And she really had no idea why I would want to wear Miners makeup or get my ears pierced. It certainly made it difficult to be a teenager. I was eighteen when I finally got my ears done – up until then I had to wear clip-ons and they were definitely not cool.

I left school at fifteen without sitting any O-levels and went straight to secretarial college. I was still convinced I would be an actress but Mum and Dad were insistent I should have some qualifications to fall back on. Even that didn't work out as they'd hoped, though. I hated secretarial college and got thrown out before I'd finished the course. Then I got a job working in the office of a shipping company called Leigh, Lineham and Sharphouse. I hated every second of that too, and to break the boredom, each time the telephone rang I would answer it in a different accent. How annoying I must have been for my boss. Not that I cared what my employer thought of me, because at fifteen, I also started going out with Paul and from then on nothing else in my life really mattered.

'Paul really fancies you,' my friend Susan said to me one evening at youth club. 'D'you want to go out with him?'

She already knew the answer to that one. I'd thought of nothing but being Paul's girlfriend for the past two years. But now that Susan was going out with Paul's best mate Richie, I was finally in with a chance.

My reply was relayed back to Paul and I became 'Paul's girlfriend'. Not that we ever went anywhere much more exciting than hanging around Churwell Park but it did mean I could call him 'my boyfriend'. I was over the moon and just as besotted with him as I had been the night he'd taken on Ellen for me.

Paul was my first love and the one I lost my virginity to. I thought he was gorgeous, handsome, funny, artistic and so, so cool. He made me laugh a lot and I totally believed he was 'the one'. Absolutely. But he was often in trouble and everyone in the village had heard the stories of him drinking and fighting. None of that worried me, though. I loved him so much I thought I could make him change. And I knew he loved me too. He said he liked me because I was different to the other girls. Maybe I was. Mum had cocooned me for so long, so I was still quite innocent in many ways.

I think Mum and Dad realised quite quickly how serious I was about Paul. They must have been thinking, 'Oh my God, what is she doing now?' They tried sitting me down and saying I was too young to get so involved with a boy, but nothing would stop me seeing Paul. Maybe part of me loved being in love – it was like living in one of the Hollywood films that I adored. Because I loved Paul so much, I was desperate for Mum and Dad to love him too. It wasn't that they disliked him, though, they just knew I was still a kid and were worried I was getting in way too deep for my age.

Then Mum read my diary. It was one of those five-year bound diaries with a padlock, but she opened it and worked out that I had been sleeping with Paul. I was mad that she had looked in my diary but my anger was nothing compared to hers. Mum was quite prudish and she was very, very upset with me. She shouted and cried but she couldn't stop me. I wasn't promiscuous, I was just totally in love with Paul.

Susan Ianson and I decided we were going to move out of home and rent a bedsit together in Leeds. We were desperate for a little independence and to be just like those girls in *Jackie*. We also loved the idea that Paul, and Susan's boyfriend Richie, would be able to come round whenever they wanted. So one day, I went home and told Mum and Dad I was leaving. Looking back, it must have broken their hearts.

I was earning a small amount in my office job and Susan was then a machinist in a factory, which I imagine was just like Baldwin's in *Coronation Street*. Susan had loving parents and so did I and we both had really good homes, so God knows what we were thinking, moving in to this little bedsit in the Beeston area of Leeds. The flat was in a converted Victorian terraced house but it was really tatty, and nothing compared to our lovely homes. Mum and Dad were worried sick about us and they and Susan's parents were always popping round to check we were OK. We thought we were so grown up, of course, and that it was great. But we had no idea what we were doing really; once we cooked a turkey and when we carved it, the plastic bag with all the giblets in it was still inside. After a few weeks it became clear that it just wasn't working and we decided to go home.

It was around the Christmas that I was sixteen that I realised my period was late. When Paul next popped round to see me, we went for a walk through the fields at the back of our house. We were walking arm in arm along a dirt track when I took a deep breath and said, 'I haven't come on yet.' Unsure quite how Paul would react, I added, 'How scary is that?'

But Paul didn't seem scared at all, in fact he was delighted. He hugged me really tight and said, 'We'll be OK. We'll be OK.'

From that moment, Paul thought we should get married. We were both convinced we were going to be together for ever, so there didn't seem any reason to wait.

Mum and Dad were less thrilled by my news. Mum marched me off to the doctor's for a pregnancy test and the result confirmed their worst fears. Mum was devastated and Dad heartbroken – it really wasn't what he had planned for his little girl. There was no screaming and shouting, Mum and Dad weren't like that, but I could see how hurt they were.

They sat down with Paul and me for a big discussion about what we should do. Mum thought I should have an abortion but I said, 'No'. I wanted to have this baby, Paul's baby. By this time, Paul and I were both determined we were getting married. Paul asked Dad for his permission to marry me, but my poor dad could only say that he really didn't want us to get married, he thought we were too young.

I was so headstrong that I was determined to go ahead with it as quickly as possible. I thought Paul and I were like Heathcliff and Cathy and were 'meant to be.' In hindsight, I realise I was so young that I didn't really understand much at all.

On 29 January 1974, two months before my seventeenth birthday, we were married, at Dewsbury Register Office.

Dad was destroyed by everything that had happened and on the morning of the wedding he could hardly talk to me. The whole thing was just awful. Mum and Dad were clearly devastated but being the wonderful people that they were, they were still there for me. There was only a handful of other family and just a few friends. It was all so rushed that I didn't even have time to buy a wedding dress, I had to borrow one from a friend. Paul wore a burgundy suit with a big fat tie and platform shoes. In the pictures we look desperately young, even though at the time we thought we were so grown up.

The ceremony was over in a flash and afterwards we went back to Mum and Dad's for a bit of a do with the family, but the whole day had a sense of disappointment about it. It certainly wasn't how Mum had imagined the wedding day of her eldest daughter. I think she always thought her girls would be walking down the aisle in a wonderful dress with a massive train, like Julie Andrews at the end of *The Sound of Music*. Whenever she saw that scene she'd say, 'Oh, oh, oh, look at that dress, isn't it beautiful?' And there was me: sixteen, pregnant and in a secondhand dress.

But none of that mattered to me, I had become Paul's wife and it was my dream come true. I was still too young to understand that very rarely do dreams last for ever.

4
THE DREAM GOES WRONG

....

Paul and I truly thought we would be great together. We found a tiny back-to-back terraced house, for which Mum and Dad put down a deposit, and we set about playing happy families.

I knew that people were gossiping about us, saying Paul was a bad lad while I came from such a good home. But I just didn't care; I was in love. It was always a volatile relationship, though. We were both feisty and passionate people and we had some terrible arguments. Usually they would start if we had been out, particularly if Paul had been drinking. But we always made it up the next day and were convinced we were right together no matter what other people said.

I loved our house, at number 6 South Street in Morley. There was one room downstairs with the kitchen area in the corner of the room, a bedroom and bathroom on the next floor and a second bedroom on the top floor. Paul decorated it all from top to bottom and we were happy there.

Then, about four months after I discovered I was pregnant, I had a period again. I went to my doctor, who examined me and then broke the news that the baby had gone. I must have miscarried without even knowing it. There had been no pain or symptoms of any kind but the doctors explained that in the early stages of pregnancy, miscarriage can happen like that.

I was desperately upset that the baby had gone and so was Paul. The fact that I hadn't had any bleeding or other signs that there was anything wrong with the pregnancy made it harder to come to terms with. We might have been young but we had both really wanted a child together so we set about actively trying to get pregnant again. Every month that passed we'd be hoping my period wouldn't come, even though I was still just seventeen and Paul was twenty.

Trying for a baby seems such a grown-up thing to do but it really wasn't an adult decision at all, we were very naïve and had no idea what being parents would be like. All I could think about was how my friend from school had had a baby girl called Samantha and she was so gorgeous. I just thought, 'I'm going to have a baby girl like her.' It never occurred to me to wonder what on earth it would actually be like when the baby came, or even that I might have a boy!

As the months passed, Paul and I partied a lot and I really loved married life. Any heated fallings-out were followed by equally passionate reunions.

Mum and Nans visited loads and despite their concerns about us being so young, they were incredibly supportive. They thought that now I was married I would automatically just take on the role of housewife, but I wasn't so sure. They were telling me I had to scrub the front step and wash the skirting boards with Flash, but I wasn't interested in any of that.

Once, Paul's cousin Maureen came round to see me and we were having a coffee when Nans popped in.

'Now listen,' Nans said to Maureen. 'Our Beverley hasn't got time to sit chatting to you. She needs to get her house-work done.'

But I was still more bothered about the latest minidress in Chelsea Girl than spring-cleaning the house!

I got a job as a receptionist for a hypnotherapist who helped people to stop smoking and overcome addictions, and the work was really interesting. He was brilliant at what he did, but he couldn't hypnotise me. He tried but I just wouldn't go under. I still smoked too, so in between dealing with patients arriving to get help to quit, I'd be in the loo, having a fag and blowing the smoke out of the window. I enjoyed the job, but even with my wage and Paul's combined, we were always short of money. Mum and Dad helped us out, buying us clothes and bags of food whenever they went shopping.

I also still saw loads of Steph; she would often come round for her tea. We were more like friends than sisters by then and could talk about anything together.

Then, towards the end of 1974, I fell pregnant again. I was desperately hoping nothing would go wrong this time but when my period was just eight days late, I became horribly ill and remained so until our daughter Rebecca was born the following summer.

I was diagnosed with a condition called hyperemesis, which means you get extreme sickness during pregnancy. This wasn't just a bad dose of morning sickness though, it lasted day and night and I lost so much weight the doctors were convinced it would probably kill the baby – and possibly me, too.

I was referred to a specialist, who said he had only come across one other case like mine in his entire career. Even after I'd been diagnosed there was nothing that could be done to ease the symptoms. I was so ill that I was being sick virtually continually and couldn't keep so much as a glass of water down.

I spent most of my pregnancy at Staincliffe Hospital in Dewsbury, being fed by a drip as without it I was suffering extreme dehydration. I became painfully thin and my hair even started to fall out because of the lack of nutrients in my body.

Mum and Dad were out of their minds with worry. Mum would come to the hospital and sit with me all day, every day. I'd hurt them both so much by going through with the wedding but when I was sick and needed them again, they were amazing. Paul would visit too, when he wasn't at work.

It was a bloody awful time. One of the sisters on the ward used to call me 'pale and passionate' because I was so white and sickly-looking. Sometimes I'd pick up for a while and be allowed home, but after a couple of days I'd be back in hospital again because, without the drip feed, I wasn't keeping any fluids in my body at all and my weight was plunging desperately low. I was terrified I might lose the baby but I felt so ill all the time that I couldn't think about anything properly. It reached a point where I couldn't even imagine having the baby, I couldn't imagine anything other than being sick every day for the rest of my life.

I lost so much weight that when Rebecca was finally born, at seven minutes to three in the morning of 3 June,

1975, I weighed 5 stone 12 pounds and could still wear size eight jeans.

The labour wasn't too bad really but I was just desperate for it to be over as the doctors had told me that having the baby was the only thing that would end my illness.

And the moment Rebecca was born, I stopped being sick. It was extraordinary. Everyone knew it was a miracle that Rebecca had survived. What was even more incredible was that she was a healthy 5 pounds 14 ounces.

The moment Rebecca was born, my entire life changed. There is no love like that you feel for your child and nothing is ever the same again.

Paul and I didn't have a car at the time, so Mum and Dad had gone round to pick him up to bring him to the hospital in Dewsbury, to see me and the new baby. They arrived two minutes after Rebecca was born. Paul instantly adored his little daughter and Mum and Dad were besotted with her.

When Mum came in to see her, it was the first time she'd seemed truly happy since Grandad died. She looked at Rebecca all wrapped up and said, 'And so life begins again.' She couldn't take her eyes off her and kept saying, 'She's our miracle baby. Look at that little face in those sheets, that little face in those sheets.'

In those days, they kept new mums in hospital for about ten days and for the first five days, everything seemed fine. Then, one day, I was looking into Rebecca's Perspex cot at the bottom of my hospital bed and I thought, 'My baby is jumping.' Her left arm and leg were clearly moving. At first I thought I was imagining it, but then it continued.

I went out into the corridor and found a nurse. 'My baby

is twitching,' I said, but the nurse dismissed me, replying 'No she isn't,' and carried on with what she was doing. When I insisted that Rebecca was twitching, the nurse said she'd come and check her in a moment, before wandering off.

I went back to Rebecca's cot and saw she was still doing it. Even more worrying, she had started turning a bluey-purple colour. I ran back into the corridor and found a senior nurse who was called Mrs Parrot. 'Please come, please, my baby is twitching,' I said.

Mrs Parrot went straight to Rebecca's cot, took one look at her and shouted to the nurses, 'Get this baby into intensive care immediately.'

After all our thoughts that Rebecca must be a miracle baby because she had survived even though I was unable to eat for nine months, now it seemed that her life was hanging in the balance again, at just five days old.

The convulsions continued in the intensive care unit, each time scaring me witless that she might not survive. One of the nurses wheeled the pay phone to my bed and I called my parents, desperately upset that they might be about to lose their first grandchild. I'd just turned eighteen and was really just a child myself, but had now found myself in a horribly adult and scary situation.

Tests showed Rebecca had been born with seriously low blood sugar – probably due to my illness – and it was that which had caused the convulsions. Thankfully though, my daughter was a fighter. I watched her like a hawk for days, desperate with worry. The doctors told me that as the weeks went by and she put on weight, the fits would stop, and thank goodness that is exactly what happened. Rebecca was kept in hospital for five weeks to be monitored and I had to stay in too because I was still seriously underweight after my illness.

So it was an incredible relief when Rebecca and I were finally discharged and were able to go home to our little house in South Street. But within weeks of having our daughter home, marriage to Paul took a frightening turn for the worse.

I always felt Paul was a great person. And I loved him and I know he loved me. Yet after Rebecca was born we became very different people. Rebecca was my everything and for me, everything had changed. Suddenly I had all these values and concerns that had never existed in my mind before. It was things like being determined that my cloth nappies were washed and on that clothesline by half past six of a morning, no matter what. (They did sell disposable nappies in those days but they were sort of looked down upon and you weren't thought to be a very good mum if you used them.)

In 1975 when Rebecca was born and again in 1976, we had fantastic summers and suddenly it was really important to me that my clothes were out drying in that sun and were whiter than anyone else's. I had to have an immaculately clean house. I was fanatical about every detail. Mum told me that when I was ironing, to make sure I pressed down the labels at the back of the baby's clothes so they didn't irritate her neck. I'd be constantly worrying, 'I hope this label doesn't scratch my Rebecca's neck.'

I really took all this stuff on board because I was determined to be a good mum. None of it impacted on Paul at all, though. I think he just wanted life to carry on exactly as it always had done. I certainly had no interest in going out partying any more and Paul really didn't like that, so he'd just go to the pub on his own. Sometimes he'd go straight from work so by the time he got home after closing time he'd be drunk.

We'd often argued when Paul had been drinking, even before we had Rebecca, but it was only after she was born that he began to get into terrible rages. At first I was more than capable of standing up for myself. Gradually though it got worse and worse. He'd come in the door and more often than not he would pick an argument with me about something. I was fiery too and so then we would have the most awful row about him being drunk again and then he'd lose his temper. He could turn into an absolute madman.

One night he had come home very late and was horribly drunk. I told him to be quiet because he'd wake Rebecca, and we started rowing. He lashed out and hit me on the side of my head, then did it again and again. At first I tried to fight back and was pushing him away from me but he was just getting madder and madder. I was crying and desperate to get away from him but I was trapped.

I ended up crouching between two armchairs pushed up against the living room wall. I had my head in my hands and I was thinking, 'I'm just going to curl up now because I can't fight any more and I can't win.'

I was crying and could feel warm tears streaming between my fingers and down my face.

Then suddenly he stopped, moved away and I could hear him saying, 'Oh my God, what have I done? What have I done?' Then he was crying and saying, 'I've got to get you up.'

It was only when he pulled me up from between the chairs and I opened my eyes and wiped the tears away with my hands that I realised it wasn't just tears I'd felt before, there was blood. I was in a real mess.

I stood in the middle of the room, utterly numb, as I watched Paul walk over to the phone and, still sobbing, ring my mum and dad.

'I'm really sorry but you have got to come over and take Beverley to hospital,' he said. 'I've done something really bad.'

God knows what Mum and Dad must have thought, but they came straight away. They had to bring my younger sister Steph too. By the time they got to the house, Mum was blazing. She was such a shy and ladylike woman but she yelled at Paul, 'What have you done to my daughter? What have you done?' Then she turned to Dad and was shouting at him, 'Now you hit him,' pointing to Paul.

Dad just shook his head, but Mum was getting more and more angry. 'Hit him. How can you stand there and do nothing?'

Dad was saying, 'No, Mavis, no. Let's just get Beverley to hospital.'

Finally, Mum and Dad got Rebecca and me into the back of their car. As we were leaving the house, Dad said to Paul, 'Just stay away from her. You can keep the house, just stay away.'

In the car on the way to casualty, Mum kept saying to Dad, 'Why didn't you hit him? Are you afraid of him?'

'Of course I'm not afraid of him,' Dad said. 'But do you want me to end up where your dad did? I want to hit him, of course I do, but it would be wrong and I won't do it.'

Both Mum and Dad were furious and devastated by what had happened. 'You can't ever go back,' Dad said.

And at that point I had no intention of going back, I really didn't.

At the hospital they said my nose was broken and they

patched up the cuts around my eye. The following morning I had a terrible black eye and I was black and blue.

I went straight from the hospital back to Mum and Dad's house to recover. I hadn't been there long when Paul turned up to see how I was getting on and from then on he started visiting daily. Of course, Mum and Dad didn't want him there, but I did. No matter what he'd done to me, I still loved him.

Every time he came round he'd be crying, saying how sorry he was and that it would never ever happen again. Within a fortnight, Rebecca and I were back home with him.

'If you go back we're washing our hands of you,' Dad said. But of course they didn't. They loved Rebecca and me too much just to abandon us. Mum and Dad still came round to visit and Steph would still pop in for her tea some afternoons.

It was about that time that Steph started getting bullied at school. She looked like our dad, with darker hair than me and grey eyes, and she was growing into a really beautiful teenager. She was also very clever and on the Morley Grammar School gymnastics team, and some of the other girls were bullying her because of that. One of them had made her do loads of cartwheels and Steph was really upset by it. Mum had tried to deal with the problem by going to the school and telling the girls involved that they were being unkind, but Mum was just too ladylike and well-mannered so I decided to take matters into my own hands.

One afternoon Mum and I went to meet Steph from her school, which was on a great long road called Fountain Street. I left Rebecca with Mum in her turquoise Silver Cross pram ('the Rolls Royce of prams', Mum called it) then marched over to the bullies and grabbed hold of one of the ringleaders.

'If you so much as go near my sister again I'll be making you do cartwheels the length of Fountain Street,' I said.

And boy, did I mean it! I was ready to batter her. Sure enough, the bullying stopped.

For a little while it was fine between Paul and me back home, but sure enough, the rows started all over again. It followed a predictable routine – Paul would go out, have one too many, come home, then start yelling at me about anything at all.

I tried to keep it a secret from Mum and Dad as I didn't want them to worry about me but I also didn't want to admit how wrong I had been to marry Paul.

It is easy for people on the outside to say that women in these situations should just walk away from a violent partner, but it is a lot harder to do when you're on the inside of the relationship.

I really loved Paul and I remained convinced that deep down he was a good person. I also felt that maybe when he hit me it really was my fault, as if I was being punished for hurting my family so much when I'd got married against their wishes. Since having Rebecca I'd learnt how much you love your child and realised for the first time just how much Mum and Dad loved me. I knew they and Steph were all worried sick about me and all I'd done was hurt them.

Another reason I stayed with Paul was that I desperately didn't want my marriage to fail, even though by then I knew it had been a mistake. I'd think, 'Everyone was right and I was wrong. I am the black sheep of the family. Why can't I be like Auntie Jean's daughters Deirdre and Deborah who got their qualifications and good jobs? I've just made a mess of everything.'

So when Paul cried after losing his temper and said, 'Oh my God, I'm so sorry, I'm so sorry, this will never happen again,' I believed him. I believed him because I so desperately wanted it to be true. Then I'd think, 'It must be true because he is crying and he loves me, I know he loves me.' It took a long while for me to realise that even if Paul did love me and did want to change, he just couldn't do it.

Once, I told my GP everything that had been going on. I said, 'But doctor, if I leave him he'll be a tramp on the street.'

My doctor replied, 'You're right, if you leave him he'll be a tramp on the street. But Beverley, if you stay with him he'll still be a tramp, and you and your daughter will be too. You can't make him better – he has to find that within himself.'

That was a real turning point for me.

One night Paul had come in drunk and we were having this awful argument in the living room. Rebecca was about eighteen months old and asleep in her baby buggy. Paul was raging about something when suddenly he picked up a 2 pound bag of sugar and hurled it across the room. The bag burst all over the floor.

Paul turned to walk away but I just snapped. I picked up the upright vacuum cleaner, which was standing next to me, lifted it up and smacked it right over the back of Paul's head. He fell to the floor and was groaning as he tried to stand up again but I didn't care any more. I'd had enough. It was the first time that I realised that Rebecca could be affected by what was going on. It was the turning point for me. Suddenly everything became crystal clear and I think we both knew that it was over. I rang Dad, asked him to collect me, and walked out the door holding Rebecca.

We never went back.

5
BACK HOME

....

Lying under the white candlewick bedspread in a single bed back at Mum and Dad's house, all I could think was, 'I've failed.' I'd been so proud, so convinced that I was right about Paul and me and that everyone else was wrong. But it was I who'd been wrong all along.

I'd spend hours wondering why I hadn't been able to make my marriage work like Mum and Dad. Years later, a counsellor suggested that maybe my parents' marriage had given me a false impression of the way the world works because they were so happy, and I thought that was normal, when in actual fact they were not really typical – they were in the minority.

Even though I'd left Paul, he was still Rebecca's dad and so he remained part of our lives. He was struggling to come to terms with the split and I knew he was watching our house. For months he seemed to know about my every move. Once he even threw a stone at one of the windows and broke it. I was scared of him because I knew what he was capable of doing. But I felt sorry for him too because I knew that despite everything, he had really loved me, and that, deep down, he was a good person.

He came round the house every few days on the pretext of seeing Rebecca, but he somehow always managed to time it for when she was asleep so he could sit and talk to me instead. He wanted us to get back together and once he even suggested I leave Rebecca with my parents and go back to him. 'We'd be fine if it was just us,' he'd say. But of course there was no way I would do that.

I still loved him and I wasn't really over him at all but I taught myself to live without him.

Rebecca was what kept me going during that time. I had absolutely loved being a mum from the very beginning. I didn't even find it particularly hard being a single mother, although I was aware that sometimes other parents would look down on me for being so young and on my own. But I was lucky because my parents were brilliantly supportive as always and they kept Rebecca and me for years.

Rebecca and I did everything together. When I joined an amateur drama group in Leeds, Rebecca would come with me and when I was invited to friends' houses for dinner, she'd be there with me too. We were a team and rarely apart.

The drama group was called the Proscenium Players and included quite a lot of semi-professional actors from Yorkshire Television. I absolutely loved it. Even though I'd become a teen bride and was now a single mum, I'd never ever lost my determination to become a professional actress. I always knew it would happen one day.

Rebecca was three and we were still living with my parents when all our lives were horribly changed again on 11 November, Remembrance Day, 1978.

I woke to feel Mum in my bedroom, gently stroking my face. I hate mornings and am the worst getter-upper in the world. My day usually started with Mum shouting up the stairs, 'Beverley, Beverley, are you ever getting out of that bed?' But that morning she was just saying my name really softly. It was so quiet and calm that I immediately knew something was wrong and I woke up instantly.

'What on earth's the matter?' I said.

Mum looked in total shock as she said to me softly, 'Are you properly awake Beverley? Have you come round yet? Because it's your dad.'

'He's dead isn't he?' I said. I could just tell by the way she was speaking.

'He is my love, he is,' she said, starting to cry.

We sat staring at each other for a few moments, both of us paralysed by shock. The previous night we had all gone to bed just as normal, and now Dad was dead.

'We need to phone people,' Mum said finally, 'but I'm not sure what we do.'

The pair of us walked out of my bedroom and as we did I could see along the landing a pair of bare feet. They were blue and motionless and I knew they were Dad's.

I remember thinking, 'Oh my God. He is just there and he is dead.'

I really didn't want to look at him but I thought if I didn't, Mum might never forgive me, so I forced myself to go over to where he had collapsed on the floor. His face was pale and waxy and his cheeks were sunken because he hadn't been wearing his false teeth when he died. And his fists were clenched tight as though he had been gripped by terrible pain in his last moments. It was awful seeing him like that, he just wasn't the Dad that I knew.

We think what happened was that he had got up just before seven o'clock and was being sick in the bathroom when Rebecca got up to go to the loo. He must have come out the door to let her use the toilet, sat down on the landing steps and then was struck down with a heart attack and fell backwards.

So poor little Rebecca had found him like that when she came out of the bathroom.

Mum was woken by Rebecca running into her room, saying, 'Grandad sick, Grandad sick.' It was November and still pitch black at that time of the morning, so when Mum came out of her bedroom, she tripped over Dad's body. It was just horrific.

Rebecca, Mum, Stephanie and I all stood around Dad's body on the landing that morning not quite sure what to do next. Stephanie had been her dad's little girl and was sobbing inconsolably. Mum was clearly utterly numb. Rebecca went off and got a pillow from her dolly's cot and tried to put it under Dad's head. I think I went into a coping mode. I knew I had to be strong for everyone else, otherwise everything was going to fall apart.

We rang the doctor, who called the police, and soon there was an ambulance on the front drive but there was nothing they could do – it was too late.

Dad had been to the doctor's two weeks earlier complaining about a pain in his arm but his GP put it down to indigestion. Since then he'd been in a bit of a bad mood, which was very out of character, but we had absolutely no idea that he was seriously ill. It was only after he died that it was discovered he'd had hardening of the arteries, which had caused a heart attack. But I'll always be convinced it was working such long hours for so many years that killed him. And he'd done all that for us.

That morning, Mum sat in an armchair, totally lost, while Stephanie was distraught. Nans, Auntie Jean and Uncle Frank arrived and waited with us for the undertakers to turn up. I remember dashing around vacuuming the carpets. I just thought I had to keep everything orderly and tidy as there would be so many people coming around and I had to stay in control of everything for all the others. Now Dad wasn't there any more I suppose at some level I felt that the role of looking after everyone had fallen to me.

When the undertakers came they lifted up Dad's body and placed it in a large, metal coffin. As they shut the lid there was a terrible clanging sound, it was like the bin men coming. 'What are they doing with him up there?' Mum said.

When they carried Dad out the front door it was like they were taking half of Mum away. For me, though, it was all so sudden that it took weeks for what had happened to really sink in and for me to start grieving. As with splitting up with Paul, I don't think I really got over it, I just learnt to live with it.

St Peter's Church in Churwell was packed for the funeral. Hundreds and hundreds of people turned out for a man who may have been just a local baker, but who had touched so many lives because he was so good, kind and moral. People used to come to his shops just to see him. I know it is easy to make saints out of people who have died but Dad really was an amazing man.

The months that followed were tough for all of us, but particularly for Mum and for Steph, who at fifteen, was at such a crucial age.

There were three shops and two bakehouses that still had to be kept going and Mum did it all. She had failed her driving test five times (on the last attempt she was going so slowly that a chicken walked under the front wheels of the car and out the side!) so every week, she would get the bus to all the shops and bakehouses to deliver the wages. At the same time she was desperately trying to keep things as normal as possible at home for Stephanie.

Mum aged twenty years in the year after Dad died. She was still only forty-seven but she had lost the two men she adored – Grandad and Dad – and she entered a deep, deep place of sadness. Her face grew old and she shrunk into herself. She'd always been quiet yet strong, but after Dad died, she suddenly seemed vulnerable and elderly. Half of her had been taken away and she never, ever got over it.

One day she said to me, 'Now your dad has gone, if anything ever happens to me you must make sure you look after Stephanie. I know Rebecca is your baby but Stephanie is mine and you must make sure she does everything she wants to do.'

I assured her that I'd always look after Stephanie but the conversation left me worried. I was terrified that in her sadness, Mum might be thinking of killing herself.

After a while we did regain some normality in our lives, though just as when Grandad died, nothing was ever really normal again.

Since splitting with Paul I hadn't really bothered much with boyfriends but I had been on a few dates with a guy called Jim, who lived with his parents in the house next door but one to us.

In the January after Dad died, Jim and I were driving home in his dad's Ford Capri after going to see a band, when we hit a patch of black ice. We were only yards from home when it happened and I can't really remember any details, but it seems the car rolled over three times before smashing into a wall. The bonnet concertinaed up, pushing me backwards from the front passenger seat and all the way out of the rear window. It was before the seatbelt law and I didn't have one on, but afterwards the doctors said that if I had been wearing a belt, I would have been killed, as the bonnet would have crunched straight up into me.

The first thing I really knew about the accident was waking up in an ambulance with an agonising pain in my back. My head was cut, I was covered in blood, the furry jacket I'd been wearing was shredded and my shoes had been ripped off.

I was taken to Leeds General Infirmary where they discovered I had damaged my right kidney, the base of my left lung and my left leg.

I was kept in overnight and sent home the following morning and the doctors told me that with plenty of rest, I should soon make a good recovery. But after a couple of days at home my leg was in agony and had become so swollen that the bandage was severely cutting into it.

I went back to the hospital and it was only when they x-rayed me that they discovered I had actually broken my leg in three places and seriously damaged the ligaments. My leg had to be broken again and reset and then I was in hospital for weeks as they monitored my progress.

I was a total mess, although Jim, who'd been driving, had walked away from the crash needing just four stitches at the base of his back. Jim was great fun to be with and although our relationship wasn't anything serious, I did like him. But for the first few weeks I was in hospital Jim didn't come in to visit me. Mum thought it was a disgrace and I was a bit annoyed, too

Then one afternoon he strolled into my hospital room with this gorgeous-looking woman he introduced as, 'Margarita, my fiancée.' He was looking at me as if to say, 'Please don't give me away,' but I was too stunned to say anything at all. There was me with eighteen stitches across my forehead, my hair matted because I had been unable to wash it, my leg in plaster and, worst of all, wearing my mum's pale blue nylon bed jacket! I looked like Morticia Adams. Then there was Margarita, looking amazing in a fox-fur jacket, drainpipe jeans and really long high-heeled boots.

I was so embarrassed that I tried wriggling my way down the bed to hide my bedjacket under the sheets, but every time I moved, the undersheet made this noise as if I was farting. 'Oh please God, make this stop,' I was thinking. My humiliation was complete! The whole situation was like something out of a comedy sketch.

With me in hospital, Mum was having to cope all on her own with Dad's death, running the business, supporting Stephanie, looking after Rebecca and visiting me. And she did it. She did it! Maybe, looking back, it helped her because she was so busy she didn't have a moment to think about anything.

It took a while but eventually Mum managed to sell the businesses and that was a big relief for her. Then after a couple more years she sold the family home, it was just too full of memories, and we all moved to a bungalow a couple of miles away in Gildersome.

When Rebecca started school I got a job on the Orlane makeup counter at Boots in Leeds. My two friends at Boots became Kay Jennings on Helena Rubinstein and Nikki Manzani on Lancôme. We all had to wear so much makeup to work that we looked like exhibits from Madame Tussauds! We had such a laugh together though and again I fell into the role of clown.

One day I was trying to explain to Kay about the old music hall star Bob Blackman, who would sing 'Mule Train' while hitting himself across the head with a metal tray. I was demonstrating in the middle of the makeup department by hitting myself around the head with a script I'd been learning under the counter when I heard the flat, broad Yorkshire voice of our supervisor, Mrs Alastair, behind me.

'Beverley, could we have a little bit of decorum please. Will you follow me.'

I was taken to her office where I probably just made things worse by going through the whole process of trying to explain about Bob Blackman bashing himself around the head while singing 'Mule Train' all over again. Mrs Alastair usually had a twinkle in her eye when she was telling me off for reading scripts for whatever play I had coming up next, behind the makeup stand, but this time I was severely reprimanded for my antics.

When she wasn't at school, Rebecca and I still did virtually everything together. Even when I had auditions or rehearsals for plays locally, Rebecca would come along with me. Sometimes she'd sit and look at her books or play with toys but most of the time she just liked watching. She already had the acting bug herself.

I dated a couple of men, usually blokes I met through the drama group, but there was no one serious. I remember one actor guy I went out with for a while even asked me to marry him but I just wasn't attracted to him. When I saw him on stage I was madly in love with him, but in the real world, the spark just wasn't there. I still wasn't ready for a physical relationship after Paul. After a while I ended it with him, saying I couldn't consider marriage again, but a few days later he sent me a letter saying, 'Oh my darling Beverley, I felt we were on a beautiful cruise together but now I find myself alone in the rapids in a flimsy canoe.'

'I think you've made the right decision, Beverley,' said Mum with a wry smile when I told her about the letter.

Then my friend Carol from drama group introduced me one night to David, the brother of her boyfriend, Mark. We were in the bar of a theatre where Mark had been appearing in a play and as usual I had Rebecca with me. I started chatting to David and he seemed a really nice guy. He was fantastic with Rebecca, too. David explained that he lived over in York although he was originally from Leeds, and came back regularly to visit his family.

After chatting for a while, David asked me out. I was really excited about the date and when the evening arrived I got myself all dressed up in a little pencil skirt, which was very fashionable at the time. But when we met up that night he said we were going tenpin bowling. In a pencil skirt! I should have realised then that we were very different people.

We started dating regularly and got on really well. David was everything that Paul wasn't and I think that was a lot of the attraction for me. He was head of economics and sociology at a school in York, politically very left-wing and really into books and the theatre. David was also teetotal, which was a huge bonus for me after having been married to someone like Paul. With David, I think we both

knew I was never going to be swept off my feet or swinging from the chandeliers, but he was a good man. After
Paul, I thought, 'Maybe this is how a relationship really
should be.'

David's dad had died when he was quite young and his
mother had brought him and his younger brother up on
her own. She was a very similar woman to my mum – they
were both conservative in every sense of the word. David had
become a member of the Socialist Workers Party and was
also active in the National Union of Teachers. Mum really
liked David's mum and she liked him too, except for his anti-
monarchy views. Mum was a big royalist (she always used to
say that the princesses Elizabeth and Margaret had been a lot
like Auntie Jean and herself!).

David was tall, dark and handsome but his greatest attraction for me was that he opened up a whole new world to me
that I had never known before. He was my Henry Higgins.
In *My Fair Lady*, Henry Higgins introduces Eliza Doolittle
to amazing new experiences and that's what David did
for me.

My parents had always been Conservative supporters and
I'd never really been political but David made me think and
question things I'd always taken for granted. He even introduced me to all sorts of new foods. Growing up, it had always
been very much meat and two veg, but suddenly I was eating
Italian, Indian and Chinese food and we were making it
ourselves, not just going out to restaurants. We'd make our
own pizzas, throwing the dough up in the air, and we cooked
loads of vegetarian food, too.

David was eight years older than me and he seemed so
much more worldly and intelligent than anyone I'd ever met.

He was sensible and serious and I guess I hoped he'd make me a bit more like that.

At weekends David would come over from York to visit, or Rebecca and I would go to stay with him. After a while though we decided we wanted to be together all the time and marriage seemed the logical step. It wasn't a Cathy and Heathcliff romance this time and there may not have been the passion I'd experienced with Paul, but David was sensible, secure and had made my life so much better. I was already divorced from Paul and when David asked me to marry him I really believed we would be together forever.

We were married at a register office in Leeds and I wore a floaty yellow Frank Usher dress. At the time I thought I looked great but in hindsight it was just awful. I suppose it was 1980, though! After the ceremony we had a big party and it was great fun, all so different from my first wedding, when I had felt I was disappointing everyone.

Mum looked after Rebecca for a week so that David could take me to Sicily for our honeymoon. It was my first time abroad and I was so excited about seeing Mount Etna and Palermo but on the second day I got severe sunstroke and was in bed sick for the next four days!

From the beginning, David and Rebecca had got on really well. David loved being with her and the pair of them would spend hours playing or talking together.

I didn't go into marriage just to get a father for Rebecca because I knew the pair of us could cope just fine on our own, but I had no doubts David would be a good dad.

He was always keen to formally adopt Rebecca, who was six when we married. David often said he didn't want children and as I'd had such a terrible time during my pregnancy with Rebecca, that was fine by me.

Rebecca adored David – and even picked up on his political leanings too. She can only have been about six when I heard her in the school cloakroom one afternoon at home time, saying to her little friends, 'Years ago children used to get milk at school and you didn't have to pay for it. Then Thatcher stopped all that.' She didn't say 'Mrs Thatcher' or 'Margaret Thatcher', just 'Thatcher' and she was still only tiny!

David, Rebecca and I lived in a three-bedroom semi in Haxby, just north of York. I got a job at the Body Shop in the city centre, which had only recently opened and was very trendy, and I also continued doing lots of amateur drama work in the evenings. It was while I was with David that my dreams of becoming a professional actress started to become a reality. He was fantastically supportive and would tell me, 'You have got to go for it. If you think you can do it, you must do it.'

A couple of months after we were married open auditions were taking place for a very early Ibsen play called *The Vikings at Helgeland*, which was to be performed inside York Minster. It was a pretty grim play and seemed like someone was dying in it every two minutes. There were loads of men in it but only two women's roles – and I got one of them. That was an amazing feeling and crucially, it helped towards me getting my Equity card, which you need to become a professional actor.

At that time, you had to do a certain number of professional contracts to get an Equity card, so I had started to do verse readings in wine bars and take any part I could get. The role in the Ibsen play was a big step forward though. After years of working wherever I could to get my Equity card, when I finally received it I was over the moon. I was now a proper, professional actress. And although I didn't have any specific ambition as to what I would do next, I was convinced that one day I would be on television and in big stage productions. David knew I could do it and he had made me believe I could do it too.

I realised I needed an agent so I rang three telephone numbers in the phone book before deciding to go with a lady called Beverley Cole in Leeds. A casting director who'd seen me in the Ibsen play offered me a role in a one-off drama for Yorkshire Television. I think I had four lines in that show, but being on telly for the first time was still an incredible feeling even though then, as now, I hated watching myself.

Lots more small parts in other things followed. I think I made it up to five lines in a sitcom with Mollie Sugden called *That's My Boy!* Next I had a small part in another sitcom called *The Bounder* starring Peter Bowles and George Cole. Afterwards George Cole rang casting and said he thought I was really good and they should take notice of me, which was very kind of him. Next I played a woman camping in the grounds of a cathedral in a series called *Hell's Bells* with Derek Nimmo. My husband in the episode was played by Jonathan Morris, who was Adrian Boswell in *Bread,* and we had great fun filming it. That role led to something in *Dear Ladies* with Hinge and Brackett, which I loved because it was filmed in front of a live audience so we had the best of both worlds – the exposure of television and the excitement of an audience.

I would get so excited about doing the television shows because there was such a thrill about being in front of the cameras but I was always very tough on myself to make sure I did the best job I possibly could. I always knew my lines inside and out and would arrive hours before filming was due to start.

David and I had been married about two years when I discovered I was pregnant again. It was a total mistake and when I looked at the pregnancy test I was shocked and scared. At that point in my life I didn't want to become a parent to a new child. David and I had everything we wanted with Rebecca. And while part of me would have liked a baby, a big part of me was terrified of becoming seriously ill again in the way I had been with Rebecca.

So, after much discussion, we decided on a termination. Abortion is an awful thing, though, and I found it affected me far more than I had ever thought it would. It wasn't so much that I had feelings of guilt for what we had done but it did really upset me hormonally and afterwards I became very low and weepy for quite a few weeks. In hindsight, I was probably suffering from depression for the first time in my life but I didn't realise it then and just kept trying to pick myself up. Gradually things returned to normal.

David was very supportive during that period when I was feeling low and throughout our marriage he backed me in everything I did. In many ways he was a very exciting person to be around because he introduced me to so many new experiences. And he was a very good man, very honest and very sensible. But as the months passed by, the reality was that I could feel myself becoming bored. I just found him a bit too sensible for me.

Once, I said to him, 'If you had to describe me to someone, how would you do it?'

He replied, 'I'd say you have frizzy hair and a blue anorak.' 'Oh, is that it?' I said. It wasn't quite the romantic or passionate answer I'd been hoping for. 'But that's how I see you,' he went on. 'I just love you for you.'

He did love me. And I loved him, in a way. But the differences in our outlooks were becoming increasingly obvious.

Once David, Rebecca and I had gone to the National Union of Teachers conference in Blackpool. It was freezing cold and all a bit grim but we made the best of it. One evening we were going out with a group of teachers who were staying in the same hotel as us. Before we went out, I sat down to put my makeup on. David said, 'Why are you doing that? You don't have to wear make up and conform to what other people look like.' But I love all that painting and preening for a night out and I didn't want to be like his teacher friends, rolling up with their bedraggled hair, dungarees and woolly jumpers. I tried to say that all his teacher mates were also conforming to a set of standards about what they should wear and how they should look, but he wouldn't have it! We could still have a good laugh together and we were doing OK as a couple but it was becoming obvious to both of us that maybe we were really very different people.

Then one day I was in York city centre and was just stepping into the road to avoid some scaffolding around a building, when I heard a voice shout, 'Beverley. Beverley.'

I turned and looked at this guy doing the building work and although I couldn't immediately place him, I knew I recognised him. 'It's me, Dave Richardson,' he said.

It was Paul's best mate, Richie, from back home in Churwell. I hadn't seen him for years so we went for a cup of coffee and talked about what we'd both been doing. Sure enough, after a while we started talking about Paul. Dave hadn't seen Paul for years either but he'd heard that he had had a difficult time and been seriously ill.

As I walked home, I couldn't stop thinking about Paul and how he was. I told myself I was worried about him because he was still Rebecca's real dad. But maybe there was already more to my concern than just that, I'm not sure.

When I got home, I told David that I was going to try to get in touch with Paul. But, to my shame, I was a lot less honest about exactly what happened next, when I finally came face to face with Paul again.

6
A REUNION AND EMMERDALE

....

'Is Paul there?' I asked, gripping the phone in my hand. I was part desperately hoping he would be and part terrified, all at the same time.

'' 'ang on,' came the reply, in a broad Yorkshire accent.

A couple of minutes later there was another voice at the end of the line. 'Hello,' he said. It was unmistakeable even after more than six years. It was Paul.

'Hi,' I replied. I knew I wouldn't need to say my name.

'Oh my God,' he said slowly.

It had taken ages to track Paul down to a gym in Bradford where he was then spending a lot of time training and working out. I'd gone on to directory enquiries to get a number for one his aunties before finally reaching his brother Andrew, who also explained that Paul had been extremely poorly but was now much better and was spending a lot of time at this gym.

Now Paul was finally on the other end of the phone, it felt weird, but good too. Paul explained what he had been up to for the last few years how he was and trying to put his life back together. He said he was off the drink – the cause of so

81

many of our rows. After about twenty minutes we decided to meet up. I think the idea was just for us to catch up after so long apart, although I'm not really sure, even now, what I was thinking when I agreed to see him again. Paul said if I got the train over from York he'd meet me at Leeds station but then we'd have to go across to Bradford as he had too many bad memories from his old life in Leeds there.

A couple of days later I was sat on the train to Leeds. I'd told David where I was going and he was OK about it. He was such a good, kind man and he accepted it when I said I was simply concerned about Paul for old times' sake.

Somehow, I'd managed to edit out all the bad parts of my life with Paul and was remembering only the good times. I actually felt excited, a bit like all those years ago when I knew I was going to see him on a Friday night at the Methodist Youth Club.

When I got to Leeds Central Station he was already stood there on the platform waiting for me. The years of heavy drinking had aged him and he was losing his hair, which was now cut short to his head. He'd also got really into body-building and his frame had filled out a lot. But to me he still looked just as handsome as he always had, and so many of those familiar feelings for him came flooding back. The strangest thing was it was almost like looking at a carbon copy of Rebecca, with the same nose and deep, dark brown eyes.

We took the train to Bradford, then went to an Indian restaurant called The Agra for a curry, over which we talked and talked and talked. We spoke about when we'd been together and stuff we'd done and we talked about what we had been up to in the years we had been apart.

I felt so sad because of the way that the drinking had driven us apart. Despite everything Paul had done I never doubted that he had really loved me. He'd been my first true love and that is a very hard thing to get out of your system. He could still make me laugh and that night in Bradford was just like the old times. There had always been great chemistry between us and it was still there.

After we'd eaten we went back to Paul's flat. And then we went to bed.

It felt completely natural, as if it was meant to be, and it was good being with him again. I didn't think the spark between us had ever gone and that night proved it.

The next morning, on the train back to York, I felt so guilty. I didn't want to hurt David and I felt really bad for what I'd done but when I got home, rather than tell the truth, I said I'd stayed over at my sister, Stephanie's. I hoped David believed me, as he always saw the good in people. But maybe he didn't, I really don't know for sure.

Certainly I started to become aware that I wasn't a hundred per cent happy in our marriage, although that's not to say I was miserable. I wasn't, and there weren't loads of rows. We were just becoming more conscious of the differences between us.

For the next few weeks Paul and I spoke regularly on the phone. Then he came over to York a few times and we met, drank coffee in little cafés and walked around the city, talking. I knew what I was doing was wrong but I went ahead and did it anyway, it was just one of those mad things. But we never went to bed again.

With each meeting it was becoming more difficult, as I knew in my heart I could never get back with Paul properly and I realised that was what he had started hoping for. It would never work with him again and I'd be stupid to try it. Our lives by then were totally different. I wasn't the girl I'd been at sixteen and to get back with Paul wouldn't just have been a step backwards, it would have been fifty steps backwards. I couldn't have let Rebecca be involved in that kind of life again, I wanted things for her to be totally, totally different and she was my priority.

David was the sensible thing for me to do. I always knew that, just as I always knew that being involved with Paul again was complete stupidity. But at first it was just so exciting. Then I started feeling worse and worse about what I was doing because I was being wrong to David by seeing Paul and I was being wrong to Paul too because I was letting him think he could have something that he never could.

One day, Paul said I was beginning to break his heart all over again because we were apart when he wanted us to be together. It was then I knew I had to put a stop to it. We were sitting in a coffee shop in York and I said it would probably be best if we didn't see each other any more. I think the spark between us was still there but I had to do the sensible thing and walk away. I could see he was very hurt but I think even he realised that it was the right thing to do.

I didn't see him again for another ten years until one day he asked Rebecca to meet him and I went along with her. But by then any feelings I'd had for Paul had died. Maybe I'd needed that brief reunion with him to lay them finally to rest.

After I finished things with Paul I really tried to focus on making my marriage to David work although deep down I knew that it probably wouldn't. We were just too different. And the fling with Paul had made me realise I was looking for something more in life, even if maybe I would never find it.

As the years went past David and I became more like brother and sister than husband and wife. We got on brilliantly well but I felt that there was no spark. Then, after we'd been married about six years, we decided to move back to Leeds. Both our mums were still there and we wanted to be closer to family. But when we went back, we found separate places to live. It sounds odd really, as there was no shouting and screaming or big drama but we knew the marriage was over. It had just fizzled out.

It took a little while to fully run its course, though. We stayed the very best of friends and missed each other terribly while we were living apart. David was still seeing Rebecca a lot and soon he was coming over for all his meals, even breakfast. So we moved back in together and tried to give things another go, but the spark still wasn't really there and after a while we went back to being on our own again. We had the same social circle though and remained mates.

David and I still get on well and he keeps in regular touch with Rebecca, even though we don't see him much because he is happily remarried and living in Singapore. I know that if I were ever in dire trouble I could phone David and he would be there for me. He is a truly good man. Ultimately he deserved better than me.

For a time, then, there was me, Rebecca, Mum, Stephanie and Nans and we did everything together. We were a family of strong women and we were very, very close. Rebecca and I were living in Headingley, in the north of Leeds, and Mum and Steph were a few miles away in Gildersome. We'd see each other almost every day and at weekends it would be all the time. Steph was still my best friend as well as my sister and she was incredibly supportive.

Mum and Nans were still struggling without Dad and Grandad around. They missed them dreadfully, we all did. Christmases could be really weird. As kids, Stephanie and I had had some amazing Christmases, with enormous Santa sacks full of pressies. There was always so much laughter in our house. After Grandad and Dad died, when Rebecca was still little, for years it felt like Mum and Nans just took it in turns to cry, all Christmas. I remember once really telling Mum off, saying, 'I know you're sad but you've got to stop crying. You're doing it in front of my child and it is just not fair.'

I think I'm a lot more understanding now of how low Mum felt for a very long time, but back then I was just interested in protecting Rebecca.

Despite that sadness, the four generations of us women did have great times together and Mum was fantastic, helping out with Rebecca whenever I had to work.

Work was going really well and I seemed to be getting more and more parts, both on stage and on television. Then around the time we returned to Leeds, I landed a part in *Emmerdale Farm*, as the show was then called. It was the biggest television role I'd yet had and I was delighted to get the part. I played a character called Angie Richards, whose dad owned the fish and chip shop. I was only contracted to do four episodes but the guy who was head of scripts at the time, Tim Vaughan, kept renewing my contract and I stayed for about six months.

We used to film on location in the Yorkshire Dales village of Esholt and there were always lots of fans hanging around and watching what was going on. I was about to start filming one day when I heard some people shouting, 'Beverley, Beverley, we think you're great!' It was the first time I had ever been recognised and it just felt weird that people who I didn't know at all knew exactly who I was. It was a good feeling. I've always believed that the fans are the people who pay us actors' mortgages, which is why I always try to appreciate them and make time for them when they write to me or ask for an autograph.

At that time in *Emmerdale Farm*, the Sugdens were at the centre of the show. Jack Sugden's son was Jackie Merrick, the show's hunk, who got all the girls in the storylines and all the fan mail in real life. And Jackie, who was played by Ian Sharrock, lost his virginity to my character Angie Richards. It was quite a big plot and I had a brilliant time filming it. When the red light went on and the camera started rolling, the thrill was incredible.

On stage you instantly know whether an audience likes you, but on television you don't. It was only weeks after we'd filmed a particular scene, when I would be out shopping in Leeds, that people would recognise me as Angie and start talking about what had happened in that episode. It was strange at first because I'd never imagined it happening to me but then I'd think, 'Oh my God, this is great.' I felt appreciated in the same way as I did on stage, just a bit delayed. In those days they would print the entire cast list in the *Radio Times* and I received letters from people requesting autographs before I'd even appeared on screen. They were the committed *Emmerdale* fans, who wanted the autograph of everyone who had ever appeared in it.

From the first scene that Angie Richards and Jackie Merrick appeared in together there was a brilliant chemistry between Ian Sharrock and me. He was a bit of a hunk at the time and very, very funny. Gradually, if members of the cast were going for dinner after filming, Ian would invite me to come along with people like Clive Hornby, who played Jack Sugden, and his wife Helen Weir who played his on-screen wife, Pat Sugden.

More and more though it would be just Ian and me chatting to each other, and about six weeks before I left *Emmerdale Farm* we started a relationship. There was no real reason for us to keep it a secret but we didn't broadcast it to the cast.

Talent is always a turn-on and Ian was a brilliant actor. He was also romantic and exciting and we made each other laugh all the time. We'd go for dinners or out to the theatre and the whole thing made me feel really alive again. He gave me such a high but I think we both knew it was never going to last. He never met Rebecca, it just wasn't that kind of relationship.

After almost six months I felt I'd had enough in *Emmerdale* because it was still early in my career and there were loads of other parts I wanted the chance to play. I could feel myself getting used to the life on a soap and in some ways it was a bit too easy – I had to make a break. I also felt that if I stayed, other people would be bringing Rebecca up rather than me because I wouldn't be at home enough, and I didn't want that.

It was a big step giving up the regular income and the security that came with that, but I was always convinced there would be other great stuff just around the corner for me. I think I was quite naïve in many ways.

Ian and I brought the relationship to an end when I left *Emmerdale* but we remained friends. Years later we did the panto *Snow White*, at Halifax Civic Theatre but we were just mates by then.

After *Emmerdale* I went back to performing in theatre and

Here I am aged 5, uncharacteristically camera shy . . .

Nans and Grandad.
They were such a
devoted couple

Me with my beloved
Grandad. He always
used to tell me I was
the apple of his eye

Mum with Nans –
two very stylish ladies

Me with Nans in 1995

Mum and Dad
on honeymoon

Cheeky shot of Mum –
look at those legs!

Family trip to
the seaside

Such a poser!

Rebecca as a little girl – she already looks like a star

Here's my Josh. I love his cheeky grin here

There was such great chemistry between me and Charlie from the start

Liz and Jim – I think, deep down, they'll always love each other

The infamous McDonald clan, with my boys Andy (left) and Steve (right)

Sarah Lancashire, who played Raquel, and I behind the bar at the *Rovers Return*

Me with Julie Goodyear and Anne Kirkbride in 1991

that way I was able to see a lot more of Rebecca. If I was performing locally she would come almost every evening with my mum and I loved that.

She even came down to London with me when I had auditions. We'd take the coach because it was cheaper than the train, and chat all the way. Before long we were both going to auditions though because Rebecca had also been bitten by the performing bug.

After being born with a low blood-sugar level, the doctors had also discovered she had congested lungs and they advised me that as soon as she was old enough I should take her to dancing or gymnastics because the exercise would be good for her. She was only three when I first started her at ballet classes and she was younger than all the other girls but she really enjoyed it, right from the start.

She had also inherited my passion for the cinema and television. Around about the time of her first dance class show, the film *Grease* had just come out and Rebecca couldn't get enough of it. She watched it so many times she knew all the songs and the dialogue. And when she took to the stage to perform 'All I Want For Christmas Is My Two Front Teeth,' she did it in the style of Olivia Newton-John in *Grease*. It was hilarious.

After a while she was doing ballet, tap, modern and jazz dancing and she loved them. While we were living in York she was selected to appear in a Christmas Hans Christian Andersen performance at the city's theatre. And soon afterwards she was chosen to be in a stage version of Roald Dahl's *James and the Giant Peach*.

I was so proud when I went to watch her but I never pushed Rebecca into performing. I don't think there is any point in doing that because although it may appear glamorous from the outside, the reality is that it can be a very hard life and unless the child really wants it themselves they will never be able to stick it. The highs in acting may be second to none, but the lows are very, very low.

But I was then about to experience one of the greatest highs in my career when I received a phone call to attend an audition – for *Coronation Street*.

7

FIRST STEPS ON THE STREET

....

Being a northern girl, there was no way I could pass up the opportunity to audition for *Coronation Street*. It was Nans' favourite programme and she had watched it from the very first episode. Back then, there had never been a show like *Coronation Street*, showing the lives of ordinary people in ordinary homes. It was compulsive viewing. Steph and I had always sat down for it as kids, every Monday and Wednesday evening, and I'd grown up watching Ena Sharples and Elsie Tanner. My favourite character was Lucille Hewitt because she was a bit of a teenage tearaway and had a tattoo that Annie Walker went mad about.

So when my agent asked me if I'd like to audition for the role of a woman called June Dewhurst, I was thrilled.

It was 1984, just a year after I'd come out of *Emmerdale Farm* and one of the Corrie casting directors had apparently seen me in that and called my agent. I still didn't want to be in a soap for ever because there were so many other parts I wanted to play, but no one in their right mind would turn down the chance to be in *Coronation Street*.

The pressure was really on when I went for the audition. I wanted the job for myself, of course, but I also desperately wanted it for Mum, Nans and Steph. For them it would be the biggest thing I had ever done and to actually watch me in the country's number one show would be amazing.

When I turned up at the reception desk at Granada Studios I immediately saw all the other women auditioning for the part of June Dewhurst and started to panic. After waiting for a while we were sent in groups of three to a corridor upstairs where we were given a script and told to familiarise ourselves with it. I was desperately trying to read the script but at the same time I couldn't help but keep looking at all the other women up for the part, thinking, 'Oh that one over there looks good,' or 'Oh, she's got jeans on, maybe I should have worn jeans,' or 'Maybe I should have straightened my hair after all.'

Then, one at a time, we went into the office to read the script in front of the show director, the producer and a casting director called Judy Hayfield. It was Judy who'd seen me in *Emmerdale Farm* and also on stage in *Billy Liar* at Harrogate Theatre.

As soon as I read the part of June, I knew I really wanted it because she obviously made an impact in the street very quickly and was a really funny character. But at the end of the audition all they said to me was, 'Thanks very much, we'll let you know.' I felt it had gone well, though of course I had no idea whether I'd get the part. But when I walked in my front door there was already a message on the answering machine. It was *Coronation Street* – and they wanted me!

I immediately rang Mum and then Nans and they were both screaming with excitement. It was amazing.

June Dewhurst and her husband Gary were a new couple to the Street who were a bit common and rather flash (in

Coronation Street terms!) and who led Brian Tilsley astray after becoming friends with him and Gail. John Bowler, who is now PC Roger Valentine in *The Bill*, played my husband, and he was brilliant to work with.

My first day on set was absolutely terrifying. All of a sudden I was surrounded by all these legends of the show that I had grown up watching. All I could think was, 'Beverley, do *not* call them by their character name, *do not* call them by their character name . . .' because like everyone else in the country that was how I knew them. I was desperate not to come across as unprofessional in any way but it was very hard not to be intimidated by it all.

When I first saw Julie Goodyear, she blew me away, absolutely blew me away. She didn't have her Bet Lynch hair, makeup and clothes on because it was just a rehearsal day and I couldn't believe how gorgeous she was and how young she looked without them. She was a huge star then and seemed way out of my league.

The first person to speak to me on set was Bill Tarmey who plays Jack Duckworth. 'Hello darling, how are you?' he said. I couldn't believe he was talking to me! He was so kind then and always has been, ever since.

In those days we did rehearsals all day every Monday and Tuesday. There was a huge rehearsal room where we did what we call 'blocking', which means there is no actual set but the rooms and furniture are all marked out on the floor with sticky tape and you practise your scenes like that.

We'd wait to go into the rehearsal room in a long, oblong green room, which had a dividing wall down the centre of it. The right-hand side of the room was divided up into individual cubicles with fabric-covered partitions, each with their own desk and chair. These were reserved for the long-standing members of the cast. The left-hand side of the room was open-plan with sofas, armchairs and a small kitchen area and was used by all the other actors who were newer to the Street.

Every time one of the permanent actors wanted to make themselves a cup of tea in the kitchenette or go to the loo they had to walk past the rest of us. John and I spent hours watching them walk past and saying, 'Oh look, there's so and so. And look who's over there!' It really was quite an experience. It was a tremendously happy atmosphere and everyone was incredibly friendly although it was a bit overwhelming, too.

Then at five to two on a Wednesday afternoon we had a tech run where we would run through the entire two episodes we were due to film that week, starting with what the viewers would see at half past seven on a Monday right through to the last scene on a Wednesday at eight o'clock.

The first time we did that, I'd never been as terrified in all my life. All the writers, directors, production crew, casting directors, costume department, makeup team and other members of the cast were there. In fact it seemed everyone from the whole show would be watching. And as soon as I or anyone else started acting there would be all these people madly scribbling things down in their notebooks. They were probably making notes about costume, camera angles and lighting but all I could think at the time was that they must be writing, 'She is total rubbish'. I spent the entire time thinking, 'I hope they think I'm good. I hope they're liking this.'

Then after all that rehearsing we would finally film the shows on a Thursday and Friday. It was only then that I saw the rest of the cast in costume and makeup and they suddenly came to life as the characters I knew and loved. Earlier in the week they'd just been wearing their own clothes but to then see Bet Lynch in her leopard skin and with her hair piled high and full slap on, it was amazing. Everywhere I looked I was surrounded by television legends: Rita, Betty, Mike Baldwin, Ken Barlow and all the rest. It was incredible but also very daunting. A lot of my scenes were with Helen Worth and Chris Quentin who played Gail and Brian and they were lovely, they were so helpful and friendly and that made things a lot easier.

It was also only when we started filming that we would really go on to the set and that was scary too. The most difficult thing of all was going into the Rovers Return for the first time. The set seemed so familiar in one way because I'd seen it a million times on telly at home, but being on the other side of the camera, it looked very different. As I walked through the pub door my body temperature seemed to shoot up about ten degrees from the sheer thrill of being in such an iconic place. I was thinking, 'Oh my God, I've been watching this room since I was a little girl and now I am here.'

Nowadays there isn't time for the rehearsal days because we have so many more episodes to film and as a result, new cast members coming in to the show are often introduced to everyone already in costume and makeup, which must make it far harder for them. And sometimes they might meet actors they are playing opposite just two minutes before shooting starts.

June and Gary Dewhurst were only initially supposed to stay for six episodes but the characters worked well and John and I ended up being there for about six weeks. I think the scriptwriters might have written for us for longer if John and I had wanted to stay but by then we had both decided we wanted to go. John's wife was in London and I had Rebecca to think about and was still desperate to try other parts in television and on stage.

Around this time, Rebecca's acting career was also taking off. She had been spotted in a couple of the children's theatre shows she had done and was asked to audition for a kids' programme at Yorkshire Television. I didn't push her into anything but asked her if she fancied going along and she said she did. She got the job and a few months later they asked for her again, to appear in quite a big role in a drama about the miners strike called *Scab*.

Someone at the BBC saw that and asked for her to audition for a drama with Daniel Day-Lewis. He played a doctor and Rebecca was his patient, and had to have a tracheotomy. It was a bit weird because she had to have loads of makeup put on her and they built a false neck around hers, which was cut into when Daniel Day-Lewis was performing the tracheotomy. I took her down to the BBC in London and she had to lay absolutely still on a table for ages while they made this false neck. I was a bit worried about her and was saying, 'Rebecca, are you OK? You must tell me if you want to move.' I didn't ever want her to feel under pressure. But Rebecca just said to me, 'Mum, I love it. I feel like Michael Jackson in *Thriller*.'

A few months after that she was asked to play the young Mary Bell in a drama about the killer's life with Joanne Whalley playing the older Mary. It was a massive role and Rebecca was earning more money than me, which was weird. I stashed it away for her for a rainy day.

Rebecca loved acting but we never had the big, 'Do you want to be an actress for the rest of your life?' conversation. It was simply that she kept being offered roles and I'd say, 'Do you want this job?' or 'Do you not want this job?' Usually she would say, 'Yes'. The work just kept rolling in for her but she was also able to carry on with her schooling at the same time, which was great.

It was while she was at school in Leeds that Rebecca made friends with another little girl called Melanie Brown. They did the same dancing classes together and went on to Intake High School, which was a comprehensive in Leeds that also offered performing arts courses. Of course, we didn't realise then that little Melanie Brown would grow up to become Scary Spice, or Mel B. Rebecca and Mel are still friends now.

I was lucky that work kept rolling for me too and over the next few years I travelled around the country for theatre roles, although I did try to stay as close to home as possible to be with Rebecca.

I was also developing a second career as a fitness instructor, which I absolutely loved. I had always been sporty at school and was on the hockey, netball and swimming teams as well as doing gymnastics and cross-country running. But it was only after the car crash, soon after my dad died, that I really became interested in fitness. Not only had I broken my leg in three places, I had also done serious damage to my ligaments and tendons, which the doctors thought might actually be more debilitating in the long term and could leave me with a permanent limp.

I was put in contact with an amazing physiotherapist at Leeds General Infirmary who did hours and hours of work to rebuild the ligaments in my leg. And it was while she was treating me that she taught me which exercises could benefit different muscle groups around the body. I found it fascinating.

I loved doing the exercises the physio gave me, and as my fitness improved I just wanted to do more and more. Around the same time, Jane Fonda was becoming really popular and introducing millions of women to the benefits of exercise and aerobics. It became a huge craze.

Once my leg was strong enough I started attending high-impact aerobic classes. It was the era of 'go for the burn', which we now know you shouldn't actually do with certain muscles in the body, but people didn't realise that then. I just found it incredible that you could work one muscle individually, then work another muscle, with the most incredible effects. I loved it then and I still love it now.

While I had been working at the Body Shop in York I had become really good friends with a colleague called Fiona Butler. So when she set up her own fitness studio, I'd go along to classes there to support her. And that's when I decided I wanted to become a fitness teacher myself.

I studied really hard and attained qualifications in fitness training, which meant I was qualified to take my own classes at Fiona's studio. Quite soon I was teaching most days of the week and I have continued almost non-stop ever since.

I think I have a natural aptitude for fitness but you have to have an even greater aptitude to give someone else the desire to get fit. But if you are a good teacher you can get someone excited about getting fit and you really can change lives. It has always amazed me that you can devise exercises that make people feel not just physically better, but mentally better too.

I call what I do in my classes 'chiselling' and it's a combination of all forms of exercise to work every major muscle group from the neck right the way down to the toes. I never do the same routine twice so if a woman comes to my classes several times a week, each lesson will be totally different. I couldn't think of anything worse than being in a class and knowing what exercise was coming up next. In my classes even I don't know what's coming up next! The greatest compliment I'm ever paid is when students tell me they never look at the clock during a lesson because they're never bored.

There has always been a great social aspect to my classes too. I like to go for a coffee with my students at the end of the class and I find that the quicker I get to know them, the quicker I can design a programme that suits their life and helps them achieve whatever it is they are aiming for. It sounds big-headed, but I know I am very good at it. I think that must be because I really do love it.

A lot of women have changed their lives massively as a result of my classes. Almost everyone who has ever attended has lost weight, although I'm not really into the idea of jumping on and off the scales and put more focus on inch loss. Looking and feeling fitter gives women a massive boost to their self-esteem and with that renewed confidence they are then able to sort out other areas of their lives that have been making them unhappy. So I have to admit I've probably caused a fair number of divorces where women who've been stuck in unhappy relationships for a long time have finally found the confidence to walk away.

When I was living back in Leeds after splitting with David I was teaching up to twenty-six classes a week at two different gyms in Leeds and another in the nearby town of Pudsey. The classes were really popular and soon I was doing morning and evening classes every Monday, Wednesday and Friday in Pudsey.

When Rebecca wasn't at school she'd come with me and we'd go for a coffee with the women from my class after the lesson had finished. We'd have a great laugh altogether. As the weeks passed, I couldn't help but notice that every time I walked into the café at the sports club in Pudsey there would be the same young-looking guy standing near the counter or just hanging around the reception area.

'I think he's got his eye on you, Bev,' the women in my class would say, taking the mickey. I was having none of it. I was thirty and he looked barely out of his teens. But week after week, every time I went into the sports club, he'd be there.

One evening Rebecca was with me in the café. She wasn't even a teenager at the time but she was old enough to see what was going on. 'Mum, he fancies you, that man fancies you,' Rebecca giggled.

'Well, he's got no chance,' I replied. To be honest, deep down I did think he was good-looking and I could sense the attraction between us but I was also determined I was never, ever getting involved with another guy ever again. I felt very young to already have two failed marriages behind me and I certainly didn't want another. From now on it was just Rebecca and me. That was it.

But the baby-faced guy in the bar had other ideas. His name was Steven Callard.

Steven was twenty-two – eight years younger than me – and still lived with his mum and dad just around the corner from the sports club where I taught. He was a very traditional Yorkshireman and worked in a local warehouse.

After a few weeks we started chatting, and we had a laugh together at a Children In Need party at the club one night, but I was still not interested in getting romantically involved.

'Do you want to go out for a drink?' he asked me one evening. But I couldn't. I explained I was divorced and my daughter was my priority. We talked a lot though and really got on.

Then one night I had an argument with a guy who worked at the club. He was a great bloke but I was unhappy that the room where I was holding my classes wasn't as clean as it should have been. I couldn't drive at that time so he would usually run me home but that night I said, 'We've just had a huge row with George, I can't sit in a car with you now, I'll call a cab instead.'

Steve overheard what I'd said. 'I'll run you home,' he offered. It was late and I was tired so I agreed. We had to walk round to his house to fetch his car and when we got there he invited me in for a coffee. We sat down and talked and talked for ages before he drove me home.

I did think he seemed really nice but he told me he had a fiancée, so now I was absolutely determined not to get involved with him. I refused to have anything to do with him if he was set to get married.

The weeks rolled by and he kept asking me out, and I kept refusing. Apart from the age gap and his engagement I was also determined I wouldn't bring another man into Rebecca's life unless it was going to be serious.

Then one day Steve came up to me at the club and said, 'I'm not engaged any more. I've ended it.'

'I hope you haven't done that because of me,' I replied.

'Well yeah, I have actually,' he said. 'You said you wouldn't go for a drink if I was engaged, so I'm not engaged now.'

But I still wouldn't go out with him, it felt too soon. It went on like that for another couple of months until finally I gave in and agreed.

I knew there was definitely a chemistry between. Most definitely. But I'd tried to fight it because I'd had two divorces and because he seemed way too young. I thought my mother would have a fit. It was just madness.

In some ways Steve reminded me of Paul but in other ways he was totally different to anyone I'd ever met before. He flattered me so much and made me feel like the most important person in the whole world. He had a brilliant sense of humour and was fantastic with Rebecca even though he had a sister a year younger than her. I kept saying, 'This can't work, it's ridiculous having this age gap and my having a daughter.' But he wouldn't have it. 'It can work,' he'd say. 'It can, it can, it can. It will.' And it did, for quite a long time.

Steve said he fell for me the first day he saw me. I couldn't say that happened to me but I loved the way he didn't accept that I kept saying 'No' and he was so persistent.

It was a very passionate relationship at the beginning and very romantic. We'd go out for dinners or he would take Rebecca and me out and we'd have great times.

At first his mum Sandra and dad Hughie were worried sick about what he was getting up to with this twice-divorced actress and single mum. But Steve's parents were fantastic people. Sandra used to make the most amazing Sunday dinners and Rebecca and I would be invited round too. One day, when I knew things were getting more serious between Steve and me, I was doing the washing up with his mum after Sunday dinner and I said to her, 'Sandra, do you disapprove of me because I'm older and I'm an actress?' They were such down to earth people that I was sure they must have been thinking, 'What does she want with our son?' But Sandra just said, 'No, I don't disapprove of you. I really like you because you make my son happy.'

Rebecca and I spent loads of time with Steve, his parents and his two brothers and sister. Rebecca and his sister Angela became good friends.

We'd only been together a couple of months when Steve first asked me to marry him but I couldn't agree. I really loved him but I was terrified of failing at marriage for a third time. So instead Steve, Rebecca and I moved in together into a little rented house in Pudsey. It was a very happy time and there was a lot of laughter in our house. Rebecca and Steve got on well and I was truly happy.

We'd been living together about a year when my doctor advised me to come off the Pill for a while because it had been making me feel a bit rough. I had no desire to get pregnant again though so Steve and I were going to use different contraception. Except one night we didn't. Afterwards, I thought, 'I bet I'm pregnant.' And I was.

8

A MUM AND MARRIAGE AGAIN

....

My first reaction when I saw the 'positive' line on the pregnancy test was one of horror. I'd been so ill with Rebecca – I could have died – and the thought of going through all that again was terrifying.

I'd bought the pregnancy test on the way to a rehearsal for a play and as soon as I got to the theatre where I was working I rang Steve and told him the news. He was shocked too but I could tell he was secretly quite pleased.

I was by then madly in love with Steve and he was with me. He wanted a child, and part of me desperately wanted another baby, too. But I was also petrified about getting seriously ill again. The doctors had warned me that pregnancy could kill me so I would be taking a huge risk. There was also Rebecca to consider – it didn't seem fair on her if I was to be in hospital for the next nine months, or even worse, if I was putting my life in danger.

Steve and I agonised for days over what to do. In the first couple of weeks my sickness didn't seem as bad as it had been with Rebecca. I crossed my fingers that the hyperemesis wouldn't recur and we decided to go ahead with the pregnancy.

I went round to see Mum to tell her the news.

'Oh my God, you're not keeping it are you?' Mum said when I told her I was expecting.

Only a mum could say that and it must sound very harsh of her but she'd been worried sick about how ill I was the first time and I understood her concerns. But by then there was no way I would change my mind.

'Yes, we are keeping it,' I replied. 'We've thought about it long and hard and we are.'

'But you nearly died last time,' Mum said. 'We can't go through that again. You mustn't, you mustn't.'

When we told Rebecca she was to become a big sister she had very mixed feelings. She was thirteen by then and the thought of a new baby arriving on the scene must have been daunting. But Steve and I were already desperately excited about the new arrival and put any concerns out of our minds. Then, no sooner had we decided to go ahead with the pregnancy, than the hyperemesis returned.

It was really extreme, all over again. I was being violently sick all day and all night. I had to give up my fitness classes, couldn't look after Rebecca properly and could barely get out of bed. It was horrific. And even though Rebecca had been born a healthy weight despite my condition, there was still the fear that this baby might not be so strong.

The sickness probably wasn't quite as bad as when I was pregnant with Rebecca but it was still very serious. Again I was in and out of hospital every few weeks, being drip fed because it was the only way they could get any nutrients into my body and prevent me from becoming dehydrated. My weight plunged and I felt horribly weak. Steve was brilliant and took over looking after the house and Rebecca as well as me.

Despite the illness, Steve and I had decided to marry before our baby was born. Steve had been asking me ever since we'd got together and now I felt it was the right thing to do. This time I really hoped I was marrying the man I would grow old with. I'd look at Steve's mum and dad, who seemed such lovely people with such a strong marriage, and I dreamed of Steve and me being like them in the future.

We married in January 1989 in my third register-office wedding. This time I wore a cream suit and Rebecca was my bridesmaid. It was a lovely simple ceremony only marred by my feeling nauseous all day long. I must be one of the few brides to have been sick throughout her wedding day.

Mum, Steph and Nans were there to support me and they all liked Steve, although I'm sure Mum thought I was turning into Liz Taylor with so many husbands! Afterwards we had a reception for family and a few friends at Steve's parents' house and it was a great day.

Then the three of us settled down to family life at number 22 Woodland Terrace in Pudsey and awaited the arrival of the baby.

Steve got a new job in Leeds, working for a chain of toy shops called Children's World. The pay wasn't great and with me unable to work, money was very tight. It was 1989 and interest rates were sky high, meaning the mortgage on our small, stone, terraced cottage in Pudsey had tripled.

My sickness continued and I was desperately skinny again from not being able to keep food down. When I had Rebecca I'd been 2 pounds under six stone; this time I was just 2 pounds over six stone when I gave birth.

Josh was born on 2 May 1989. Rebecca and Steve were both with me for the labour, which was wonderful. For years it had been just Rebecca and me together and we were incredibly close, but having found a whole new family in the Callards and with a new baby on the scene, I was determined that Rebecca should never feel pushed out. I didn't want her to find out she had a new brother or sister over the telephone. So Rebecca came with Steve and me to the hospital when I was going into labour.

'If at any point you don't feel happy about being here that's absolutely fine, you can leave,' I told her.

But she stayed for the whole thing. When the contractions came she was holding my hand and saying, 'Squeeze me, Mum, squeeze me.'

I had an epidural so the labour wasn't too bad and Rebecca was the first to hold baby Josh, which was wonderful.

Josh weighed in at 6 pounds 4 ounces so again, despite all the doctors' concerns that the child might become malnourished in the womb, I had a healthy baby. After years of thinking I would never have a second child, I was over the moon to have him. All three of us were crying with happiness as we looked at little Josh. It was just amazing and Steve was the proudest father you could imagine. Thankfully, as with Rebecca, almost the moment I gave birth, that awful sense of nausea disappeared.

We returned home to Woodland Terrace a very happy family. Josh was a very, very cute baby. The only difficulty we had at first was with his feeding. I couldn't breastfeed because I'd lost so much weight during pregnancy and it became clear he was allergic to formula milk because he was being so sick after every feed and failing to gain weight. Once we got him onto soya milk, though, he was fine and was soon sleeping really well. But Josh was only two or three weeks old when

I got my first glimpse of what the future might hold for my marriage.

The company Steve was working for, Children's World, was about to have its grand opening in Leeds. To mark the occasion they were throwing a big party at the Queen's Hotel in the city centre one Friday evening. Sandra and Hughie had said they would babysit so I could go with Steve and I was excited at the thought of a big night out after so many months of feeling lousy.

Then on the Friday teatime, Steve came home to change for the party and announced that partners weren't invited after all, it was for staff only.

'Oh, oh all right then,' I thought. 'But you're telling me a couple of hours beforehand, that's not very nice.'

I cancelled Sandra babysitting and stayed in on my own while Steve went off to the party. When he wasn't home by midnight I wasn't particularly worried. But when he hadn't appeared by two o'clock in the morning I was starting to panic. It was before most people had mobile phones so I couldn't even call and say, 'Where they hell are you?' When another hour rolled by and there was still no sign of him I called the Queen's Hotel but with no success. Then I rang Hughie and Sandra but they hadn't heard anything either. I couldn't work out what was going on, I thought he must have had an accident.

The next morning I kept ringing Children's World over and over again until finally they put Steve on the phone.

'What happened?' I asked, more shocked than angry at that point.

'I just got really drunk and didn't make it home,' he said.

Now I knew he wasn't laying dead in a ditch somewhere I was seething with him. I've got a vile temper when I lose it and I certainly lost it with him then.

'What do you mean you didn't come home?' I screamed. 'I've got a two-week-old baby here. This is outrageous.'

'I can't talk, I'm at work,' Steve said. 'I'll explain when I come home.'

But I wasn't having any of that.

'If you don't come home right now then I will be coming straight round to that store and I will wreck the whole place,' I yelled. And boy, did I mean it!

I don't know what he must have said to his boss but Steve came straight home and we had the biggest row you can imagine. Sandra and Hughie had taken Rebecca and Josh for me so there was just the two of us at home.

Oh my God, it was a terrible fight. I kept asking if he had been up to something with a woman but he totally denied it. We were both screaming at each other. I wouldn't let it drop though – I was boiling with rage. Steve walked out the house and I chased him down the road.

I admit I'm not always the easiest person in the world to live with because I can be very demanding, but I felt I didn't deserve what he had done to me that night. The most upsetting thing of all was that we'd just had a baby and he had disappeared for an entire night without telling me where he had gone. I felt that he didn't care about me. It all just seemed so out of character, or certainly out of the character that I knew. I knew Steve liked a drink, but he would only go on the occasional big session. And up until then he had never done anything like this and had always appeared to completely adore me. Even when we were screaming at each other that day he was still saying he adored me.

That was the first big row we'd ever had and it all came as a bit of a shock to me.

It was hours before Steve returned to the house after I'd chased him down the street, and things were strained between us for weeks before they gradually returned to normal. But with our mortgage repayments spiralling ever higher we were getting more and more worried about money. Steve wasn't earning much and he didn't like working at Children's World so it was vital that I got back to work as quickly as possible.

Josh was just a few weeks old when I went back to teaching fitness classes. I also got a receptionist's job at weekends in an estate agent's office called Local Properties. On top of that I worked Wednesdays in a friend's clothes shop. When Local Properties asked me to start going in during the week too, I had to take it – we needed the money. They let me take Josh with me and they were lovely people but I was working seven days a week and it was exhausting.

Then, just as I was battling to cope with a new baby, a teenage daughter and three different jobs while also trying to regain all the weight I'd lost during pregnancy, I got an incredibly lucky break.

One day the phone rang. It was my then agent, who explained that Mervyn Watson, who had been the producer of *Coronation Street* when I was playing June Dewhurst, had left the show but recently returned. And he wanted me to audition for the role of a new Street regular, Liz McDonald.

'So are you interested?' asked my agent. 'The thing is they want someone who will be in it for quite a long time.'

'Oh yes, I'm definitely interested,' I said.

I put the phone down and thought, 'Thank God. We so need the money.'

Steve came with me a couple of days later when I went over

to Manchester for the audition while Sandra looked after Josh and Rebecca.

I felt the reading for the part went well and by the time I got home that evening there was an answering-machine message for me, saying they wanted me to go back and read with the people they had shortlisted for the role of Liz's screen husband, Jim. By this point they had devised the characters of the new family but they still weren't certain whether Jim would be a Scottish or an Irish McDonald.

When I returned to Granada three days later there were four possible Lizs and four possible Jims waiting to read the lines with each other. I knew instantly that Charlie Lawson would get the job of Jim because he was just so charismatic. When I walked into the office he was already there and as he started talking to me I could barely understand what he was saying because of his broad Belfast accent.

'So are you good for the craic?' he said to me. I thought, 'Oh my God, he's a drug addict!' I'd never met anyone who talked quite like that before. Then, while we were waiting to be called in to read our parts together, Charlie suddenly turned to me and said, 'What size are your feet?'

'Er, about two and a half to three,' I replied.

'How the f*** to do you stay upright?' he said, booming with laughter.

He was so funny and I thought, 'He is going to be so good. I so hope I get the job with him.'

We were called in to read in front of Mervyn Watson, a director called Ian White and a casting director called James Baine. As soon as we started reading our parts it felt right. Charlie is a fantastic actor and we just clicked. Afterwards Mervyn Watson called me into his office. 'How do you fancy being in *Coronation Street* for the next ten years?' he said.

'Absolutely yes,' I replied. 'Yes! Yes! YES!'

I couldn't really celebrate yet because nothing was definite until I got the call from my agent. For the next couple of days every time the phone rang I'd be thinking, 'Oh my God is this it?' But then it would be Mum or Stephanie saying, 'Have you heard anything?' I'd be desperately trying to get them off the line as quickly as possible in case my agent was trying to get through, and thinking that if he couldn't then they might give the part to someone who answered their phone immediately instead.

'I'll call you as soon as I know,' I kept telling Mum and Steph. They were as excited as I was.

When the phone call to say I'd got the part finally came, I was just over the moon. And so were Steve, Mum, Steph, Rebecca, Hughie and Sandra. We were all just thrilled to bits. I was told that the contract would be for a year and that the McDonalds were the first people to go into the show on an annual contract. I was bursting with pride.

I was due to start filming in September when Josh was still only four months old so it was going to be very hard work. I'd have to commute every day from Pudsey on the train as I didn't drive but I didn't want us to move to Manchester then as Rebecca had her GCSEs coming up and I didn't want to disrupt her schooling.

I knew that all the difficulties would be worth it. Financially it solved all our problems and for an actress it was a dream job.

9

THE MCDONALDS ARRIVE

....

Liz McDonald was first seen teetering down Coronation Street, wearing skin-tight ski pants and a black cowl-neck jumper, on 27 October 1989. She knocked on the door of number 11, Alf and Audrey Roberts' house, which she had come to view as a possible home for her family. It was to be an incredible new beginning for both Liz and me.

In the show, Liz was the first McDonald to arrive in Weatherfield. Her husband Jim was about to leave his post as a sergeant in the army and her fifteen-year-old twin sons, Steve and Andy, were staying with her mother.

The background to the family was that Liz Jayne McDonald, who was originally from the north, had fallen pregnant by Jim at just sixteen. After getting married she'd followed her husband around, living in army accommodation and bringing up the boys pretty much single-handed. Now she was thirty-one and preparing for a life on Civvy Street with Jim, a fiery Ulsterman.

On our first day, Charlie and I went into hair and makeup together. Charlie was getting a classic short army haircut. The makeup lady looked at my mass of curls, trying to decide what to do with them. I think she must have thought I had a perm and she'd be able to do all sort of nice things with it but when she picked up a brush and ran it through my hair, all the curls stuck straight up. I was left with one section totally frizzed out, and nothing would make it go down again. I had to keep it like that for weeks for continuity. So there was my big first moment on *Coronation Street* and I looked awful!

After filming that first scene at the door of number 11, I was in the green room and Brian Mosley, who played Alf Roberts, was chatting to me.

'How long are you here for?' he asked me. I told him the contract was for a year.

'Oh, do you buy our house then?' he said.

'Yeah,' I replied, not knowing then that the cast are generally the last to know what is going to happen to their characters.

'Oh, right,' Brian said. He must have wondered what on earth was about to happen to Alf and whether he was going to get killed off but fortunately it was only that he and Audrey were to move to a posh semi in Grasmere Drive.

Lots of my scenes in the first few weeks were with Brian Mosley and Sue Nicholls who plays Audrey and they were both wonderful, showing me where the camera would be and the best place to stand.

With our one-year contracts, Charlie Lawson and I both knew we really had to make our characters work within that time if we were to stay on the Street. Viewers find it hard to warm to new characters and every other complete family that had been introduced into *Coronation Street* in the past had failed. In those days there were very few new characters at all compared with now. I think the last new cast member before us was Curly Watts.

We were determined our family would work, but for that we had to seem believable to the viewers, so Charlie and I spent ages thinking about how we would play our characters. I even went to meet army wives to talk to them about what it was like being married to a serviceman and living in army accommodation. These are women who are only ever in a place because of their men and so you might think they are subservient. But in fact the women I met were the total opposite. They were strong, feisty women who were quite competitive with each other. I thought, 'Right, this is what I have got to get into Liz.'

One of the best bits of advice I was ever given was by Brian Mills, who directed *Coronation Street* for years. He could be quite scary if he was in a bad mood but he was brilliant too.

'Beverley, I am going to tell you something and I want you never to forget this,' he told me. 'Normally as an actor you get the text and you have your character and that's that, but this job is very different because you can inspire the writers. The show is ongoing so the writers will watch what you do and that will affect the way they write for your character.'

An actor in the show will never change the dialogue they are given because the writer has given it their all to create it. But there are fifty ways to say any one line and that is what you have to work with to develop your character.

In the beginning, Jim was written as a very strong, hard-drinking Irishman who was definitely the boss in the marriage, whereas Liz was a 'Yes Jim, no Jim' character. But Charlie and I thought this was slightly too stereotypical and we wanted to give Liz more strength. She'd been bringing up the boys on her own most of the time since she was sixteen, so she must have had true grit. We also wanted to give Jim a vulnerability that would make him more real and interesting for the viewers.

So once we had our scripts for the weeks ahead Charlie and I would meet up or spend hours on the phone talking about how we were going to play our characters to make them as realistic as possible. We did things like make sure Jim never left the house without giving Liz a peck on the cheek – after all this was a couple who'd been together sixteen years. And we'd say things like, 'Maybe Jim could look a bit upset when Liz says that.' As we couldn't change the dialogue it all had to be done through facial expressions and how we moved. We had to make it seem as though Jim and Liz had been together for a very long time, even though Charlie and I had only just met.

Once Charlie and I were established, we were then asked to go along to auditions to select our twin sons. We had to do improvisation sessions with twelve teenage boys who'd already got through the first two rounds of auditions. We all met in a big rehearsal room: me, Charlie, Mervyn Watson the producer, the casting director James Baine, a couple of directors and one of the writers. Then, after doing the scenes, we each wrote down which boys we would like. Every single one of us wrote down the same names – Simon Gregson, who became Steve, and Nick Cochrane, who became Andy. There were no arguments – we all knew who fitted as Liz and Jim's sons.

In the show the two boys are very different characters. Steve takes after Liz in that he has a self-destructive element that means that just as he is about to get mega-happiness, he does something stupid and blows it. Andy takes after his father. Just as Jim had the grit and determination to become a soldier, he has the determination to do well academically.

Once the boys arrived on set we worked really hard all over again to make sure their relationship with their parents and as brothers appeared realistic. They too would never leave the house without giving their mum a kiss and almost instinctively they picked up mannerisms from each other that made them seem like real brothers.

The boys were quite modern characters for the Street. They were always getting into trouble, particularly Steve. There was the time they both nicked a JCB then drove it through Alf Roberts' shop window and another time when Steve got caught selling stolen car radios.

Off screen, the relationship between the four of us became very strong. I was always the boring one who would give them a bollocking, just like a real mum, saying things like, 'You were late today and I'm just not having it!' And I'd be the one in the green room saying, 'Come on, let's just run through these lines one more time.' Charlie was so laid back though and would say, 'Don't worry. We'll be fine when it gets to the take.' Charlie was much more of a wild influence on the boys! But I think it was good for Simon and Nick that Charlie and I were so different because they learnt both sides of the business.

One day, Mervyn Watson called for me and said, 'Beverley, Nick and Simon are swearing a lot in the green room.'

'Well most actors swear, Mervyn,' I replied.

'I think it might offend some of the older members of the cast,' he went on. 'Can you have a word with them?'

'I'm not their real mum you know Mervyn,' I said. 'I'm trying to build a relationship with these boys because hopefully we're going to be working together for years, so I don't want to be nagging them all the time.'

In the end I did have a word with them but a while later Mervyn sent for me again.

'The boys are smoking and they're only young,' he said. 'Can you talk to them again?'

'No, Mervyn,' I said. 'No. No. No. If I keep nagging them it'll jeopardise the way we work together.'

That was the end of that.

They could be very mischievous though. Once, my script notes said I had to deliver my line then drain my mug of tea. But when I opened my mouth and started drinking the tea I saw this disgusting green slime at the bottom of the mug. I thought I was going to gag but I just about managed to keep it together in front of the cameras. The boys had bought the slime from a joke shop and thought it was hilarious to drop it in my tea.

We all played terrible tricks on Charlie. Both he and his character Jim were Protestants from Belfast but in the next-door set to us lived Ivy Brennan, who was a Catholic. We'd nick pictures of the Pope from Ivy's wall then hang them up on ours so Charlie would walk in, see the picture and choke, 'What's the Pope doing on the wall in the McDonalds' house?'

At one time there was a storyline that Steve McDonald had run away to the Lake District with a young girl. Liz was determined to bring him home and had borrowed Rita's Ford Fiesta to drive up there and find him.

We filmed lots of scenes in the Lake District and then had to shoot a scene in the dark where Liz was driving Steve back down Coronation Street and then parking outside the McDonald's house at number 11.

Simon Gregson and I were sitting in the car just around the corner of the Street waiting for the director to say 'Action'.

We were getting a bit bored and started messing around and rummaging in the glove box, where we found these really funny sunglasses that had a button on them which, when you pressed it, made lights start flashing all round the frames.

'I'm going to wear them,' I giggled to Simon.

'Yeh, yeh, do it,' he replied, egging me on.

The director was called Richard Signy and when he said 'Action', Simon and I suddenly appeared around the corner in the Ford Fiesta with me wearing flashing sunglasses. We couldn't stop giggling.

But of course it was night-time and pitch black and me wearing sunglasses made it very hard to see where I was going. The next thing we heard was a loud crunch. I'd driven the car straight into the post box outside Alf Roberts' corner shop!

Around about that time it was coming up for Nick Cochrane's eighteenth birthday. Charlie and I spent ages thinking about what we could do to mark the occasion – it had to be something special.

After a lot of thought we decided we'd do a bit of a Jeremy Beadle-style prank on him. We got all the cast and crew involved and started a rumour that his character Andy was about to get his first girlfriend.

We told one of the storyliners, Tom Elliott, what we wanted to do and he said: 'Fantastic. Leave it to me.'

A few days later Nick received a script that said:

Andy McDonald is walking down a school corridor where Candice, the cleaner, is mopping the floor, her large rear end sway-ing from side to side. Andy grabs hold of her hand and says: 'I cannot contain myself any longer, I'm in love with you and I want us to run away together.'

Candice then turns around and says: 'I can't, I go to WeightWatchers on a Wednesday!'

Nick was just ecstatic because he thought it was going to be a great storyline and he'd be getting off with some gorgeous girl!

'But it says she's got to go to WeightWatchers,' Simon Gregson said to Nick when he showed him the script in their dressing room (Simon was in on the joke too!).

'Oh mate,' Nick, who was still only seventeen, replied. 'Don't you know anything about women, they're all worried about their weight!'

Me, Charlie, Kev Kennedy and Mike LeVell were outside their dressing room listening to the conversation and killing ourselves with laughter.

For days every time an attractive girl walked past the studios Nick would be saying: 'Do you think she is going to be playing Candice?'

Then one afternoon after we'd finished filming a McDonalds scene they said they wanted Nick to do some publicity stills shots with the actress who would be playing Candice. He was beside himself with excitement.

But we'd persuaded this lovely lady, who was in her sixties and who occasionally appeared in a non-speaking part in the Rovers, to pretend to be Candice.

When she walked into the room she was wearing a yellow crocheted jumper, a turquoise anorak and thick glasses!

Nick took one look at her and his face just dropped – but only for a split second. He is so kind that he hid his disappointment and just said: 'Hiya! Pleased to meet you.'

Then they were making 'Candice' sit on Nick's knee for the publicity shots and kiss him on the cheek – at which point me and Charlie jumped out, shouting 'Happy Birthday Nick'. It was hilarious. The director Brian Mills actually fell off his chair because he was laughing so much. Nick says he'll never forget that present!

As Simon and Nick got older they certainly learnt how to party but it wasn't easy for them growing up in *Coronation Street*. I think it is harder for young men than it is for young women because suddenly they appear on screen and all the girls fancy them because they're on telly and all the boys want to punch them because the girls fancy them. It must be very, very difficult but Simon and Nick have both managed it well.

Charlie Lawson and I became great mates and we still are now even though he isn't in the show at the moment. We couldn't be more different though. I am paranoid about getting anything wrong. If I'm called for a 7.15 start, I'll be there at 6.45. I might be late for everything else in my life, but never work. And I really worry about whether I am doing everything properly. I'd know my lines inside out, which Charlie always joked about. If someone said, 'I don't know this scene,' he'd say, 'Just ask Bev, she's learning next f****** December's!'

So while I was very hard on myself, Charlie was the most laid back guy ever.

I could always tell when Charlie had come into work drunk from the night before and I'd cover up for him so no one else guessed. In one way it was hysterically funny but I did worry that he was going to get into trouble.

When you are filming a scene the producer can watch you on a monitor in his or her office but if Charlie was still a bit drunk in the morning, we'd persuade the vision mixer to fade the producer's screen to black so they wouldn't be able to see what was going on.

Thanks to Charlie's antics, the McDonalds were the first *Coronation Street* characters to appear on *It'll Be Alright on the Night*. We'd filmed a scene one day with Charlie still drunk, and he was so funny like that because he'd be happily drunk rather than falling down drunk. In the storyline, Andy had got a girlfriend and in the scene we were filming he came downstairs into the McDonalds' dining room, all ready for a date. Liz had to say to Andy, 'You smell nice, have you got aftershave on?' And Jim was supposed to say, 'Och, yeah, I suspect there is a woman involved here.' Except it came out as, 'Och, yeah, I suspect there is a vol-au-vent involved here.'

After he'd said the line we just carried on normally for a couple of minutes and then everyone thought, 'Did he just say vol-au-vent?' *Vol-au-vent*? It was hilarious.

Another time, the McDonalds were supposed to be having a massive row (of which there were many) and Jim had to walk around the dining table, behind where I was sitting. But as he did it, he got his shoe caught in my handbag. He was saying, 'Steve, I've told you I won't put up with it. And I won't put up with it because . . . I've just put my foot in your f****** mother's handbag!'

Once, I was in my dressing room early one morning getting ready to film when I heard the most awful noises coming from the dressing room next door, which Charlie shared with Geoffrey Hinsliff who played the cab driver, Don Brennan.

When we arrived on set in the morning we'd be given the key for our dressing rooms and inside our clothes would be laid out for us. I was putting on one of Liz's miniskirts but all I could hear was Charlie stomping around next door, coughing, jumping up and down and shouting, 'What the f*** stupid idea is this?'

Then there was this banging on my door and Charlie saying, 'Can I come in?'

He stood in the doorway wearing a pair of trousers that were pulled tight round his legs and just reached down to his calves.

'I know the f****** McDonalds are skint but this is f****** ridiculous,' he said.

'Charlie,' I replied. 'They're not Jim's clothes. They're Don Brennan's.'

Charlie had got so pissed the night before he'd put the wrong costume on.

Soon after Liz and Jim arrived in the Street we were both given leather jackets but they looked so new and were still so stiff that they squeaked when we walked. We looked like Barbie and Ken! So Charlie got his, rolled it into a ball then jumped up and down on it to make it look more lived in.

It was fantastic fun working with Charlie. He is a great actor and also totally unpredictable. I was constantly thinking, 'How is he going to play this line?', which kept me on my toes. While I knew my lines inside out, Charlie would get by on a wing and a prayer, but it worked between us brilliantly. On screen, it was a very passionate yet volatile relationship. Charlie and I always said that if Liz and Jim had a row it would be incredibly heated, almost violent, but when they made up it would be just as passionate.

I always imagined that Liz would have really tarty underwear. Even if she became a millionaire she wouldn't spend loads of money on clothes. She'd have lots of clothes but they'd all be cheap because she'd be thinking, 'I've got a bargain from Bury market here!' And her underwear would be red and black or shocking pink and maybe one size too small. She would always have a visible panty line and the only person in the world who would find that attractive was Jim McDonald! Because of course Jim was obsessed with Liz and that is what made the excitement.

The first ten years for Liz were all high drama. There was always an undercurrent of violence in the rows she had with Jim, even before she became a victim of domestic abuse. And then, in 1992, Liz gave birth to a baby girl called Katie who was premature and only lived for a couple of hours. Those scenes, written by a guy called Julian Roach, were just amazing and fantastic to act. After he saw the finished episode, Julian wrote me a letter that said, 'When a writer tells an actor that you made him cry, it is not usually a compliment, but you made me cry with your performances.' It was a very kind thing to say.

We were inundated with mail from viewers who were moved by the storyline, but despite the sadness of the episode, there was still a funny side to filming it. The scenes were shot on location in a freezing cold, disused hospital, so I was sitting on a bed, shivering in a nightie and crying my heart out over a Tiny Tears doll wearing a bonnet! I never found crying on demand difficult. Once, a director asked me, 'When you go for a take will you really cry or do you need a tear stick to fake it?' Charlie said, 'Will she really cry? She could fill a f****** bucket.'

In the storyline about baby Katie, Bet came to visit Liz in the hospital with this big bunch of flowers. Liz worked for Bet at the Rovers and she adored her boss. So Bet was supposed to walk up to the hospital bed and say, 'How are you kid? Come on, you can get through this.' But Julie Goodyear was such a joker and she came up to the bed and said, 'How are you kid? Oh, you've got shit down the front of your nightie!' Then she gave me this bouquet of flowers and in the middle of it was a giant cucumber! She was so funny and I was thinking, 'I'll never be able to do these scenes now without laughing.'

I know there have been stories in the past about Julie being difficult to work with and a bit of a prima donna but she was never, ever like that with me. She was fantastic and we became great friends.

Julie was, and still is, an icon. She is a great actress and she taught me so much about camera technique. With each inside scene it is normally 'multiple camera', which means first of all they do a master shot, the wide picture, then they might do a mid-shot with two cameras over the shoulder and then finally a close-up. So if you were doing something like a dead baby storyline you could sob your heart out three times before they even got to the close-up and by that time you'd be spent emotionally. It was Julie who taught me what to do in that situation. She'd say, 'Right, this is your scene Beverley but save your tears for the close-up when you really need them.'

Julie also taught me about lighting and that if maybe you moved just two inches in a different direction you could find your light so much better without putting anyone else in shadow. If other people were giggling or talking nearby she would say, 'Switch your brain off to them and concentrate.'

When Liz got a job behind the bar at the Rovers I was working almost every day with Julie, Roy Barraclough, who played Alec Gilroy, Bill Tarmey who plays Jack and Betty Driver who plays Betty Turpin. Betty is the most amazing actress – she has made that character completely believable. Even now I still do quite a lot of scenes with Betty and I am in complete awe of her. She is ninety this year but her skin is amazing and she has such a happy disposition.

When Liz first got her job as a barmaid it was fantastic because I had the drama of life in the McDonald house then the humour of the Rovers. And it was really important for Liz's character too because that was the first job she had ever had and she was gradually starting to assert her independence from Jim.

Roy Barraclough is one of the funniest people I have ever met. Once, we were filming a scene and he kept making quiet asides and slightly changing his words until we all started laughing. We were going with the scene over and over and over again but each time one of us would start laughing and then we all became hysterical. The director was saying, 'Come on now, we're short of time,' and it was like being in trouble at school but we couldn't stop. In the end they had to break from filming completely until we'd pulled ourselves together. All four of us got a blue memo from Mervyn Watson (blue memos were always about something very important!) saying we had to get it together because we were making everyone get behind in the filming schedules. We really were like naughty kids.

Another time, Julie made me laugh so much that I cried all my makeup off, and I had to drop to my knees behind the bar of the Rovers and hide because I knew Mervyn would be watching us on the monitor in his office.

Then there was the time that Alec had to tell Liz he was leaving her in charge of the pub because he had to rush away as his daughter and son-in-law had been killed in a car accident.

It was a really serious scene but we did take after take because Roy kept laughing and during one close-up he was saying his lines but out of shot he was using a knife to break into a Sooty the Bear charity box sat on the bar of the Rovers!

One of the funniest days was when Jack and Vera had borrowed a motorbike from Jim and gone off on it all dressed up in leathers. Vera was even wearing a leather miniskirt! Liz Dawn, who played Vera Duckworth, is a lovely woman and was amazing to work with. I think Vera and Bet have to be my very favourite *Coronation Street* characters.

In the scene, Jack and Vera were pushing the motorbike back into Coronation Street alongside a police car, because they had just been arrested. It was getting late in the day and we had to film it quickly before the light went. Except, just before we started shooting the scene, the guy playing the policeman said, 'I can't drive!' After a bit of faffing around we sorted that out by getting one of the crew to drive the car but then, when the policeman got to the door of number 11 Coronation Street and said, 'Are you Mr and Mrs McDonald?' we realised the actor had a really bad speech impediment.

He had to say, 'They had no tax, no insurance and were driving the wrong way down a one-way street,' except it sounded like, 'They had no takshhhh, no inshhhhuranchhhh and were driving the wrong way down a one-way shhhhhhreeet.' Kev Kennedy was standing next to me and going, 'Uh-oh!' and then we all started giggling but we didn't want to be cruel to the actor so were desperately trying not to show it. The light was getting worse and worse but we had to shoot the scene a dozen times before we could do it with straight faces. But then we still had to film the inside shots when the policeman came into the McDonalds' house and carried on lecturing us.

By this point we were in hysterics. Bill Tarmey delivered his line then, out of shot, stepped onto the McDonalds' sofa and jumped off the set so he could get out of the room because he was laughing so much.

About eight years later, Bill Tarmey rang up to me one day saying, 'Beverley, you're not going to believe it. He's back!'

'Who's back?' I said.

'The "no takshhhhhhh, no inshhhhhhhuranchhhh" policeman,' he said. 'And I've got to serve him in the Rovers!'

This time the actor was playing a guy in the Rovers and his line was, 'I'm not one to boil me cabbageshhhhhhhhh twice.' And he still spoke exactly the same. What that actor must have thought of us! I hope he didn't think we were bitchy because we're really not, we just couldn't help giggling.

It seemed for a long while that I was never out of big storylines. Liz made such a good impression with the brewery that she was given her own pub, the Queens, which Jim hated. Then he became convinced she was having an affair with a boss from the brewery called Richard Willmore and they split up. And then she really did have a fling with Des Barnes' brother Colin and almost got involved with Des, too.

Scenes at the Queens were filmed inside a real pub called the Pig and Porcupine on Deansgate in Manchester. We'd have to shoot there really early on a Sunday morning and it was always freezing cold but it was a great time for me in the show because I had so many fantastic storylines. And it was a good time for Liz too because she was becoming an independent woman at last.

Throughout all Liz's traumas in *Coronation Street*, her best friend has always been Deirdre. And if Liz wasn't going through some drama then you could guarantee Deirdre was, and Liz would be comforting her.

I think the scenes between Liz and Deirdre are 'proper' *Coronation Street*. In my opinion the strength of the show has always been its women and the characters you most remember are all women; Hilda Ogden, Annie Walker, Elsie Tanner, Bet Lynch and Vera Duckworth. There have been fantastic male actors too but at its heart are strong women and that is why I so love those scenes with Liz and Deirdre just talking.

Anne Kirkbride, who plays Deirdre, and I have been great friends in real life since the very first time we met in rehearsals and just clicked. I was immediately struck by how beautiful she was and how very different she was to Deirdre. In my early days we would go out once a week for a 'Chinese and a chinwag night' and just chat about girlie stuff. But my best mate from *Coronation Street* was always Charlie Lawson. When I started there was a much bigger social life that came with the job and the two of us would go out with a group of people for drinks after we finished work at around seven. Granada Studios used to have its own bar called the Stables and we would go in there, but then that closed and the bar moved across the road to the Old School, which became our new regular stop-off. Often there would be me, Charlie, Johnny Briggs who played Mike Baldwin and Lynn Perrie, who played Ivy Brennan. Lynn was like a stick of dynamite. She was hilarious and a fantastic actress.

Now that we're filming so many more episodes there isn't as much time for going out. Some of the cast still go to a pub around the corner occasionally but I'm not really part of the social scene any more.

In my early days in the Street I was still living in Pudsey

and Charlie was living in Stratford so if we were first on set in the morning then we'd stay over at a pub that did bed and breakfast, called The Commercial, at the back of Granada Studios.

One night we were both staying there with another actor called Vincenzo who was playing a former army mate of Jim's who'd had an affair with Liz years before. It was a great storyline and Liz's killer chat-up line when her ex-lover returned was, 'Still like your eggs turned, do ya?' You'd only get a line like that in *Coronation Street*!

Charlie insisted on calling Vincenzo, 'Vincey Baby' and every time he walked in the room he'd say, 'How ya' doin' there Vincey Baby?'

Normally when we were staying at the Commercial I'd be the boring one who'd say, 'Right, we've got an early start in the morning we should all be getting to bed.' Or, 'Charlie, don't do that because we will get sacked.' Or, 'No, don't do that either. We *will* get sacked.' But Charlie would get so pissed he really wouldn't care what he was doing.

That night though, I'd decided that every time Charlie had a Bushmills whiskey (which was his drink at the time), then I'd have a vodka and bitter lemon. After a while I was off my face. Charlie was saying, 'She's been f****** unfaithful to me with Vincey Baby. This is f****** outrageous.' We were all having a hysterical time.

The more I drank, the more outrageously flirty I became with this Vincey Baby guy. I'm not usually like that but he must have thought, 'Yes, I'm in here.' He was coming on to me big style and I was thinking, 'Oh great.' Then this Vincey Baby said to me, 'Shall I take you upstairs?'

I lurched round to Charlie and slurred, 'Charlie, I'm just

going upstairs with Vincey Baby. I won't shag him, we're just going to cuddle.'

Charlie was having none of it. 'No you're f****** not,' he said.

'I am, I am, I am,' I was saying, even though I really didn't know what I was doing. And then it all started getting a bit heated between the two guys.

Vincey Baby, who was a bit of a cockney, said, 'You alright Charlie?'

'No, I'm not,' Charlie said. 'If she does anything with you she'll be so f****** sorry in the morning. She's married with a wee baby. You can't do this.'

'Well actually, it's none of your business,' Vincey Baby replied.

Now Charlie was boiling. 'Right, I believe tomorrow we are on set at 7.15 and we've got big scenes together. Do you want to play those f****** scenes with a f****** broken jaw? You are not taking her to bed,' he said.

At that, Vincey Baby disappeared off, leaving Charlie to pick me up, carry me to my room, plonk me on the bed and leave. I was saying, 'Oh Charlie, don't leave me, don't leave me.' But he is a very honourable man and went back to his own room.

He'd only just shut the door though when there was this knock, knock, knock on it and a voice calling, 'Char-lie, Char-lie.' It was me – wearing nothing but a white thong and white socks. He knew I'd regret it in the morning if anything happened, so he took me back to my room again, put me on the bed then laid next to me all night with his arms folded and still wearing his jeans, leather jacket and Timberland boots! How rough did I feel the next morning? Oh my God!

Looking back I still can't quite believe how outrageous I was that night. It was really out of character and like Charlie said, I would have been mortified the next morning if I had gone off with another man.

Another outrageous night we had was when Charlie, Mike le Vell who plays Kevin Webster, and I went over to Liverpool for a leaving party for Sue Johnstone and John Mcardle who had played Sheila and Billy Corkhill in *Brookside*. We were all good friends with the *Brookside* lot and Lewis Emerick, who played Mick Johnson in the show, is one of my best mates.

One of the Granada drivers called Roy Powers, who was a lovely man, took us over there and on the way he said, 'You're a bit quiet today Beverley. I wonder if you'll be this quiet on the way home?'

'Oh, I will be Roy,' I said. 'I've got work tomorrow so I'm going to be sensible.'

'Well I'm not going to be f****** sensible,' said Charlie.

So we got to this party and again, every time Charlie had a Bushmills, I had a vodka and bitter lemon. I think I've only been that drunk with Charlie about four times but this was the worst. There was this great jazz band playing and for no reason whatsoever I got up on the stage and started doing backing vocals, knocking over a massive speaker in the process.

In the car on the way home, Charlie was having a cigarette and I was chattering away when suddenly I collapsed on to his knee. A couple of minutes later, Roy the driver was saying, 'Charlie, is Beverley all right back there? I can smell burning.'

No reply from Charlie.

'Charlie, Charlie, I can smell burning,' said Roy, becoming increasingly anxious.

What I'd done was fallen asleep onto Charlie's cigarette, which had caught light to my hair. Charlie was frantically banging my head with his hands, trying to stop it smoking, while I was still totally out of it.

Charlie was staying with Steve and me that night. Apparently I banged on our front door looking like Wurzel Gummidge and said to Steve, 'Hi, we're home, now Charlie wants a drink but don't just give him water because he's an alcoholic', then I ricocheted down the hall to bed.

The next morning I was first on set and had to do a scene with Brian Mosley in the corner shop. Liz was buying toilet rolls. I felt like death. I was halfway through the take and I went to run my hands through my hair when a great big clump just fell out in my fingers. I thought, 'Oh my God, I've drunk so much vodka my hair is falling out!' It was only later Charlie told me what had happened.

We had such a laugh together and despite my daft come-on the night I was paralytic, there never ever was anything romantic between us. We were both married for one thing. We were just great mates then and still are to this day.

Being in *Coronation Street* was tremendous fun but I also learnt that there were downsides to life in the public eye. While I didn't mind people coming up and asking for autographs and pictures with me, Steve hated it. Understandably, it was annoying for him that almost everywhere we went, someone would recognise me. Still, life felt good. I had no idea that a new, huge challenge was just around the corner.

10
CANCER

....

For a while it felt as though I had everything I could ever possibly want. I had a dream job on *Coronation Street,* I was happily married to a man I adored and who adored me, we had a beautiful baby and Rebecca was doing well both in her acting career and at school.

There were some niggles though. The commute from Pudsey to Manchester every day was a grind and I missed Josh, who was looked after by a nanny when I was working. She was a lovely woman but it wasn't ideal for me. I liked having him near me and when he was very little I'd bring him into the *Coronation Street* set and even bottle-feed him in the green room and my dressing room.

At the same time, Steve still wasn't enjoying his job at Children's World.

One day he said to me, 'Look, you earn more money than me, why don't you carry on working and I'll stay at home and look after Josh.'

It seemed a sensible solution, so I agreed.

With Steve no longer working in Leeds, we were free to move to Manchester and we found a three-bedroom flat in the city centre. It was the term before Rebecca took her GCSEs, so for six weeks Steve drove her back to school in Pudsey. Then after finishing her exams Rebecca enrolled to take her A-levels at college in Manchester.

We sold our little house in Pudsey to Debbie McAndrew, who was in *Coronation Street* playing Angie Freeman, a design student who was big mates with Curly. Then after a while we found a big old-fashioned town house on three floors in Chorlton, just south of Manchester.

At first, Steve seemed to enjoy being at home looking after Josh but after a few months, he became touchy that he wasn't bringing in a wage and decided he did want another job. Then he spotted a furniture shop for sale near our house and he put an offer in on it. We got the shop and found a nursery for Josh so Steve could concentrate on turning his hand to the furniture trade. But it was harder than he thought it would be and business was slow. With our finances precarious, I threw myself into work – it was vital that Charlie and I made the roles of Jim and Liz McDonald work.

Maybe it was because I was working so hard that I didn't pay as much attention as I should have done when I started feeling a little under the weather.

Ever since Josh had been born in May 1989 I had suffered problems with my periods. They were really irregular and never fell back into any kind of pattern after having the baby.

I started to feel abnormally tired. At first I thought it was the pressures of starting a new job with big storylines plus looking after a baby and a teenager. But although I wasn't in any pain, I also had a nagging worry that something wasn't quite right.

While we were still living in Pudsey I went to my GP, who

decided to send me to a gynaecologist at Leeds General Infirmary. By the time the appointment came through in the autumn of 1990, we'd moved to Manchester, but I drove back over for the examination. Afterwards the gynaecologist said he thought I needed a D&C to remove excess tissue in my uterus, which might be causing irregular periods. I didn't want to cause a fuss at work, so I just had two days off for the op and then was back filming again.

I was due to have a follow-up appointment with the consultant but I was in the middle of really big storylines at the time so I phoned and said I wouldn't be able to make it. I assumed it was just to check everything had gone OK with the op and as I felt fine, I was sure it must have done.

It was a Wednesday lunchtime, just before the tech run where we ran through the entire week's episodes, when I was called to the studio telephone. It couldn't have been at a worse moment. By then we were doing three episodes of *Coronation Street* each week and it was our busiest day. At the other end of the line was my consultant's secretary, chasing me up to rearrange the appointment for as soon as possible.

'Well, I'm working really long hours for the next three weeks,' I said. 'I've got three solid episodes a week to shoot but I'll give you a call when things get a little quieter.'

I thought that would be the last I heard of it, but just twenty minutes later, I was called back to the telephone. This time it was the consultant himself. But it still didn't occur to me for a moment that it was anything unusual or that there might be anything wrong with me. I was one of the healthiest people I knew, I ate well, apart from the occasional blow-out I didn't drink much and I taught three fitness classes a week as well as working full-on at *Coronation Street*.

'Look Beverley,' said my consultant, 'I really need you to come and see me as soon as possible.'

'Why?' I asked. 'I don't mean to be difficult but I am very busy at work right now.'

He must have realised that if he was going to get me to miss filming for another appointment he would have to spell out the situation to me on the telephone.

'We've studied the tissue that was taken away during your D&C,' he explained. 'And I'm afraid we've found some abnormal cells.'

Of course, now I know that when doctors say 'abnormal cells' they probably mean cancer. But back then, although I knew it didn't sound good, I wasn't totally sure what it meant. And the only thing I could think about at that point was Wednesday afternoon's tech run.

'I'll call you back at the end of the day,' I said.

I was word perfect for tech run although I was by then feeling very uneasy. When we'd finished, I rang my doctor back and said I would go over to Leeds to meet him face to face.

Steve came with me and sat next to me in the office as my consultant spelled out the seriousness of what had been discovered – that the abnormal cells meant I had cervical cancer. When I first heard the word 'cancer' I felt utterly numb. How could this be happening to me? I ate healthily, I was fit and I was only thirty-two. It was all too much to take in and I just refused to believe it could be all that serious.

My consultant said he wanted to carry out a colposcopy, which is a more detailed examination of the cervix, as soon as possible to see what the extent of the problem was.

A few days later I had the colposcopy, which showed quite a large number of cancerous cells. I would need laser treatment to burn them off. It was horrible to know that something had been growing inside me for ages and I'd had absolutely no idea. I felt as though I had something dirty inside me, and I wanted it out.

I was able to schedule my laser treatment appointments around filming and barely needed any time off at all. My way of dealing with any kind of problem is to immerse myself in work, and on this occasion, I was no different. I was determined to prove that this illness wasn't going to beat me and that even with cancer, I could still be on set twelve hours a day, still teach my fitness classes, still keep my house immaculate and still be a good mum. Looking back, it might have been better for me in the long term to talk about how frightened I was feeling. But instead I just carried on coping. I had a family to support and a demanding job that I couldn't afford to lose. Steve was really supportive and was worried about me but I didn't want to make a big fuss about it all. I just wanted everything to continue as normally as possible. The laser treatment caused terrible bleeding but I still refused to take any more time off work.

I hoped the treatment would kill the cancer but after the final session, my consultant broke the news that it had been unsuccessful and some of the cells were still there. The next option was a cone biopsy, which is an operation to remove an area of the cervix where the abnormal cells are. But the consultant said that might still not get all the cells. By then I just wanted the cancer out of my body. I hated the idea that there was something growing inside me that shouldn't be there and I wasn't going to take any chances that any part of it might be left inside me. I couldn't have anything putting my life in danger – I needed to be around for Steve, Josh and Rebecca.

So I told the consultant I wanted a full hysterectomy.

Steve and I had already decided we didn't want any more children. Josh had been our miracle. I never thought I'd be able to get through another pregnancy and then he had arrived, the most gorgeous baby you could hope for. After years of it being just women in our family, him being a boy made him extra special. I felt very lucky to have him and Rebecca but I had no wish for more children, so a hysterectomy seemed to make perfect sense.

Steve was fantastic throughout and said he wanted me to do whatever was the best thing to get rid of the cancer. But although I was adamant that a hysterectomy was the right answer, the thought of it was still traumatic. I was just thirty-three years old, with an eighteen-month-old baby and I was about to have an operation that I thought would turn me into an old lady. One night I lay awake crying, thinking, 'Is this the end of womanhood?' I didn't admit it to anyone but I was scared.

At work, I only told Charlie Lawson, Julie Goodyear, Anne Kirkbride and Amanda Barrie, who played Alma Sedgwick. They were all incredibly supportive.

Julie Goodyear was completely fantastic. I'd had loads of people saying, 'Oh, you poor thing, having to go through a hysterectomy,' and that just makes you feel worse than ever. But Julie had a very different approach.

One day I was in my dressing room and I heard this knocking on the door. When I went to open it, Julie was standing there wearing a balaclava.

'What are you doing?' I said.

'Just thought you needed something to make you laugh,' she giggled.

Of course I burst out laughing.

Julie came and sat down in my dressing room and said, 'Listen, I've had a hysterectomy and you're going to be fine, but let me tell you this, afterwards you're going to shag like a snow leopard.'

And I said, 'Oh, right. And how do snow leopards shag, Julie?'

We both fell about giggling. Then she told me that when she had discovered she needed a hysterectomy, her mum had rung her auntie and said, 'Oh bad news, really bad news. Our Julie's been to the gynaecologist and she has to have a complete ex-directory!' Julie was so funny like that.

Even knowing that I needed a full hysterectomy to deal with the cancer, I continued to focus on work. It was my way of coping. I even insisted on waiting five months before I had the operation, because I was involved in big storylines and didn't want to upset the filming schedules.

It was the time when Andy was threatening to go into the army and I didn't want that spoiled. Liz had also recently split up with Jim and was on the verge of having an affair with Des Barnes, and I thought I couldn't just disappear for three months or however long it would take to recover. With hindsight I realise I was just stupid and I should have had the operation as soon as possible but at the time, although I still felt tired and my periods were erratic, generally I was OK.

Whenever you have an operation there is always someone with a horror story to tell about when they, or some friend, had their op. It seemed that everyone I mentioned the word 'hysterectomy' to had some story of doom. One woman said to me, 'You'll always have a fat tummy afterwards!' Another said, 'You can't do so much as lift a kettle for three months!' And another told me I'd go straight into the menopause and start growing a beard! It really wasn't what I needed to hear.

The thought of not being able to work or do any physical exercise after the op worried me far more than the hysterectomy itself. So that winter, in the run-up to my operation, I threw myself into my fitness training. I wanted to be in the best possible physical shape before I went into hospital. I hoped it would make up for any exercise I wasn't able to do afterwards and I thought it might also mean I recovered more quickly and get me back to *Coronation Street* sooner. I also found it good for me mentally, as it kept my mind off the cancer.

That winter, I would be in the gym before work and then I'd go again later in the day if I had a break from filming. It reached the point where I could do the abdominal routine of an Olympic athlete.

On 11 March 1991, I went in to have the hysterectomy at Leeds General Infirmary. And the operation was nowhere near as bad as I'd thought it would be. In fact on the afternoon of the day I had surgery I was sitting up in my hospital bed painting my toenails. So much for all those horror stories I'd been told about not being able to even move for weeks afterwards!

Amanda Barrie was off work having a hysterectomy at the same time as me. She was in a different hospital but we had lots of phone conversations about how we were feeling and where it hurt.

Just thirteen days after the operation, I was back in the gym.

Because I'd had to take time off work for the surgery, both Liz and Jim McDonald were written out of *Coronation Street*, briefly. So while I was recovering in hospital, Charlie was sunning himself on holiday in Africa. We'd been off a couple of weeks when the *Daily Star* wrote a story saying 'Flame-haired Beverley Callard' (they always called me that!) had gone mad with Charlie for not knowing his lines properly, jumped over the bar of the Rovers and punched him. It was total rubbish, we weren't even at work! I was still in hospital when Charlie rang me.

'You don't 'alf pack a f***** punch then,' he said. 'You're in Leeds General Infirmary and I'm in Africa and you're supposed to have decked me, eh?'

We couldn't stop laughing about it.

It did bother me a bit that I was now fair game for the press, even if I was having to get used to it. I always thought of myself as a jobbing actress, not a national treasure like Julie Goodyear, and it took me a while to learn to live with the interest. Little did I know how much more intrusive it would become.

Despite being told I'd need three months off work, I took just five and a half weeks. I knew *Coronation Street* wouldn't want me to be away for a full three months and I didn't want to be either. By the time I went back, I honestly felt fine.

The only real downside of the operation was the effect it had on our sex life. For six weeks after you've had a hysterectomy you're not supposed to have sex and so maybe Steve felt a little neglected. And in the run-up to the operation I had been working long hours on big storylines, keeping as fit as I could in the gym and trying to be a great mum to Rebecca and Josh. Perhaps I didn't spend as much time then with Steve as I should have done. But if he was feeling forgotten about, I didn't realise it at the time. I adored Steve and thought he adored me. Which is why what happened next came as a total shock.

11
BETRAYAL

....

'There's a story going in the Sunday papers that your husband is having an affair,' said the voice on the end of the phone.

I wasn't so much shocked at that point as totally confused. 'That's ridiculous,' I said.

There couldn't be a story like that going in the papers because it wasn't true. Steve couldn't possibly be having an affair. He didn't go out in the evenings, there had been no suspicious behaviour and we knew everything about each other's lives. Or so I thought.

The phone call had come from the *Coronation Street* press office during a rare Friday afternoon off, just four months after my hysterectomy.

It was a warm summer's day in 1991 and I'd managed to nip home early after a photo shoot for a magazine. I'd called Steve, who was at work at the shop, and told him I'd pick up Josh from nursery. I'd just got stuck into a pile of ironing when the phone rang. Graham King, a *Coronation Street* press officer, had received a call from the *Sunday Mirror* saying they were running the story and would I like to comment. I made Graham repeat what he was saying several times. I just couldn't get my head around it.

'They say they are definitely running the story that he's been seeing another woman,' said Graham.

'But he hasn't,' I repeated. 'He works in the shop, he comes home, we've got a baby, we've just got back from holiday. When could he possibly have been seeing another woman?'

In the end, Graham said Carolyn Reynolds, who was the producer, was going to call me back.

I put the phone down and thought it through. We'd only recently returned from a week in Spain with Deborah McAndrew, who played Angie Freeman, and her husband Tim. Steve's mum and dad had looked after Josh while we were away and we'd had a brilliant time. It was true that since then, Steve's mood had been low. The Saturday afternoon that our flight landed, he had gone straight out to check on the shop and when he got home he'd stood at the sink in our kitchen and cried.

'What on earth's the matter?' I said.

He said the business wasn't working and he'd given it his best shot but it was losing money, he was behind with the rent and he didn't know what to do. It was the first I'd had an inkling there was a problem with the shop, but I reassured him everything would be fine and we'd sort it out. He was still crying though and was acting very out of character. For the next few days he was very down and not really himself, but I just assumed he was worried about the business. It didn't occur to me that there could be any other reason for his bad mood.

After putting the phone down to the *Coronation Street* press office, I immediately picked it up again and called Steve in the shop. I repeated everything Graham had told me.

'What?' he said in his broad Yorkshire accent. 'What are they talking about?'

'Apparently you've been seen with another woman,' I repeated.

'Well, who? Who?' he shouted.

I said I didn't have a clue but the papers had this story about him and they were threatening to run it. I still had absolutely no doubt it was total rubbish.

Then Carolyn Reynolds rang me. 'Beverley, they *are* running this story on Sunday,' she said. 'They say they've got evidence.'

I rang Steve back and he shut up the shop and came home. By this time it was mid-afternoon.

'What are they talking about?' he said, appearing totally baffled at what was going on. He kept saying it over and over again and I really didn't have the slightest thought that the story might be true. I had no doubts about Steve at all. He hadn't been staying out late and apart from when we were at work, we were rarely apart. Even if I went to the gym he would pop in for a coffee. Everyone we knew thought we were the perfect couple. It just could not be true. There had been that one night when I'd be very drunk and joked about going upstairs with the 'Vincey Baby' actor but I would never have gone through with it. I was totally faithful to Steve and believed he was to me too.

A really good actress friend of mine called Maria, who I'd worked with on stage years earlier, was married to a barrister, so I rang them to see what they thought we could do if a newspaper was about to write a load of lies about us. Maria and her husband Paul came straight round.

We were talking to them when Graham King rang back and said, 'I don't want to talk to you Beverley, can I speak to Steve?'

I put Steve on the phone but was standing next to him and heard Graham say, 'Can you get Beverley to go out of the room?'

Steve said, 'Er, yeah, yeah, 'ang on.'

'No, I'm not going anywhere,' I said.

Then I could hear Graham saying down the phone, 'They've got photographs of you, Steve.'

'No, they can't have, they can't have,' Steve replied. At this point I still believed him.

Then Steve became totally monosyllabic. All I could hear was him saying, 'Right.' Then, 'Yep' and 'No'.

When he put the phone down, he turned to me and said that the *Sunday Mirror* had photographs of him with a woman.

'What woman?'

'Elaine,' he said, totally matter-of-factly.

'Who's Elaine?' I asked. I didn't even know this woman existed. I'd never even heard her name before.

'She works in the shop next door but one to mine and sometimes she comes in if she needs change for the till,' he said.

'But how come you've never mentioned her to me before?' I asked, feeling more confused than ever.

'Because I hardly know her,' he said.

I always talked to Steve about my day and there was no one at work or in the gym who I wouldn't have mentioned to him, but I still believed what he was telling me. There had been that one night soon after Josh was born when Steve didn't come home, but since then he had never done anything like that again.

Next, I called our friends John and Judy Capello. John trained me at the gym and Steve often went there too.

'What complete rubbish,' said John. 'Steve worships the ground you walk on. He wouldn't do anything like that.'

The conversations and phone calls seemed to go on all night. The press office was trying to get the story stopped, Steve was trying to get the story stopped, but still the *Sunday Mirror* said they had evidence and were going to run it. By the following morning we hadn't had any sleep and Steve was saying that if the paper printed anything about him and Elaine, he would sue for libel.

'Well, we need to tell this Elaine that a story is about to appear about her in the Sunday papers,' I said. 'She's got a right to know. Is she married? Has she got a family?'

'I don't know,' said Steve.

By this point though, something was niggling me so I got in a taxi and went to the shop. Steve said he'd speak to her but I was determined to do it myself.

The shop where Elaine worked sold secondhand clothes and it was really grotty. When I opened the door a woman looked at me and gasped. She clearly knew exactly who I was and what I was there for.

'Elaine?' I said.

'No, she's out the back,' the woman said. 'I'll give you some privacy.'

The back of the shop was filled with secondhand shoes. It was scruffy, dirty and pretty smelly too. And standing there was this really skinny woman with dyed, jet-black hair and pale skin.

'Are you Elaine?' I said.

'Yeah,' she replied, in a strong Scouse accent. 'And I know who you are.'

'Oh,' I said, then explained that a newspaper was going to be running a story about her and my husband.

'Yeah, right,' she said, when I'd finished.

'So what do you feel about it then?' I asked.

'I'll tell the truth, he talks to me.'

'He talks to you? What do you mean he talks to you?'

'Well I know what you've been through.'

'What do you mean, you know what I've been through?' I said.

'I know you've had a hysterectomy and couldn't have sex for six weeks.'

'Oh, Steve talked to you about that did he?' I said, totally shocked that he could have discussed something so private with someone who was a total stranger to me.

'Yeah,' she said. 'He needed somebody to talk to. Somebody his own age.'

It was such a nasty thing to say but rather than being angry with her I was just confused about why Steve had been confiding in this woman. I kept her talking a bit longer, though, and she told me she had a long-term boyfriend and a young son.

'Well, you're going to have to tell the newspapers that what they're saying is not true,' I said and left her.

But by then I was having serious doubts myself about whether it wasn't true. I had to find out what had really gone on.

Steve's parents had taken Josh to stay with them and Rebecca was down in London where she was appearing in *Romeo and Juliet* at the Regent's Park Theatre, so fortunately they were both out of the house that weekend.

When I got home, this Elaine was still in my head and I couldn't shift her, so I rang her and asked her to come round to the house so we could work out what we were going to say to the papers. Then I asked my friend Maria to keep Steve in the kitchen while I talked to Elaine in the lounge.

As soon as she sat down on the sofa I said, 'Steve has told me what's happened so now we've got to sort it out.'

It was a complete bluff but I needed to know.

Elaine looked down and said, 'It was just the once.'

Now she had admitted it, I felt physically sick, but I couldn't let her see it.

'OK,' I said and walked back into the kitchen to confront Steve.

But still he wouldn't give in.

'She is f****** lying,' he kept saying, but I refused to believe him a moment longer. Finally, he agreed he had been to bed with her, but he claimed it had only happened once.

Then I went back into the lounge and was standing talking to Elaine when I heard this incredible banging outside – my front door was being kicked in. A minute later a huge guy had stormed into my house and barged into the lounge. He was well over 6 feet tall with a massive build.

'I'll f****** kill you,' he was yelling at Elaine. 'I'll kill you and I'll kill him too.'

This guy was seriously scary but I was too stunned at the time for the situation to really sink in. He totally ignored me and carried on yelling at Elaine, 'Is it true? You slag. You total slag.'

Then Steve came into the lounge and this guy, who I later discovered was, bizarrely, called John Lennon, began shouting at him. Steve didn't react. Elaine was screaming and crying and then she dashed out into my hall, dialled 999 and called the police while I managed to get between Steve and this John Lennon guy. Finally, I made him stop and sit down in a chair under the window. But he was still yelling, 'You f****** slag' at Elaine, then shouting at Steve, before he finally turned to me and said really politely, 'I'm sorry about this love, I'm really sorry.'

Then the guy was saying to Steve, 'What did you do it for? You're with this beautiful woman who's an actress and famous – why did you do it?'

Elaine just sat there, looking at the floor.

It was the most surreal situation. I had this massive guy shouting and swearing in my lounge, Steve was sat on the floor and then there was a skinny woman sitting on my sofa, just staring at the floor.

'Oh my God, what have I come to?' I thought. 'Yesterday my life was perfect. I had a husband who I adored and who I thought adored me, a dream job, the most gorgeous daughter being directed in a play by Judi Dench and a miracle baby son. Today my life is a total mess.' I kept saying to myself, 'Don't react. Don't react. I've got children to think about. I've got a baby.'

Then John Lennon asked Elaine if she loved Steve.

'No,' she replied.

I was so angry then. 'You don't love him and you did it anyway when you knew I'd got a daughter and a baby son. So why did you do it?'

'He bought me presents and really spoiled me, it made me feel good,' she said.

So all the while that I'd been paying to keep his furniture shop going, he had been wasting his time taking her here, there and everywhere in a brand new car and showering her with presents that had all been bought with my wages.

I was thinking, 'I've got to get these people out of my house.' But it wasn't over yet because then the police turned up. They came in the front door and were clearly intrigued when they recognised me from *Coronation Street*. They asked what had been going on and checked everyone was OK. We convinced them there wouldn't be any more fighting and so they left again, soon followed by Elaine and John.

I turned to Steve. 'You've broken my heart,' I said. 'You had better go.'

I was still completely in love with him but I was angry and so hurt by what he had done that I didn't want him anywhere near me. He packed a bag and went off to his dad's house.

I had to ring Rebecca in London and tell her what had happened. I was worried that a journalist might break the news to her before I did. She was boiling when I told her, and when she got Steve on the phone she went mad at him.

Steve never gave me any more information about his affair with Elaine and everything else I know about what really went on came from what I read in the paper that weekend and from other people. It turned out that it certainly wasn't just a one-off thing as Steve had claimed, and that in fact the affair had been going on for several months. A press officer from *Coronation Street* brought me the *Sunday Mirror* that weekend and I felt sick as I read the story and looked at the photographs. There were pictures of Elaine and Steve all over the place and I spent hours afterwards looking at them, trying to work out where they had been together. One picture had a set of railings in the background and those railings tortured me for ages afterwards. Years later I would be driving along a road and see some railings and think, 'I wonder if this is where they were together.'

The next few days were horrific. In those days, *TV-am* was on every morning and when I switched it on early on Monday, every half an hour it was flashing up, '*Street* Star's Love Rat

Husband'. I felt like the whole world was looking at me and wondering why he'd done it. It was horrible.

Everyone at work was fantastically supportive. It had been in the papers and all over television so there was no way anyone couldn't have known what had happened.

Julie Goodyear was fantastic. One day she turned up at my front door with a huge bottle of pink champagne and crystal flutes to drink it from. 'Come on Beverley, you're not going to sink,' she said. 'Tell the bastard to f*** off. You're far too good for him anyway, I always knew it.'

And Charlie was a rock. He was there for me all the time and said he never wanted to speak to Steve again. Nick and Simon came to visit me at home and they said they wanted to kill Steve. They'd become good friends with Rebecca as they were about the same age and they were angry on her behalf, too. I remember Ken Morley, who played Reg Holdsworth, coming up to me and saying, 'Oh, you really are going through it, aren't you!' If one of the cast is having a tough time, everyone else really does rally round. I suppose because we spend twelve hours a day together, five or six days a week, we do know each other very well.

It turned out that Elaine had tipped off the papers herself, so that showed how much she thought of Steve. In the weeks that followed, she admitted more about the affair to John Lennon and then he in turn would ring me and tell me about what had gone on. One of the most shocking things for me was that it turned out that when we'd sold the house in Pudsey to Debbie McAndrew, Steve had kept a set of keys and taken Elaine back there. They'd also used a flat in Manchester that belonged to a friend of Elaine's.

A lovely guy called Derrick, who'd worked for Steve in his

shop, also came to see me and said, 'I told him she was bad news and not to get involved with her but he wouldn't listen. I'm so sorry.'

Steve's parents were both really mad with him but they too had split up the previous year, which had come as a terrible shock to everyone. But then I always felt that Steve's Dad blamed me for the break-up because I wasn't a 'proper' wife, staying at home with my baby while my husband brought home the bacon.

I was gutted. Firstly, I didn't feel I had changed Steve when we met. The Steve I'd known had always been the same person. I didn't make him fantastic and I didn't make him a horrible cheat either – both things were down to him.

Later I started to worry, maybe if I had been a 'proper' wife this wouldn't have happened. I was from a very traditional background myself, where Dad had gone to work and Mum had stayed at home, but my marriage had been very different to that. And I knew that when I was involved in a big storyline at work I could be very full-on and wouldn't be able to think about much else. Maybe I had been so busy at work, keeping fit and trying to be a great mum that I hadn't been a great wife. Maybe I hadn't juggled things as well as I should, but I had been so worried that his business was sinking that I was determined to hold on to my job. I'd send myself mad thinking about what had happened and what I could have done differently. But then I'd send myself even more crazy, thinking about where Steve and Elaine had been and what they had done together.

For the next few months all I would do was get up in the morning, take Josh to nursery, drive to Granada, film all day, go to pick up Josh again, bath him, put him to bed then sit down and learn my lines. The next day I'd do it all over again. But I just got on with it. What else could I have done?

Elaine and John later got back together and said in a newspaper that I'd acted like a perfect lady throughout the whole thing. But if it ever happened to me again, I swore I wouldn't be a perfect lady.

12
SUSPICION AND SADNESS

....

'I don't think Steve's very well,' his mum told me down the phone.

I trusted Sandra and knew she wouldn't be saying something like this unless she had very good reason. And no matter what Steve had done to me, I still cared for him.

'What do you mean?' I asked.

'He can't be, otherwise he would not have done what he did,' said Sandra. 'He has never been a womaniser and he adored you – he still does. If he were OK there is no way he would have put everything with you, Rebecca and Josh at risk.'

He hadn't taken the break-up well and since I'd kicked him out he had seemed very low. He'd lost loads of weight and I began to worry that Sandra was right. He didn't seem himself. I still loved Steve though, and he was the father of my son. I hated to think of him suffering. And part of me thought that we had so much that was worth saving. But I just didn't know what to think anymore.

I agreed to meet him, so he travelled over to Manchester one day, on the train. We talked and he said he also thought he was depressed and ill. He still wouldn't tell me anything about what had happened with Elaine but said he couldn't understand why he had done it.

We met a few times after that and finally I said he could move back in – so long as he went to the doctor's to try to get to the bottom of what was wrong with him. If he was ill I wanted to help him get better. And I really didn't want to fail at marriage yet again.

Josh was coming up for seven and was desperately excited about the idea of his dad coming home. Steve had a fantastic sense of humour and really made Josh laugh and he had missed him terribly while he had been away. But all my friends thought I was stupid taking him back. Mum agreed. 'If he has done it once, he'll do it again,' she said.

I took Charlie Lawson to one side at work one day and told him that I'd let Steve come home. The news was bound to get out and I wanted him to hear it from me first.

'What?' he said when I explained what had happened. 'Steve is back?'

'Yeah,' I said.

Then he took hold of my hand and led me outside to what we called the croquet lawn, but which was really just a patch of grass. We went right into the middle of the grass so no one could hear us and were standing underneath the big, old chimney that towers over stage one.

'Are you mad?' he said. 'You are the strongest woman I know—you're like that chimney up there. You even came to work a couple of hours after having laser treatment for cancer, but you still did your scenes. You're also faithful, kind and sensitive. He is a piece of shit.'

But I didn't listen. I wanted my marriage to work.

To me, Steve's behaviour seemed totally out of character. He had been quite low for a while and I partly blamed myself for what had happened because I hadn't been at home all the time as a 'proper wife'. Perhaps if I had been there more, he wouldn't have felt the need to look elsewhere.

Steve was really struggling to come to terms with the impact his affair had had on our relationship, and I felt I ought to try and support him, even though I was still angry and hurt by everything that had happened. Plus, he's Josh's father and I wanted to make it work for his sake.

But it wasn't easy . . . Steve stayed at the top of the house, because although I wanted to try to save my marriage, I still wasn't ready to sleep with him. However hard I tried to put what had happened behind us, I just couldn't do it. I couldn't forgive him for what he had done and there were days when I wished he would disappear off the face of the earth.

He had never given me any detail about what had happened during the affair – how often he'd slept with her, where they'd done it, what gifts he had given her – so my imagination went into overdrive. I would torture myself for hours thinking about what she and Steve might have done together. I began doubting everything about myself. I would think about what Steve had found in Elaine that he couldn't get from me. I became more and more insecure about the way I looked and what people thought of me. My sense of self-esteem crashed around me. Even though we were trying to put it behind us and move on for Josh's sake, I couldn't help screaming, 'Why? Why have you ripped our entire lives apart?' Or we'd be sitting watching television and I'd suddenly say, 'Why won't you tell me where that flat is that you took Elaine to?'

'Give it a rest,' he'd reply and then we'd have another massive row.

With hindsight, we should probably never have got back together but I felt I couldn't give up on him and deep down I still loved him and desperately wanted to save the marriage. I wanted to believe that he still loved me.

The constant tension at home was making me feel really low. I was desperately unhappy and my weight dropped to seven and a half stone.

'You're getting too thin,' Julie Goodyear told me one day at work.

Things rolled on and very slowly we returned to something a bit more like normality. But I was pretty messed up by then. Steve's affair had badly dented my confidence and to be honest it turned me into an insecure f***-up. I became demanding and paranoid and was constantly doubting Steve and thinking he was having other affairs.

He couldn't understand why I was unable to put the affair behind us but I couldn't do it. So that just led to more rows.

We were still living in Chorlton and I felt as if *that woman* was just around the corner the whole time. To try and get away from her and all the bad memories, we decided to move to Bolton. We bought a brand new, five-bedroom detached house in the Smithills area of the city, thinking a new house in a different city would be a new beginning for us.

But however much I wanted us to start afresh and for our marriage to work, I was still struggling to get over the affair. I was suspicious every time Steve was as much as five minutes late home and I couldn't stop torturing myself by thinking about him and his mistress together. As a teenager I'd tried to cover up my insecurities about the way I looked or about being a bit of an outsider by trying to be the class clown but now it was harder to hide those feelings of low self-esteem that were only building up more and more inside me. I blamed myself for things going wrong in our marriage.

At that point, our marriage seemed doomed and after a couple of months we split up again. But I had never stopped loving Steve and after a short while we decided to give the relationship another go.

Steve didn't work when we were living in Bolton but we had a great life. Steve had archery lessons and was driving one of just sixty-five Lotus Esprits in the world. And a Jaguar too! We also had a lady called Karen who was a good friend of mine and worked as our childminder and cleaner, so he didn't even have to do any of that.

Meanwhile, I was getting up at the crack of dawn every day to drive to Manchester (I'd passed my test by then!) to do *Coronation Street,* as well as teaching fitness classes three times a week and doing personal appearances in shopping centres and places to earn a bit more cash.

But for all that, I stuck with Steve and increasingly felt I was to blame for what had happened. The affair had really impacted on my self-esteem. Gradually the good periods between Steve and me started lasting longer than the bad and things got back on an even keel. It wasn't long before my life was plastered all over the tabloid newspapers again, though, and this time, the shock had even greater consequences.

A *Coronation Street* press officer rang me late one Friday afternoon to tell me a Sunday newspaper was running a story claiming I had a 'guilty secret'. 'Well what is it?' I asked, totally bewildered.

'That your grandad killed someone,' the press officer replied.

I felt instantly sick that all this was going to come out all over again. I'd never kept what happened a secret and had talked about it to people who knew me but having it in the papers again would be horrendous for Mum, Steph and Nans.

Nans was in her eighties then and still living on her own in the back-to-back terrace in Morley, so we arranged for her to go and stay with Mum for a few days. When they read what went into the paper, they were furious – there were thirteen inaccuracies. There was a group of journalists sat outside Mum's door and she was desperate to speak to them.

'They're telling lies about my dad and I'm going to go out there and tell everyone the truth,' she said.

'But you can't, Mum,' I said. 'It doesn't work like that.'

Later, with the help of the Granada press office, I did an interview in reply to the piece that set the record straight. But it still came as a shock to see our family in the newspapers just because I was in *Coronation Street*. All the cast were really supportive and Julie Goodyear and Anne Kirkbride in particular were amazing. They'd say, 'Don't worry, it's just tomorrow's fish and chip paper!'

But the damage had already been done, particularly to Nans. She'd got through the trial and managed to still hold her head up high, then she'd got through Grandad's death and the television campaign to clear his name, but now it was all being raked up again and it was too much for her.

She'd had asthma years earlier and after the story about Grandad was printed, it came back. When she went to collect her pension on the Tuesday after the story appeared, a couple of people said they'd seen it and she got really upset. She didn't want to go out again after that. Shortly afterwards she had a heart attack and died. Nans had been such a strong woman that it took me a long while to really accept that she had gone. We'd often been sparring partners but were so, so close. When I did come to terms with her death it was devastating. Mum was heartbroken all over again and she was convinced that the newspaper story about Grandad had brought on the heart attack.

So in the end, the fight in the mill that night led not only to the death of Paul Suchar but to that of Grandad and Nans, too.

Fairly soon after the upset and sadness of Nans' death we had a new challenge to deal with, when Josh was diagnosed as dyslexic.

When we had first moved to Bolton, Josh went to the nearby Horwich Parish School. He loved it and his teacher told us he appeared very bright and we should put him forward for the entrance exam for Bolton School, which is an excellent independent school. We took him for the exam and he sailed through it. But after he'd been there a few months I realised there was a problem. At Bolton School there was a spelling test every Friday, and soon every Thursday evening Josh was complaining about being ill – he clearly wanted to avoid the test.

It was becoming apparent he had a problem with spelling. Each night I would put him in our big corner bath and we'd do his spellings together. I tried to make it fun, saying, 'If you get this right you can splash me.' But although he might get a word correct once, a couple of minutes later he'd spell it completely differently. He was also getting lots of letters the wrong way round in his writing.

I talked to Josh's teacher and she was convinced he had dyslexia. His reading was amazing but when he had to copy things down from the blackboard into his exercise book, they wouldn't make any sense at all. Before that the school hadn't been sure he had a problem and I think they thought that Josh was simply lazy.

I knew Josh was clever though, and had a real problem. I was also concerned because Steve had been trying to get him to play football but Josh's hand/eye coordination was very poor, whereas when he had swimming lessons he was fantastic.

During all of this, Steve and I split up again. I had been working long hours at *Coronation Street*, teaching fitness classes and doing personal appearances all around the country. I spent any spare time visiting educational psychologists and experts in dyslexia trying to find the right help for Josh. I contacted the Dyslexic Institute and Josh started going there two afternoons a week in addition to school but Steve found it difficult to accept that anything was wrong with Josh. We still had my friend Karen working as our childminder, and another great friend Sarah helped out with the admin work. Steve would spend day after day sitting in front of the cricket on telly.

We were getting further and further apart and in the end Steve said he was going. We got an agreement drawn up by a solicitor. Steve moved back to Leeds and at that point, my main concern was finding the very best support for Josh.

When Josh was seven and a half he was formally assessed and the report showed he had a very high IQ but also chronic dyslexia and dyspraxia, a condition affecting coordination, which is sometimes called clumsy child syndrome.

Then an educational specialist suggested I consider moving

Josh to Giggleswick School in North Yorkshire because it was an amazing school that would be brilliant at stimulating his high IQ while also catering for his dyslexia. The only problem for me was that Giggleswick was a boarding school. People like me from ordinary backgrounds don't send their kids to boarding school. Rebecca hadn't even gone to private school and I liked having my children near me. I'd taken Rebecca to my auditions and rehearsals when she was little and I'd bottle-fed Josh in the *Coronation Street* green room, so the thought of sending him to boarding school when he was so young was very tough.

At first, I think Steve might have thought I was only considering it because I worked such long hours and was now living on my own. That wasn't true as I had the childminder for Josh at home, who could look after him whether Steve was there or not. In the end, Steve agreed Giggleswick School probably was the best place for Josh and we got him all prepared. First he spent a couple of days there and then a weekend and he loved it.

On the day he started properly, Rebecca, who was then acting in London, came home and went with Steve and me to drop off Josh. It was horrendous saying goodbye to him and after we left him there, all three of us were crying. Back home it was desperately quiet and I missed Josh terribly.

At Giggleswick they had 'exeat', which was a weekend off once every three weeks. It was very hard because you could bet your life that if Josh was at home for a weekend, I'd be called in for filming *Coronation Street* on a Sunday. That was a killer.

Josh loved his new school though and he came on in leaps and bounds after starting there. He made some brilliant friends and developed a wicked sense of humour.

Josh was tall for his age and very blond, but his best friend at Giggleswick was a boy called Arthur who looked young for his age and was quite dark. They couldn't have appeared more different but they became great mates and together they were unstoppable.

On one occasion there was a huge inter-school sports day and lots of boys from the posh schools, Ampleforth and Sedbergh, had travelled over for it. One of the main events was meant to be a cross-country race.

Later that day I received a call from a member of staff at Giggleswick School.

'I'm afraid Josh has been in some trouble,' he said. 'We're treating it very seriously and he and his friend Arthur are going to have to be suspended for a few days.'

I was horrified. He was only eight years old!

'I'm so sorry,' I said. 'What has he done?'

'He and his friend turned around all the markers for the cross-country race,' the teacher explained.

Afterwards I couldn't help laughing. Josh and Arthur had pointed all the arrows in the wrong direction and had these terribly posh boys running halfway round the bloody Dales!

Josh became like me, the class clown. He had a brilliant sense of humour.

By this time I had filmed my first fitness video – *Real Results* – and it had been massively popular. I had previously been asked by lots of different companies to make a video but each time I said, 'Absolutely not.' I thought they were only interested in me because I was in *Coronation Street*, and I wanted to keep my fitness work and my acting work very separate – I didn't teach the *Corrie* cast aerobics and I didn't go to teach fitness dressed in one of Liz's miniskirts!

But one company called VCI kept on asking me to shoot a video and in the end I said someone from their firm could come up and watch one of my classes in Bolton. I wanted them to realise I only dealt with real women, not stick insects and supermodels. I didn't think they would be interested in that but after watching a couple of classes they were keener than ever.

I said I'd only go ahead if I could use normal women in the videos rather than models, which we did. We shot it one summer and it went on sale around Christmas time.

Soon afterwards, I was at work and Bill Roache, who plays Ken Barlow, came up to me and said, 'Beverley, I believe you've done a video with exercises and you're jumping up and down?'

I said, 'Yeah, that's right.'

'Well, it's just been on the radio that you're number one in the charts.'

I couldn't believe what I was hearing but Bill was so sweet and kept saying, 'Congratulations.' The video's sales in England had beaten the film *Heat* – and the stars of that were Robert De Niro and Al Pacino! Liz Dawn, who played Vera Duckworth, bought me a magnum of champagne and the biggest arrangement of flowers. Everyone was so kind.

Charlie asked me, 'Why are you going up jumping up and down every night? Do you need the money?' But it wasn't that. I did it because I loved it.

After the success of the first video, we made *Ultimate Results* and *Rapid Results*, which were also big hits. I think all three of my videos and DVDs were successful because before me no other actor apart from Jane Fonda had ever made an exercise video. These days it seems that anyone can bring one out, even if they don't know the first thing about fitness – they just get a personal trainer to devise it for them, go on a crash diet, release the DVD then put all the weight back on again afterwards.

I devised all the choreography on my DVDs myself. I'd be up until two o'clock in the morning timing each routine to make sure it fitted the pieces of music.

I think my DVDs also worked because they featured real women and were based on the sorts of exercises that would help ordinary, busy women at home. I truly loved making them and even now I get dozens of women coming up to me telling me how much they enjoy exercising to my videos.

Meanwhile, Steve and I had got back together again. Even after he moved out, we had carried on talking, partly because of Josh, and then we started seeing each other again. Sure enough, he was soon back at home in Bolton and we really did seem to be getting on better this time than we had in years. With money from the videos and my *Coronation Street* wages, we were financially secure. We had a beautiful big home, Steve had his two flash cars and I was driving a Mercedes SLK. Josh was loving school and Rebecca's career was flying after she'd appeared in two series of a television production of *The Borrowers*, which won a Bafta. I was fit and had a body many women would die for and we were all in good health.

So, to the outside world my life must have looked great. Which was why I couldn't understand why I was feeling so flat and empty. At first I thought it was solely that I was missing Josh, but increasingly I felt low and tearful a lot of the time. I felt worthless and as though nothing I did was good enough. I was also incredibly tired and when Josh was at home for holidays I'd go to bed at the same time as him. But then I wouldn't be able to sleep or would wake up panicking that I was going to miss my alarm for work.

I wondered whether it was a hormonal problem because I was suffering terrible mood swings and felt old, ugly and exhausted. Nothing was helping me get better and I thought maybe I was going through the menopause because of the hysterectomy.

When it carried on for a few months, I knew something was wrong with me so one day I went to the doctor. He diagnosed me with depression and prescribed me with Seroxat antidepressants. I'd always been a fighter and a coper and I didn't like the idea of depression. I didn't want people thinking I was a wimp and couldn't cope.

Every month, I'd go and pick up my repeat prescription for the tablets, hoping they would help, but they didn't. In fact, I was feeling worse than ever. I was still struggling with the idea of Josh being away from home at boarding school, I was losing weight again and my self-esteem was at rock bottom.

Sometimes Steve could be supportive but at other times I felt that he played on my insecurities. If we went out for dinner and I joined in with everyone at the table telling funny stories, when we got home Steve might say, 'You know when you told that story at dinner and everybody laughed? Well you weren't funny really, you know.'

Sometimes I'd argue with him but inside I was thinking, 'Maybe I'm not funny, or interesting or a very nice person at all. Over time I started to think that Steve was right and I began to put myself down too, and the feeling that I had nothing to offer grew stronger.

I became very withdrawn at work and would arrive at the

studios in the morning, go straight to my dressing room, do my scenes and go home. I wasn't unfriendly but I kept myself to myself. I didn't feel I had anything to say that people might want to hear. I wasn't feeling sorry for myself though, if anything I was being too hard on myself. I think Charlie Lawson saw what happened next coming because I'd become so withdrawn and the spark had gone but I managed to hide it from everyone else.

Then one day I woke up and I couldn't go to work at all. I couldn't stop crying, my hands were shaking, my hair was wet with sweat at the back of my neck and I felt sick. I thought I was having a heart attack.

I rang my mum, who came straight over from Leeds on the train and called my GP. The GP said he was referring me immediately to Dr Pasterski at the Priory in Altrincham.

Dr Pasterski was incredible. I couldn't find the words to explain how I felt but he did it for me. He ran through a list of twelve symptoms, including tiredness, emptiness and feeling unlovable, and I was saying, 'yes', 'yes', 'yes' to all of them. It was as if he was a mind reader. At the end of the consultation he said, 'Beverley, you are very poorly. You have clinical depression.'

I still wasn't entirely sure what that meant, although I know now that it means that your brain makes less of the chemical, serotonin, than it should, which can lead to feelings of depression. The idea of antidepressants is that they improve the brain's ability to produce and respond to serotonin. But finding the right antidepressants for someone can take a lot of time.

Dr Pasterski wanted to admit me to the Priory immediately so they could start trying to find me the most suitable medication but I didn't want that at all. 'I can't,' I said. 'I've got to work and at weekends I've got my son to look after. And if I go to the Priory it'll get in the papers and there will be all that attention all over again. I'm not having other kids at my son's school reading stuff like that about his mum.' I really couldn't face going to the clinic, so Dr Pasterski put me on a course of anti-depressants.

Denise Welch, who had spoken publicly about her own battle with depression, was by then also in *Coronation Street*. Rebecca had worked with her husband Tim Healy in the TV series *The Grand*, so she called him and told him I was struggling. Denise came to visit and it was such a huge relief to speak to someone who had some idea what I was going through. Denise said to me, 'When I was ill, if someone came to my front door and told me I'd won the lottery and I was going to be really rich, happy and healthy and so were all my children, for all of eternity, or if someone came to my door and said my children had just been burnt to death, there would be no difference in the way I felt.'

And that is exactly how I felt. I was sort of emotionless.

I followed Dr Pasterski's prescription to the letter but the drugs still didn't make me feel any better. Then he tried me on a different medication but that just left me feeling utterly emotionally numb. I didn't feel sad any more but I didn't feel happy either. It was as if everything that was happening was going on a long way away from where I was standing.

I was on the antidepressants when I had to go down to London between Christmas and New Year to film the commercial for my latest fitness video. The video producer was a woman called Jacky Moini and after a short while in the studio she called me to one side.

'Beverley, what are you on?' said Jackie. 'Are you taking something?'

I explained I was on tablets from my doctor.

'You've got dead eyes in the camera,' she said. 'They're dead.'

The tablets weren't making me feel any better either so when I returned home to Bolton I decided to ditch them. I gradually weaned myself off them over a few weeks but the withdrawal symptoms were still horrific. I had hallucinations, creeping scalp, where it feels like you have spiders crawling all over your head, and cold sweats in the middle of the night.

Dr Pasterski is a brilliant doctor and he was doing everything he could to get me well again. There are tons of different kinds of anti-depressants available, and as with the contraceptic pill, different pills suit different people. Unfortunately this particular drug really didn't suit me. I told Dr Pasterski I'd given up the drugs and though he was disappointed that the treatment hadn't worked, he prescribed me something different again called Venlafaxine. He also sent me to see Dr Helen Buckler, an endocrinologist, who specialised in hormone problems. She discovered I had no oestrogen at all and was very positive from the beginning that she would soon have me feeling better once she had my hormones more in balance.

I also went to a counsellor and I found seeing her really helpful, as for the first time in ages someone seemed to think I had something to offer and something interesting to say. I just didn't feel that from anyone else at the time, particularly not from Steve, the person who was supposed to be closest to me.

Within a few weeks I finally started to feel better again.

Throughout the whole thing I'd only taken three weeks

off work and only Denise Welsh, Charlie Lawson and the producer Brian Park knew how ill I had been. Gradually the feeling of emptiness left me and I began to enjoy work and home again. I was on the road to recovery.

13
LIZ LEAVES THE STREET

....

The sun had finally dropped below the horizon but it was still a gorgeous warm evening. Steve and I were sitting with our friends Nicola and Alex outside our rented Spanish holiday villa. I had a glass of chilled white wine in my hand and felt utterly relaxed.

'Can you imagine how wonderful it would be to live here all the time?' Nicola said.

'Maybe we should try it,' Alex joked.

'But maybe we really should,' I joined in.

Within a few minutes, Alex, Nicola, Steve and I had hatched a plan that was to lead to an amazing new chapter in all our lives – moving to Spain.

I'd first met Nicola when she had come to one of the seminars I ran for fitness trainers. She taught exercise classes near her home in Durham and had come along to the session I was running in Newcastle. As soon as she walked in I thought, 'Oh my God, that woman has a figure to die for and the most beautiful, smiley face.'

After the seminar a group of us sat and had a cup of coffee and I got talking to Nicola. 'I'm going to use you in my next fitness DVD,' I said. I took her number but I'm sure she thought I'd never ring. But the following year, when it was time to film the DVD, I called her and she came down to be in it.

We quickly became great friends and Steve, Josh and I went on holiday twice to Spain with her and Alex, their daughter Leigh and son Adam, who was a year younger than Josh.

Everything about the Spanish way of life appealed to us: the weather, the laid back attitude and the outdoor life. Steve was a little bit less excited about the thought of moving out there permanently but Alex, Nicola and I talked about it and talked about it and soon we were treating the idea very seriously.

For me, the hardest decision was leaving *Coronation Street*. I loved my job but I thought moving to Spain might give me the chance to be a proper mum to Josh and a proper wife to Steve. I felt very guilty that I wasn't seeing Josh as much as I should. It felt to me that whenever he had a swimming gala, I'd be at work. And the nativity play, I'd miss that. Whatever it was, I never seemed to make it. The weekends he didn't come home from boarding school were the worst. I'd be thinking, 'He should be here now, he should be here now.' It felt as if he was growing up without me. I thought how wonderful it would be if I wasn't working and we were all together in Spain – then I could see him every morning, every evening and every weekend.

I also thought that by giving up my long hours at *Coronation Street* and starting a new way of life in Spain, I would be able to get my marriage firmly back on track. The hours on *Coronation Street* at that time were really tough. I did thirty-three weeks of six days a week and it was all heavy drama and totally exhausting.

Steve still really didn't like me being recognised everywhere we went, and it certainly took me a while to get used to too. Being in a soap doesn't make you a star – we don't get paid millions of pounds or anything like that – but it does make you a household name. And because you're on the telly in people's front rooms three or four times a week they really do feel like they know you, so when they see you they want to stop for a chat. I hoped that being in Spain where hardly anyone would recognise me might mean there was one less pressure for the both of us on our marriage.

I was also coming up for my tenth year in the Street and felt ready for a change. I still wanted to try other things and I feared that if I didn't leave soon, maybe I never would.

I'd had an incredible time in *Coronation Street* with some amazing storylines. Liz had developed so much in the time I'd played her, going from someone dominated by her husband to an independent woman with her own life and career. She had also been a battered wife, which had led to literally binbags full of letters pouring in from viewers who were affected by the scenes. What neither they nor the rest of the cast knew was that I'd been through similar problems myself in my first marriage. There was a huge poignancy to those scenes for me. Liz had also been held hostage at gunpoint, lost a baby and had an affair. It had been ten years of high drama!

I was once talking to the show archivist and I said, 'I so want to do comedy.' I had loved working with Bet and Alec and Jack in the Rovers and I wanted more of that.

'No, it won't happen,' he replied. 'Liz and Deirdre are at the high drama character end of the scale, they'll never get comedy.'

It had reached a point where I really wanted to do some different roles and, particularly, play a part that would make people laugh.

The previous year I had thought about leaving the programme and had ended up staying. But the following March, when I and the rest of the crew got our letters saying they would like to renew our contracts, I thought, 'No. I'm going to go. If I don't do it now I never will.'

I went to see the producer, Brian Park, who had already announced he would soon be leaving himself.

'I'm really flattered you've asked me to stay but I'd like to leave at the end of this contract,' I said. Honest to God, he nearly fell off his chair!

'Are you serious?' Brian said, in his strong Scottish accent.

'Yes,' I said.

'Do you want more money?' he asked.

'No,' I said. 'If I wanted more money I'd ask for money.'

'Well, has someone upset you then?'

'No,' I said. 'I just want to leave. I love it here, I love it and I so hope you don't kill Liz off but I just want to do other things.'

'Well, is there anything I can do to make you change your mind?'

'No,' I said. 'I don't think there is.'

There was a series of meetings with the casting director Judy Hayfield and the then executive producer Carolyn Reynolds, but I had made up my mind. I think they understood that mainly I wanted to go because of Josh. I needed to spend more time with him and while I remained in *Coronation Street* I couldn't. It was a factory there – we had one day off a week and just three days off at Christmas. And everyone at work knew that me and Steve were having a few problems in our marriage and this was my chance to try to put things right. It was hard breaking the news to Charlie and he was sad about it, but he knew I wanted to try to fix things at home and he understood.

My plan was that once I was settled in Spain, I would return to England for short spells when good acting jobs came along and I'd also do fitness training out there with Nicola. She and Alex were making their plans for the big move to Spain, too. Alex was an electrician and singer so we thought he would be able to find work quite easily. Steve was the only one of us who might struggle to find work but we thought he could help Alex doing up a property once we'd found somewhere to buy.

My last few weeks on set were really sad. Phil Middlemiss, who played Des Barnes, had also handed in his notice and it was weird knowing that soon neither of us would be part of *Coronation Street* any longer.

In the storyline, the McDonalds had split up but then Jim and Steve had a really big fight on a building site and Jim had fallen from some scaffolding. No one was ever quite sure whether Steve had in fact pushed him. Afterwards, Jim couldn't walk and was in a wheelchair so Liz took pity on him and went back to him. Except then she started having an affair with this young, handsome physiotherapist called Michael, who was coming round the house to treat Jim. Jim was about to propose to Liz again when he found them in bed together, went ballistic and told Liz to get out.

My last scene was in the McDonalds' living room in November 1998 when Liz said to Jim, 'I'm going.' It was really, really sad but we knew we had to keep it together until the scene was in the can. As soon as it was finished everyone started crying. Charlie and Simon Gregson and I were all really upset. We'd been a family for almost ten years and been through so much together and now it was over.

That evening, *Coronation Street* threw an amazing party for me.

Nick Cochrane had been written out by then but he came back for the party and everyone from the cast was there. Even Victoria and David Beckham came because he was still playing in Manchester at that point and I'd met Victoria a few times through Rebecca's friend, Mel B. Paul O'Grady came along and compèred the evening, Russell Watson sang for me and Cliff Richard sent a massive bouquet of flowers.

My only disappointment was that Rebecca was abroad filming the TV series *Sunburn*. It was being produced by Tony Wood, who used to work at *Coronation Street*, and I was a bit annoyed that he had been able to fly back for my party but hadn't allowed Rebecca to do the same.

Then, a magician came on stage and started performing some tricks and suddenly he magicked Rebecca out of a box. It was fantastic.

Simon Gregson had a speech prepared but he couldn't deliver it because he was crying constantly. Charlie cried. I cried. Everyone cried.

Then they presented me with a cobble from the Street with a red stiletto mounted on it. They'd also had one of Liz's miniskirts framed, with some lines from the script carved around it. Above the skirt it says, 'Liz: "Bet, do you think I dress like a tart?"'

And beneath it is written, 'Bet: "No, some days we can't see your knickers at all."' I keep that in my dining room and I'll always treasure it.

The only two days in my life that have been more emotional than my last day on Corrie were the births of Rebecca and Josh.

When I got home it felt strange that a big part of my life was over but as usual I didn't give myself any time to dwell on it. Two days later I began rehearsing for panto, which I'd arranged to do before we moved to Spain the following year.

Rebecca was living and working in London by then but we knew we would be seeing a lot of her when we were in Spain because she was still filming *Sunburn* in Portugal.

When we arrived in Marbella in 1999, we rented a big house about ten minutes from the beach for Steve, Nicola, Alex, the kids and me. It had a massive pool and was just beautiful. Antonio Banderas and Melanie Griffith lived at the top of the road. We'd chosen Marbella because we'd been on holiday there together and I loved it from the very first moment I set foot there. I adored the sunshine and the outdoor life but most of all, I loved being able to take Josh to school at the English International College in the morning and to pick him up in the afternoon. After years of missing assemblies and nativity plays, at last I was a full-time mum.

It took a few weeks to get used to the different pace of life in Spain. At first it drives you mad because you are still trying to function the way you did back in England whereas over there, everything is so much slower and more relaxed. Once we had wound down a bit and got used to it, it was brilliant. I do think the Spanish way of life is fantastic, particularly for children because they can be outside all day long.

When we'd spent a few months working out where we wanted to live permanently, the four of us bought a plot of land in La Cala on the outskirts of Marbella, where we intended to build a house. We were hoping that in the short term we would also be able to buy the house that we had been renting. But with neither Steve nor I working, we soon found our finances were going down fast. So I took a part in a sitcom with Jim Broadbent called *The Peter Principle* and returned to England to film that. Then, after a bit more time off, I did a feature-length episode of *Casualty*.

Nicola got a job selling timeshare apartments but it wasn't right for her. Then she got a job in a really nice restaurant as a waitress and she enjoyed that. Alex was also working as an electrician. So apart from Steve, we were all busy working, trying to put enough money together to build our dream home.

I think a lot of people who move abroad make the mistake of treating it like a holiday, but you can't afford to lose your work ethic. You still have to get up in the morning and go to work, otherwise things can go very wrong. Steve hadn't had a steady job in years, so it was left to me, Alex and Nicola to bring in the money. The problem was, even with all three of us doing our best, our savings were rapidly diminishing.

And then Steve started to behave differently, really differently. He started going out on his own a lot more and was drinking much more than he had in England. In Spain there are bars everywhere, even in petrol stations. They serve all day and all night and the shots are triples.

As well as going out more, I noticed that Steve also became very moody. Nicola, Alex and I would get up in the morning and have breakfast around the dining table with the children, but often Steve would still be in bed. Then Nicola and

I would take the kids to school and when we got back, he still wouldn't be up.

If we were all going for dinner in the evening, Steve would say, 'No, I'm not coming, I'll get a takeaway later.' He stopped joining in with the rest of us at all. Then, when he did go for the takeaway he'd be gone three hours and get back having had a few drinks.

We all started taking Spanish lessons but Steve dropped out after only the fourth one. The rest of us were meeting new people and making friends, both Spanish and English, but Steve just didn't seem interested. On one occasion we were all invited out for Sunday lunch but Steve just said, 'I'm not coming.' Alex was really annoyed. 'Why not?' he said. 'We've come here to meet people and to start a new life. What's the matter with you?'

While the rest of us were mucking in with cooking, cleaning and decorating our rented house, Steve wasn't helping out at all. There was one massive row between Steve and Alex because he wasn't pulling his weight at all. Alex tried to get through to him that he was letting us all down but Steve wouldn't listen.

Another time we were all in the car going somewhere with Alex driving and Steve in the front seat and they started rowing. Suddenly Alex slammed on the brakes and jumped out of the car, shouting, 'Come on then, let's sort this out right now. Come on.'

Steve backed down and apologised and we all tried to put the row behind us but I think Nicola and Alex were getting more and more fed up with Steve for his behaviour. Now that we were sharing a house, they realised he could be very hurtful, chipping away at my already very fragile self-esteem.

One day, Steve was sitting in the office of our rented house. I walked into the room but as I did, I saw him drop his mobile phone.

'Who was that on the phone?' I said.

'I wasn't on the phone,' he replied.

'Oh, OK,' I said, 'so why don't you give it to me to look at then?'

So then he went on the offensive. 'You're a f****** psycho you are,' he yelled, 'I wasn't on the phone.'

That sort of thing would happen quite often if we rowed about him disappearing for hours on end or going out drinking. When I challenged him about his behaviour he'd say I was paranoid and sometimes I did think, 'Yes, it's me. I am going mad. I can't get over the affair and I'm just imagining all these things. He doesn't even know anyone here, so how could he possibly be cheating on me again?'

Nicola's mum had by now also moved out to Spain and one day she had a big row with Steve because she didn't like his attitude or the way he was treating me. But Steve didn't seem to care about any of us. He was getting more and more moody and it was awful for all of us to live with.

I felt so sad that my dream of saving our marriage with a new life together seemed to be collapsing around me.

At the same time, Josh was struggling at school. The college he was going to wasn't able to cater for his dyslexia in the same way as they had at Giggleswick. We found a tutor for him, but everything was making me feel that things just weren't turning out to be the happy-ever-after I'd hoped for. Then they took a turn for the worse.

I was still taking the Venlafaxine antidepressants and every month I would go to my GP in Spain for a repeat prescription. One afternoon I picked up the tablets and they were in different packaging but I didn't think too much about it, went home and swallowed the pills as normal. A day and a half later I couldn't stop crying. I felt flat and empty all over again, as if nothing in my life meant anything. For a week I felt like that. I had a dressing room attached to our bedroom upstairs and I would just sit in there for hours on end, crying. I honestly felt like I didn't want to be alive any more, I just couldn't see the point in it.

After about ten days I went to my GP, desperate for help to make me feel better. It was only then that he worked out that I had been given the wrong medication and the chemicals in my brain must have been turned totally upside down. After a couple of weeks I felt more normal again.

Steve's moods were only getting worse, though. If we went outside to the pool, he'd stay indoors. He refused to take Josh to his tennis lessons, which I'd hoped would help him with his coordination. There still seemed no chance that Steve might get a job, even though our savings were virtually gone. I just kept hoping that once all the paperwork was done on the land we were going to buy, maybe the house-building project would give him a goal and he would return to normal.

I was being sent lots of scripts to read in Spain but I was very choosy because I didn't just want to play the character of Liz McDonald again in a different show. I also didn't want to leave my family in Spain to return to England to film unless it was something I really wanted to do.

Then I was offered the part of Floella in the BBC 2 comedy *Two Pints of Lager and a Packet of Crisps*. The writer, Sue Nickson, said that when she heard I was leaving Corrie she thought I'd be perfect for the role. As soon as I got the script, I thought, 'I can't say no to this. I've got to do it.' It was a brilliant part because Floella was outrageous and even more brash than Liz McDonald.

Initially, we had a workshop with all the actors who were going to be in the show and Maxine Peak, who later appeared in *Shameless* and *Dinnerladies*, played my daughter, but when we came to do the series, Natalie Casey played that part. We all got on really well and it was brilliant fun to do. It amazed me that the writer, Sue Nickson, who was only eighteen when she wrote the first series, could write so well for the youngsters but also for the older character Floella.

Towards the end of 2000, *Coronation Street* asked me to return to England for a while because Charlie Lawson was leaving as Jim and they wanted me involved in the storyline, which would be screened around the time of the show's fortieth anniversary at the end of that year. They flew me over to Manchester for a meeting and I said I'd love to come back for a while but I didn't want to just cry next to a coffin for two weeks.

In the end the storyline was that Jim had been sent to jail for manslaughter for attacking drug dealer Jez Quigley, who'd tried to kill Steve. Then Liz, who'd split up with her handsome physiotherapist, started visiting Jim in jail and in November 2000 they remarried. It was Liz's way of showing Jim that she was certain he was going to be found innocent at his trial.

Commuting back and forth from Spain was fine and I loved being back in the Street for a while and working with Charlie again. I think he also enjoyed me being back because he felt they hadn't written well for him since I'd gone, which was partly why he wanted to leave the series. He also wanted to do other things himself because he is a fine actor.

We had to film a lot of those scenes actually inside

Strangeways Prison in Manchester, so we'd go early on a Sunday morning to do it. When you looked across you could see some of the inmates through their windows and it always made me think, 'How on earth does anyone survive in prison? It is so awful.'

For the fortieth anniversary we were also filming an entire episode totally live. It was fantastic fun to do although pretty scary as there was absolutely no cheating, it was all live and even Prince Charles had come to watch it.

Liz was working in the Rovers again for the new landlady Natalie Barnes, who was played by Denise Welch. Denise had only just started when I had left the show but I knew her because she had been so kind to me when I'd been hit by depression. I'd always thought that our characters would be really good together because they would either love or hate each other. When we did finally start working together we had a great rapport but we also found it hard work because we would laugh so much. For me, it was like the good old days again when I'd worked with Julie Goodyear, Bill Tarmey and Roy Barraclough. It was just brilliant.

During the live episode, Vera Duckworth was in a coma and the set they'd built for that scene was right next door to the Rovers set. They were filming a scene with Vera and then the next bit was to be Liz and Natalie Barnes in the hallway of the Rovers. But as we stood there waiting for our moment we heard this terrible creaking noise – the coat rack on the wall as you walk into the living room was starting to fall off the wall!

Denise and I were going, 'Oh f***, what are we going to do?' So Vera was in a coma in one room and the other side of this paper-thin wall, the coat rack was collapsing. We were in hysterics, trying to lower it to the ground really gently so it didn't make any noise. And then we were racing to hang all the coats back up on a few old screws still sticking out of the wall, to cover up the big gap where the coat rack should have been before the cameras got to us. Oh my God, that was hilarious.

It was a really busy time for me because I would shoot all my scenes for *Coronation Street* on a Sunday, then travel down to London that evening, arriving at about two in the morning. All week I was doing *Two Pints* during the day and in the evenings I was recording a radio series *Stockport, So Good They Named It Once*, which had won awards. We needed the money, so I was trying to earn as much as I could before I went back to Spain.

Then, one Monday morning, I was in a taxi on my way to the BBC to film *Two Pints* when my phone rang. It was Nicola.

'I've got some really, really bad news,' she said.

14
ALONE

....

She may have been 800 miles away but the telephone line was crystal clear and there was no mistaking what Nicola was telling me.

'Steve has been seeing another woman and he brought her back to the house last night,' she said slowly I felt like someone had punched me in the stomach. But the news was getting worse.

'I'm so sorry, but Josh saw them together,' Nicola said. 'He went into your bedroom and they were there.'

I felt angry, devastated and stunned all at once. This time, there was no part of me that couldn't believe what I was hearing, even though on some level I thought, 'I should have seen this coming.' Steve can't honestly have thought he would get away with taking another woman back to my bed and no one else in the house noticing. Maybe he just didn't care any more if I found out or not.

I was desperate to jump on the first plane to Marbella but I knew I couldn't because I was in the middle of three jobs and if I let down the BBC, Granada and BBC Radio I would probably never work again. From the moment Nicola told me what had happened, I knew I'd be bringing up Josh on my own from then on, so I was going to need every penny I could get. So I told the cab driver to keep going and I went straight on set for *Two Pints*.

I didn't cry at first, I think I was too stunned, but my emotions were swinging from feeling broken-hearted to thinking I was going to smash Steve's face in.

When I got to the studios I told the director and a couple of the cast what had happened and they were all so kind. Natalie Casey and Sheridan Smith were a lot younger than me but they were so supportive as I spent every spare moment of the day on the phone to Steve, Nicola, Mum and Steph.

When I rang Steve I went mad down the phone at him. I was screaming, asking him why he'd done it but he couldn't even offer a reason. This time we both knew there would be no going back, our marriage was over.

When I told Mum, I think she was relieved that I was determined to leave him this time; she had always thought that I shouldn't have taken him back after his first affair.

Alex and Nicola were devastated too – moving to Spain had been our joint dream and now Steve had ruined it for all of us. We had to abandon the plan of buying the house we were renting and set about selling the land we'd bought in La Cala. Everything was a mess.

Over the next few days I found out through friends in Spain that the 'other woman' was a nineteen-year-old Russian girl. Again, Steve never told me what had gone on or how long it lasted, but I think it must have been at least two or three months. I suppose he had been with her every time he said he was going for a takeaway or for a drink. Although I had been struggling to overcome my suspicions ever since Steve's previous affair, somehow I still couldn't quite believe he'd done it again. We didn't even think he knew anyone in Spain well enough to have an affair with.

Over the next few days I was also on the phone to Josh at every opportunity, trying to reassure him that everything would be all right. He was only ten years old and God knows what he must have thought when he walked into his parents' bedroom and saw his dad there with another woman. We've since talked about it a lot and the whole thing has been very, very hard for him.

I also spoke to my solicitor in London. There was no doubt in my mind that this time it was the end and no amount of crying and pleading by Steve would persuade me to give him another chance. I still loved him but now I hated him as well. I wanted a divorce. I had to go back to London because of my job, leaving Josh behind with Steve.

'What the hell am I going to do?' I said to my solicitor. 'I'm in the middle of three jobs that I can't just walk out on but I'm worried about Josh. I can't leave him with Steve.'

'You've got to get Steve back here,' said the lawyer. 'You've got to get him back to Britain.'

'But how am I going to that?' I said.

'You'll have to make him think it will be worth his while.'

The next time I spoke to Steve, we were both a bit calmer.

'This marriage is over,' I said.

'Yeah,' he agreed. 'It is.'

'I'll book you a flight and you can come over and we'll talk it through,' I said. 'Nicola and Alex will look after Josh while you're away. I'll get John to pick you up from the airport and bring you to the flat.' John was this great guy who had driven for me for years when I was in London and I'd become good friends with both him and his wife. So I rang John and asked him to collect Steve and bring him round to mine but not to tell him that he would wait outside to drive him on to his mum's house in Leeds.

The plane was due to land at ten o'clock at night and I was so tense as I saw it getting closer to the time. Then just after eleven o'clock there was a knock at the door – it was Steve. He was barely inside the flat before he started crying all over again.

'I'm sorry,' he said. 'I'm so sorry. I still love you, I still fancy you. I don't know why I did it.'

I was really calm and just sat there listening to him even though I was dying on the inside. I still loved him and was heartbroken it had come to this but this time, no part of me wanted him back. In fact I wanted to lean across and punch his lights out but I knew I had to be strong for the kids and myself.

I said, 'Look, you've had a long journey, why don't you have a cup of tea and a bath and then we'll talk about it.'

So he went and ran a bath but while he was in there I picked up his holdall and started rummaging through it. My hands were shaking and I was terrified he was about to find me. At the bottom of the bag I found his passport. I took it into the kitchen, cut it into tiny pieces then hid it in the microwave. I couldn't think where else to put it! It sounds an awful thing to do but at that time I felt it was the only way I could prevent Steve from going back to Spain and arrange for Josh to come back as soon as possible.

I was still shaking when he came out of the bath. I know he thought I was going to go to bed with him when he came back into the room, but he couldn't have been more wrong.

'Did you make the tea?' he said.

'No,' I replied. His passport was destroyed and I was now able to speak my mind. 'I didn't make the tea and I have to tell you, I hate your guts. You are never doing this to me again. You're not getting anything from me. There is a car outside to take you to your parents in Leeds. Now f*** off, I don't ever want to see you again.'

And that was it.

'You don't mean it, you really don't mean it,' Steve said. 'You won't get away with this.'

'I've done it,' I replied.

Rebecca and her boyfriend were living in a flat upstairs at the time and I had their number on redial on my phone so I could call them at a moment's notice if Steve got angry. But rather than start screaming and shouting, he stayed quite calm, picked up his bag and walked out the door.

A few days later he rang me and said, 'Did I leave my passport there? Can you send it up to me?'

'No I can't,' I said. 'I've cut it up into little pieces so you can't go back to Spain.' He was furious.

It was only a few days until I finished filming *Two Pints of Lager* and my part in Jim's departure from *Coronation Street* and then I was able to fly back to Spain to be with Josh. That was an incredible relief but Josh was heartbroken by what had happened. For a long time he was a very sad little boy.

It was tough being back in Spain because everything we'd dreamed of had turned sour. We'd all had to move out of the big house we'd rented. Alex and Nicola had found somewhere smaller and they let Josh and me stay with them while we worked out what we should do next.

Mum and Stephanie were both saying I should come back

to England and they'd help me get back on my feet, and I knew my only chance of work was at home. But it wasn't as easy as just moving back. I'd taken Josh to a different country and he'd just got settled in school, had made friends, was enjoying tennis and now had a great tutor for his dyslexia. He loved it there and it just didn't seem fair to say, 'Sorry son, we're off again,' and to uproot him back to England. So we decided to stay.

On 18 December 2000, Josh and I moved into a small three-bedroom flat in Marbella. I had hardly any money at all by this point and was still waiting to be paid for all the work I'd done while I was in England. I had no other jobs lined up and was now a single mum living in a foreign country. I thought to myself, 'F****** hell. What next?'

That Christmas, Rebecca came over to spend it with us in Spain. We tried to make it as jolly as we could for Josh but I still felt that there was a terrible black cloud hanging over me. Then for New Year, Josh flew back to England to see Steve, who was living with his dad. I paid for the flight, thinking I had to keep my feelings out of it and try to ensure Josh kept a relationship with his dad. While he was there, Josh and I spoke on the phone a few times and I could tell something wasn't quite right, but it was only when he got home he told me that the nineteen-year-old Russian girl had been there too.

'I didn't want to tell you on the phone because I knew you'd be upset,' Josh said.

I felt so sorry for him. It turned out he'd had the most miserable New Year ever. Josh spent most of the holiday watching Cartoon Network.

I was bloody boiling that Steve had the Russian girl staying at the same time as our son and rang him up, shouting and screaming like a madwoman.

'So? So? It's not your problem,' Steve kept saying. He just didn't get that he had done anything wrong at all.

We began divorce proceedings on the grounds of adultery and I gave Steve ten thousand pounds as a payoff and agreed to take full financial responsibility for Josh. All Steve had to do was get a job, hold on to it and support himself.

After a while, Josh and I moved into a rented house a bit closer to Puerto Banus. The rent was quite low because I helped maintain the house but things were still tight financially. Then one day, I got a letter from a solicitor in Pudsey saying Steve Callard wanted a one-off cash payment. Apparently that was based on his estimate of the equity on a small flat we owned in Kilburn, north London. He was demanding maintenance and a percentage of my future income. I was reading the letter and thinking, 'Is Jeremy Beadle about to jump out on me here? He cannot be serious about this.' Josh was living with me, I was paying all his school fees and everything else. I had no money and wasn't even able to work back in Britain because now that I was on my own I couldn't leave Josh. My only income was from fitness classes but that wasn't much at all.

I rang my lawyer thinking he'd just laugh at the letter, but instead he said, 'I'm afraid you might have to make him a payoff, Beverley.'

I was gobsmacked. He had barely earned a penny during the whole time we'd been married and I was still expected to pay for him now we were getting divorced.

'No,' I said. 'If I give him a fiver he has won and I won't let that happen.'

So I fought it. The case went on for ages. By the time the

case got to court, my legal fees were £49,000 but I still wasn't going to give in.

On the day of the hearing, Steve and I came face to face for the first time in months, outside the courtroom.

He started trying to talk me round. He hoped we could settle our dispute and he was being really nice to me and for a second I believed the things he was saying but then I came to my senses. He couldn't sweet-talk me any more.

After hearing the evidence in court, the judge concluded Steve wasn't entitled to anything further from me. He said the money I had already given him was enough and now Steve had to find his own way in life. I was so relieved. I couldn't afford the money Steve was asking for but even if I had been able to, it seemed so wrong that he should get a payout when he was the one who'd had two affairs.

When the divorce became final I felt sad but relieved. I wasn't just closing another difficult chapter in my marriage this time, I was closing the book. I felt sad because I'd lost my parents-in-law, Hughie and Sandra, and they were such good people.

I also still had to find £50,000 for the legal fees for the court battle with Steve. And by then Josh and I were totally broke.

I knew I was going to have to take more acting work in Britain if we were going to stay afloat as it was clear I couldn't earn enough in Spain from my fitness classes to support us. But Josh didn't want to leave his new school and friends to move back to England and after everything he'd been through, it didn't seem fair to upset him. So I said that if Josh wanted to stay in Spain I would commute backwards and forwards every weekend and I would either employ a childminder to take care of him or he could go to a boarding school locally, where he already had friends. Josh said he wanted to go to the boarding school with his mates, so that is what we did. I hated being away from Josh again but by then he was feeling happy and very secure in Spain and I didn't have the heart to pull him back to England again just because I was going back to work.

I got more work in the second series of *Two Pints* and they were brilliant about arranging the work schedules around me so I could make the flight back to Spain on a Friday. I made sure that any other work fitted around my weekends in Spain, too. So gradually, a bit more cash started coming in. Josh loved his new school and both of us were meeting new people and making friends. I was still on a mixture of HRT and Venlafaxine and I was feeling better in myself than I had done in years.

And so, slowly I started the climb back up again.

15
FUN IN THE SUN

....

For almost the first time since I was sixteen, I was single and an independent woman. Life was good.

I was teaching fitness classes in Spain and flying back to England when work came up that interested me. I filmed a second series of *Two Pints of Lager* and did a theatre tour called *Mum's The Word*, in which six women including Tina Malone from *Shameless* and Julia Watson from *Casualty* performed monologues about being a mum. It was so funny and I loved it.

Every time I got two or three days off I would fly back to Spain to see Josh or if I were working over a weekend, he would come and visit me. While I was working in England I was also able to see more of Rebecca who in 2001 married her husband, Gideon. The pair had been cast together as the lovers in a *Midsummer Night's Dream* and they feel hopelessly in love themselves. It was all terribly romantic. I loved spending time with Rebecca and Gideon because I could see how happy they made each other.

I was also building up a great social life in Spain. I'd never really been into wild nightlife, concentrating on working rather than partying. Yes, there had been the odd occasion when some friends and I had gone on big nights out, but most of the time I was quite boring. If I had an early start I was always in bed early.

For the first year after I split up with Steve, all I did was work and look after Josh, but as the months passed by I began going out in the evenings with friends I had met locally. I'd also become good friends with Denise Welch during the time that I'd returned to Corrie and when she told me once that she'd never been to southern Spain, I said, 'You've really got to come out'. So she did and she absolutely loved it.

Denise and I can both be absolutely outrageous and very bad influences on each other, but we get on brilliantly. We can have really deep conversations about the meaning of life and depression and all sorts of serious things but then we can go completely the other way and be really mad.

Before Denise first came out to visit me, I'd heard there was great nightlife in Puerto Banus with piano bars and clubs, but I had never been to them. So when Denise arrived, we got our glad rags on and went in search of the bright lights. The first time we went out we arrived in a piano bar at about eight o'clock and of course it was totally deserted because in Spain no one goes out until about eleven and the peak party time isn't until about two o'clock in the morning. So we went back a second time, much later in the evening, and we found this nightlife in Puerto Banus that I'd known nothing about. It was so much fun.

In England, things are very much geared towards couples and if you are a woman on your own it can feel as though you are lacking in something. But in Spain, the focus is on the whole family and there isn't the same pressure to be with a partner all the time. At first it is a shock because you'll be in a restaurant, thinking, 'Oh my God, it's nearly midnight and there's a baby in a pushchair over there.' But then you get used to it and it's great.

One day when Denise was staying, the two of us and my friend Nicola decided we'd hit the beach. We agreed it'd be baseball caps on, no makeup and no one would ever know it was us. So off we went in our big baggy shorts and t-shirts and at first no one recognised us at all and it was just fantastic.

We kept going backwards and forwards to the beach bar for more jugs of sangria until there we were, five jugs later, all three of us on a pedalo singing songs from the shows at the tops of our voices! I was lying upside down on the slide at the back of the pedalo, absolutely paralytic. Denise and Nicola were at the front but we were just going round and round in circles because only one of them was pedaling.

At one point we were singing 'There is Nothing Like a Dame' while more and more people were lining up on the beach staring out to sea at us. It was like that moment in the film *What Ever Happened To Baby Jane?* when Bette Davis goes mad on the beach and there is a whole audience of people watching her. People were saying, 'Oh my God, it's Liz and Natalie. What are they doing?' They were all pointing and taking photographs. Before, I would have thought that was just terrible, but Denise taught me not to worry what people thought and that I was allowed to have a good time, too. What we were doing wasn't awful at all, it was just fun.

Denise came over quite a few times and then she bought

an apartment out there herself. And then so did Liz Dawn who played Vera Duckworth and Kevin Kennedy who was Curly Watts. At one point a newspaper ran a story saying, 'Weatherfield is moving to Marbella!'

Another time, Denise came out to Spain to do a magazine photo shoot with some of her *Coronation Street* friends and I agreed to be in the feature, along with Gabrielle Glaister, who played Natalie Barnes' sister, Debs.

We were due to do the shoot on a Sunday so we decided we'd go out for dinner on the Saturday evening with the journalist, Steven, the photographer and lighting guys. We were really sensible during dinner and hardly drank, but afterwards we thought we'd just quickly pop into our favourite piano bar, which was called Marvellous. Then we started on the vodka Red Bulls.

At Marvellous we bumped into a friend of ours who at around three in the morning offered to take us all out on his yacht. 'Why not?' we thought. So there we were in the middle of the night on this luxury yacht in the Med with music blasting out and us all singing along. Then we decided it was the perfect time for a swim. We all jumped in and paddled around a bit and then most of us got out again, at which point Denise and I thought it would be hilarious to turn the boat on and drive it a few yards. Except of course we didn't realise you can't go just a few yards in a massive luxury boat. When we turned the ignition on, the boat sped off for what seemed like forever. And Gabby and Steven were still in the water!

At first we were laughing hysterically like naughty schoolgirls but when we realised how far we'd gone, we were going mad. It was pitch dark on the sea and we couldn't see a thing. 'Oh my God, we've killed them,' I kept saying. 'Oh my God.'

We turned the engine off, the music off and the lights off in the hope of seeing Gabby and Steven but there was no sign of them. Then we switched them all back on, hoping they would be able to see us. I was convinced we'd killed them.

Then, after what seemed like an eternity, we heard these voices. 'For f***'s sake', Steven was saying and Gabby, who is wonderful and terribly posh, was saying, 'Don't worry, I'm an incredibly strong swimmer, hang on to me.' Eventually they got to the edge of the boat and we hauled them up. 'We're so sorry,' we kept saying, 'we're so sorry.' and I think they were both terrified. Denise and I felt awful.

The next morning, we had to do the photo shoot with crippling hangovers. We looked like Crufts champions and the poor makeup woman really had her work cut out to make us look passable.

In Spain I also found a social life with friends I had made through teaching fitness classes. There were Spanish, English, French, Belgian and German women in my classes but we all became really good friends and on a Friday and Saturday night we'd get our glad rags on and go out. We had some great times.

One night a group of us went for a big night out in Puerto Banus. We were out until very, very late and I was hitting the vodka Red Bulls big time. It was about six o'clock in the morning when I started staggering home with a friend of mine who was a keyboard player in one of the piano bars. We were very, very drunk and decided to stop off for a kebab. As you do!

I'm not sure what started it but we began having this food fight with the kebab and there were bits of meat and pitta bread flying everywhere. We must have looked awful.

That morning I was supposed to be teaching my fitness class at ten o'clock so I just got home, threw on a tracksuit and went straight out again. And I made it on time, even though I think I was still tripping on the vodka Red Bulls!

In the class I was warming up with all my ladies and was shaking my head around when all of a sudden a piece of kebab flew out of my hair! It was so embarrassing.

But we had such a laugh in those classes and often once we'd finished the lesson we would all go down to one of the beach bars for a real girlie lunch and several jugs of sangria!

After I'd been single for a while I started dating a guy out there called Terry. He was divorced, originally from Yorkshire and a bit older than me – and he was a millionaire! We were friends for quite a long time and eventually it developed into a relationship. But after a couple of months I felt he was looking for someone who'd be content to fit into the role of a little wife, being looked after by him. He certainly didn't want a woman who kept going back to England to work. Once I agreed to go back to England to a party organised by OK! magazine and Terry was furious about it. He couldn't understand why I was going to a party in England without him. Terry was a good person but I could never give up work and just live off him, so we agreed it wasn't going to work between us and split up.

My next boyfriend in Spain was an Italian guy called Paulo who worked in a local bar. And truly, Italians are *the* most romantic men in the world! Paulo was very handsome with a huge physique and an amazing sense of humour.

He made me laugh so much. One day he came to take me out and he kept saying he couldn't believe I had such small feet. In the end he made me take my shoes off and he hung them on the rear view mirror like a good luck charm. He was so, so romantic and if we were going on a date he would book us into amazing hotel suites where there would be smoked salmon, strawberries and champagne waiting for us. He treated me to amazing dinners in fantastic restaurants, was kind, interesting – and even bought me gorgeous shoes!

Paulo told me he was separated from his wife and he had a son who he doted upon. I met his little son a couple of times and he was obviously a great father. Paulo even came over to England to see me in the *Mum's the Word* theatre tour so it was becoming really quite serious between us. I had fallen madly in love with Paulo, or at least, I thought I had.

There was just one problem. People kept saying to me, 'He is married you know' and I'd reply, 'Yes, I know he's married, but he's separated.'

I never visited him at home but I was convinced he lived alone because he'd tell me things like he'd had to go round to his wife's house to pick up his son. I never doubted that he and his wife were separated and living apart.

Then, after we'd been seeing each other a few months, more and more often I'd hear people say things like, 'She's going out with a married man,' and I'd say, 'Hang on there, no I'm not.'

I spoke to people who knew him and they confirmed he was definitely still living with his wife. That was a total no-no for me and I ended it immediately. But even then Paulo still denied everything. Looking back I can't believe I didn't realise what was going on sooner, but Paulo was a very convincing liar. For a couple of weeks I was heartbroken. And then I got over it! I think I'd reached that stage where you think, 'F******* hell, all men are bastards.'

Then Josh and I found ourselves someone who really needed

our love – our little dog, Tilly. I was filming in London one day when the phone rang. It was Josh, who was then twelve, and he was sobbing so much I could hardly work out what he was saying.

'A little dog has turned up here at school, Mum and someone has tried to hang her. She's still got the rope around her neck. Can we keep her, Mum? Please, can we keep her?'

There are hundreds of strays in Spain and lots of them have a disease which is the equivalent of AIDS in humans and if this dog had that, she would have to be put down. And how would we be able to look after a pet anyway, if I was to-ing and fro-ing to England for work?

'We can't keep her, darling,' I said. 'How would we look after her?' But Josh wouldn't take no for an answer. 'OK, if she's still there on Friday when I pick you up for the weekend, I'll take a look at her,' I said, feeling certain that some other gullible parent would have rescued her by then.

But come Friday, the scrappy grey-haired dog was still at school when I went to collect Josh. And when we climbed in the car to go home for the weekend, Tilly, as we called her, came too.

She was in an awful state. She had thirty-seven ticks on her, was stick thin and had a deep gouge around her neck where she had been hanged. We think she must have been strung up from a doorway because for more than a year she was so terrified of going through doors that we had to put her lead on and pull her through if we wanted her to go from one room to another. She was terribly nervous and at every opportunity she would run away into bushes in the countryside near our apartment and we'd have to go and find her. But we loved having her. Josh, Tilly and I were a great team and I was more than happy to keep it that way. The single life suited me. But some of my friends had other ideas.

One of the girls who came to my fitness classes and our girlie chats afterwards was called Tracy. She was originally from Luton but now ran a hair salon in Spain.

'I know just the fella for you,' she kept saying, week after week.

Tracy and her friend Beverley kept going on and on about this bloke called Jon McEwan. 'He is the nicest guy,' they'd say. 'He's good-looking, he's got three kids, he's a great dad, he's funny, really intelligent, plays the drums and he lives on his own in an apartment overlooking the beach.'

'No, no, no,' I replied. I really was not interested in men any more.

But they kept nagging me about it and then they invited me to a party on New Year's Eve 2002, saying Jon was going to be there. Finally I cracked and agreed to go along but at the last minute I rang up and said I'd been invited somewhere else with Josh and wouldn't be going. Tracy and Beverley still didn't give up – in fact they arranged for us three to go out for dinner one night with Tracy's husband Bradley, Beverley's husband Gary – and Jon. The date was set for January 11, 2003.

'What have you got to lose?' the girls from my class kept saying.

'A lot,' I replied. 'I'm single and independent for the first time in my life and I'm having a great time – I do not want a man!'

Tracy said that if I backed out of the dinner party at the last minute like the previous time, she would never speak to me again. She was joking but I knew I was going to have to go along this time, even though as I was getting ready that evening all I could think was, 'Why on earth have I said "yes" to this?'

I wore a black knee-length skirt, long black boots, a black sleeveless polo neck top and just a bit of makeup. To be honest, I'd made the minimum amount of effort. I arrived at Beverley's house, where we were meeting before dinner, was handed a glass of Bucks Fizz and saw a guy standing in the corner who I guessed must be Jon, even though no one had introduced us.

My first impressions? 'Oh my God,' I thought. 'He has a shaved head, a tattoo and a gold tooth! What am I doing here? I'm going to kill Tracy in the morning.'

After about twenty minutes, Jon and I introduced ourselves to each other and started chatting. Beverley's little Yorkshire terrier jumped up onto his knee but rather than make it get down, he stroked it. 'Oh well, he likes dogs,' I thought. 'That's something!'

When we arrived at the restaurant it felt like everyone in there knew him. He owned a very well respected building company and had done a lot of work for the restaurant owners. He obviously ate there regularly. We chatted loads during the meal and afterwards we all decided to go on to a bar called Vibes. Jon had built the bar and every time he went in there, all the staff and customers would say, 'Oh, it's Jon the builder,' or 'Hi Jon,' or 'How's it going Jon?' So he must have been thinking, 'Great, I'm going to know everyone there, she's going to be really impressed!'

When we walked into Vibes it was full of English people and they all suddenly started saying, 'Oh my God, it's

Beverley Callard. Oh my God.' And Jon was thinking, 'Oh. How many people does she know? She must have the biggest fitness class ever!'

Jon only knew me as a fitness teacher. He knew I'd done some acting back in England but he didn't know I'd been in *Coronation Street* so he couldn't understand how all these people recognised me. He'd lived in Spain for sixteen years by then and had never even seen Liz McDonald!

In Vibes, this gay guy came up to me who was so obsessed with *Coronation Street* and desperate to have his photograph taken with me that he literally fell off his seat. Jon was obviously thinking, 'What the hell is going on here?'

When I explained I'd been in *Coronation Street* for nearly ten years he was stunned. 'I'd better start watching it,' he laughed. But it was great meeting someone who knew nothing about me or Liz McDonald because I could be taken for exactly who I was, not who people thought I was.

We had such a lovely evening that I didn't want it to stop. That area of Spain is often called the Costa del Crime and there are quite a lot of dodgy people there, most of whom have shaved heads, tattoos and gold teeth, which was why I'd been so horrified by my first glance at Jon. But when we started talking I realised he wasn't anything like that at all. He was wonderful to talk to, he made me laugh and was fascinating company.

Jon had been married very young and served in the army before settling in Spain. He'd been separated from his wife for six months.

I didn't want to give him the wrong impression and invite him back to mine so we ended up drinking coffee and talking,

talking and talking in a petrol station opposite Vibes until five o'clock in the morning. Then Jon got a taxi and dropped me back home. As I was getting out he said, 'Would you like to go out again some time?'

'OK, yes,' I replied.

'When are you free then?'

'Tomorrow?' I replied. I think he was expecting me to say the following Saturday but I didn't want to wait until then. And neither did he!

Jon said he'd pick me up and take me somewhere authentically Spanish where I wouldn't be recognised by a soul. So the next night we drove off into the hills to this place where Jon said we would be able to eat in peace. We arrived at this amazing restaurant that looked like someone's living room with hardly anyone in there, just a few Spanish couples – and an entire table of Irish golfers!

'Oh for f***'s sake. It's Liz McDonald,' they all bellowed across the restaurant. They even sounded like Jim McDonald! 'We can't f****** believe it,' they were laughing, 'here we are in the mountains in Spain and we run into you!'

It's not that I don't like being recognised, because I do, but sometimes it isn't quite the right moment and that was one of them.

'Is it always going to be like this then?' Jon asked, smiling at me.

'Yes, I think so,' I said.

We had a fantastic night and saw each other again on the Tuesday and the Wednesday, when we met for a coffee and he took me to the bar that he and his brother Andy were working on. Jon had told Andy that he'd met me but threatened him that he must not embarrass him in any way. But sure enough, as we turned up, Andy was up a ladder whistling the *Coronation Street* theme tune. Jon wanted to kill him!

I started taking Jon and Andy bacon butties to work and very soon Jon and I were seeing each other every day. Each time we met it seemed to get better and better.

About a week after we first met, Jon invited me round to his apartment. It had an amazing view over the sea and was really lovely but in the middle of the lounge was a Scalextric and in the corner was his drum kit. 'Oh right,' I was thinking, 'this really is a bachelor pad!'

He cooked me spaghetti bolognese but he was too nervous to eat his. Afterwards we were sitting on his sofa and we leaned in to kiss for the first time but the seat cushion had come over the edge and I ended up collapsing onto the floor.

'She's fallen for me,' he insisted on telling everyone afterwards. 'Literally, she's fallen for me!'

At that time Jon had his children living with him week on, week off. One night he rang me saying, 'You've got to help me. I've got the hairbrush stuck in Danielle's hair and I can't get it out. What do I do?' I had always said I would never get involved with anyone who had children because I wouldn't want the responsibility of helping to bring up someone else's kids, but after meeting Jon the idea didn't bother me at all. It felt so right us being together that nothing would upset that. We were like best mates from the beginning and we still are today.

It quickly reached the stage in our relationship were we wanted to meet each other's children. Josh can be a bit like a mad scientist and the first time Jon met him, Josh just said, 'Hello, meet my salamander.'

'Er, hi,' Jon said, staring at Josh's slimy-looking pet.

I think Josh, who was then thirteen, was trying to gauge his reaction!

Jon's daughter Danielle was then twelve, his son Jonathan was thirteen and Ben was sixteen. I first met Danielle and Jonathan at a restaurant on the beach and it was totally nerve-racking. I so wanted them to like me and I wanted to like them, too. I already knew that it was going to be a long-term relationship with Jon so it was vital that we both got on with each other's kids. Thankfully we all got on brilliantly from the very beginning.

Things were becoming so serious that I also took Jon back to Leeds to meet my mum. I rang Mum from Spain and said, 'I'm flying over to see you and I'm bringing Jon with me so you can meet him.'

'Oh, well, I shall look forward to it Beverley, I shall look forward to it,' she replied. 'Now, you'll not be sleeping together though will you?' she went on.

'But Mum, I have been married three times you know,' I said.

'Yes, but you're not married to him and this is my house,' Mum replied.

It seemed funny and old-fashioned to Jon and me, but that is the way she was. She had been a virgin on her wedding night and she and my dad were both very moral people.

Steph was desperate to meet Jon too because I'd told her so much about him on the telephone. She was desperate to know if he was going to be *the* one.

So I was really excited and a little bit nervous as we arrived at the airport for our flight back to England. But if I'd known what was to happen next I would have been more than just a little nervous!

As we lined up to go through passport control, Jon was standing behind me and behind him were what seemed about a thousand diehard Corrie fans all staring at me and nudging each other. I went up to the counter first, showed my documents and was waved past. But when Jon walked up to the glass window, things seemed to start moving in slow motion. The Spanish official stared at Jon's passport for ages, then kept tapping things into his computer and looking Jon up and down. Something clearly wasn't right. Then he started talking to Jon really fast in Spanish. The next thing I knew Jon was surrounded by airport security and was being arrested.

'Oh my God,' I thought. 'What now?'

The only word that I could make out that the officials was saying was 'Traffico, traffico.'

'Oh no, he can't be,' I thought. 'He can't be a drugs trafficker! How on earth am I going to explain this one to Mum?'

All the *Coronation Street* fans in the queue were now beside themselves with fascination at what was going on as I stood there like a lemon seeing my new fella being led away to jail.

I immediately called Lorriane, one of my best friends in Spain.

'Hiya, are you there already?' she asked when she heard my voice.

'No,' I replied. 'I'm still at the airport and Jon is on his way to Malaga jail!'

After much confusion I was finally reassured that Jon wasn't a drugs trafficker after all and that what the security men were talking about was a traffic offence – Jon had been involved in an accident on his motorbike and after his divorce hadn't informed the authorities about his whereabouts and that was why he was in trouble.

But they still kept him in prison for two nights while they sorted it all out.

The worst bit was ringing Mum to say we weren't coming to visit after all – although I didn't tell her the real reason why!

When Jon did return home it was with some very unpleasant new companions – fleas! He picked them up in jail and they infested our flat. We tried everything to get rid of them but nothing worked. In the end we had to move!

Thankfully when Mum and Steph did finally meet Jon they liked him instantly.

'He's "the one", Beverley,' Mum said to me afterwards. 'He's a good man and he is going to bring you happiness.' She'd never said that about any other man I'd ever been with and I knew she was right.

Jon and I had only been together a couple of months when we moved in together. We were barely ever apart so it made perfect sense. We rented a little house at first and then a larger one so there was room for Josh and Jon's younger kids when they were with us. Ben used to visit sometimes too but he was then seventeen, so he was much more independent. The kids are all quite different and in different circumstances they probably wouldn't be friends, but they all got on incredibly well from the start.

In Spain there are twelve weeks of holiday in the summer and the kids would be in the pool the whole time or down at the beach, which was only ten minutes' walk away. In the evenings we would have barbecues all together and it was fantastic.

I became like a stepmother to Jon's children and although I'd always thought I'd hate the role, I loved it. We tried to predict all the problems we might come across with the kids but they never materialised.

Then the children's auntie died very suddenly at just twenty-four years old and they stopped coming as much because their mum needed them around. After that it became harder for us to have the kids, although we still saw them as much as we could.

Then, around that time, in 2003, *Coronation Street* asked me back again. They had invited me back previously to take part in a 'soap bubble' episode, which was filmed on location in Cornwall and shown late at night, but I hadn't been keen. This time they said the storyline was going to be filmed entirely on location in Blackpool but shown as part of the normal show over about six or eight weeks.

Tony Wood had become producer of the show and I'd known him for ages, ever since he had been an associate producer. He'd left *Coronation Street* for a while and had produced *The Grand*, which Rebecca was in. Then he'd cast her in *Sunburn* when he worked on that. Tony told me that when he returned to *Coronation Street* he had two ambitions – first, to get Liz McDonald back and then Leanne Battersby – and he achieved both of them. Granada flew me over to the UK and we had big meetings. I thought the Blackpool idea sounded good, so I agreed to do it.

It was great being back in *Coronation Street* even if I wasn't actually filming at Granada Studios. The storyline was that Liz was running a pub called the Black Dog in Blackpool and Jim had escaped from prison to see her because he thought she was having an affair with the bar manager. Then Bet, on her way to a pub landlords' conference, turned up in the Black Dog. Their first scene together again was in the ladies' loo and Bet said to Liz (who was wearing one of her usual miniskirts), 'By gum, I'd recognise those legs anywhere.' In the storyline, Liz and Jim were planning on fleeing to Ireland but the scheme went wrong and Jim was recaptured and returned to prison.

It was great fun working with everyone again and usually I was still able to fly home at weekends to see Jon and Josh, or if it was difficult because of filming schedules, they would come over to see me in England.

With the Blackpool storyline over I wasn't sure what would happen next but Tony Wood asked me to stay and return to Weatherfield permanently. At first I said I'd do it for a while and see how it went. I'd enjoyed taking on other roles in the time I'd been away from the Street but time away had also made me realise just how much I loved being in it. By then the routine at *Coronation Street* was very different from the first ten years I'd done on the show. We'd gone from four episodes to five episodes and there was no rehearsal time any more, which meant you were either there or you weren't. There wasn't so much hanging around, which I preferred.

If I was going to stay in *Coronation Street* indefinitely though, I knew I couldn't carry on commuting backwards and forwards to Spain and I would have to move back to England. For me it was a wrench and I knew I'd miss Spain. Not for a single day that I was there did I ever take it for granted. I loved the weather and the relaxed way of life. And as much as I love Manchester and its fantastic buzzing vibe, it does seem to rain and look grey almost every day. But I felt the time had come to return home.

Jon and I hated being apart for any time at all and his

eldest son Ben was also returning to England, so after a bit of thought Jon said he was coming with me. 'Well, I'm a builder in Spain, I can be a builder in England,' he said. Jon's younger children stayed with their mum but he arranged that at weekends he would either fly out to visit them or they could come and stay with us.

Josh had just a few more months before his GCSEs so he stayed at boarding school until he'd completed them, then enrolled to do his A-levels in England.

First, Jon and I rented an apartment in a converted mill overlooking Canal Street, in the gay village in Manchester. I was already in the flat the first time Jon came over from Spain. He'd never even been to Manchester and didn't know there was such a thing as the gay village. So when he got dropped off in a cab outside the apartment he looked around thinking, 'Where on earth am I?' Although, with his shaved head and earring I'm sure some of the guys in the street were looking at him as if he fitted in perfectly! I was looking down at him from the window of our apartment and it was hilarious.

We had a fantastic time living in Canal Street. It was a real party life for a while and it was great catching up with old friends who I hadn't seen for ages while I was in Spain. There was a bar called Eden, which we went to most Friday and Saturday nights and which did amazing food before turning into a fantastic disco at 11pm. One weekend, Jon's mum Crystal, who lives in Kent, was staying with us and we took her to Eden. She was seventy-four then and we thought that after dinner she would probably want to go home for an early night. But not at all. When the disco started she was up and dancing on the tables! She was fine getting up there but then she couldn't get down again afterwards so we had to get two of the big burly doormen to come and lift her off. She is an amazing woman!

After a few of months I decided I wanted to stay in *Coronation Street*. I'd loved being back and Liz was getting some great storylines. Jon and I were having a ball, going out every night and making new friends, and he didn't have any problem with me being recognised by fans of the show. He realised it came with the job.

As we were planning to stay we bought a big, six-bedroom detached Victorian house in Ellesmere Park near Eccles.

We'd been out there to visit Nick Cochrane, who'd played Liz's son Andy, and his family one afternoon and we really liked the area. Nick helped us find the house and we set about doing it up. It was a massive project for Jon though because it was almost entirely derelict and needed to be totally restored. We put everything we had financially into the house and Jon worked on it fifteen hours a day. He restored the ceilings and we bought and fitted antique fireplaces. It looked amazing.

Coronation Street was going well, Josh was happy at his new college, Jon's son Ben had moved in with us and was studying music at college in Manchester, and Danielle and Jonathan came over as often as they could. Life was going brilliantly. Then, just as Jon was finishing the house, I noticed a sign outside the local pub saying the tenancy was available. It was five minutes from our house but we'd only been in there once before, with Jon's brother Andy and his wife Mae. They didn't do food and there had been hardly any customers, which seemed a real shame because it was a great spot for a pub.

'We should do that,' I said to Jon, pointing at the 'tenancy for sale' sign. And so, after years of working behind the bar of Britain's most famous boozer, The Rovers Return, I was about to find myself landlady of my very own pub.

16
REAL LIFE LANDLADY

....

People thought we were mad. An actress and a southerner taking on a pub in Eccles? We knew our critics thought it was bound to fail, but we were determined to make the White Horse a success. Jon had run a small bar in Spain before we were together and we are both 'people people', so we thought we could really make a go of it and were so excited about the idea.

The White Horse was a 1970s building, and inside it was very tired-looking, so once we'd signed all the brewery paperwork to take on the tenancy, we set about transforming it. I took my holidays from *Coronation Street* and for three weeks we worked eighteen-hour days, painting, decorating and cleaning.

When we opened the doors to our first customers, it looked amazing. The bar was all done out in gold and red and it looked like a proper, classic pub. The toilets were decorated in black and ivory and everybody said we had the best toilets of a pub anywhere! I'm really finicky about things like that and was very proud.

The locals loved it and we had soon taken the White Horse

from bringing in £1,500 a week to taking £15,000 a week. People would queue in the car park on a Saturday night to get in and they'd get all dressed up for it. We never had any trouble with customers. We even started a talent competition called the Eccles Factor, which was hugely successful, and sometimes I'd get Simon Gregson or whoever I could persuade from the *Coronation Street* cast to come along and be one of the judges. We did proper homemade pub food too – none of your ping-and-serve rubbish.

Jon was in the pub day and night and I'd go straight there to help out when I got back from *Coronation Street* in the evenings. We were working seven days a week and it was tiring, but we didn't mind because we loved it and we had fantastic staff and fantastic customers.

Life was good. Then in 2006, I landed the best role ever – as a grandma! The moment I set eyes on Rebecca's first baby Sonny, I was besotted. I'd been so worried about Rebecca throughout her pregnancy because she was still my baby, but seeing her as a mum was wonderful. Then just over a year later Rebecca had another gorgeous little boy, George. I hated being in Manchester when they were down in London but I'd nip down whenever I could to see my grandsons. Rebecca and I had always been close but when she became a mother herself the bond only got stronger.

After about two years we felt we had taken the White Horse as far as we could for the size of the building. Then one day, Jon and I were driving through a village called Hale Barns, which is quite a posh village near Altrincham, southwest of Manchester, where a lot of the footballers live.

I was looking out of the window when I saw a huge, old-fashioned pub with a sign up saying, 'Tenancy for sale'. Just like last time, I didn't hesitate. 'Oh my God, we have got to have that place,' I said.

'No, we're fine as we are,' said Jon.

'But we could just have a look inside,' I went on.

'No, no, no,' replied Jon.

Within a few hours, we were being shown round by a manager from the brewery that owned it. The pub was massive, at least six times the size of the White Horse, and we both knew that it would give us the scope to do all the things we wanted – an area for fine dining, a piano bar and a larger pub section too. By the end of the tour, I said to the brewery rep, 'Yes, we want it.'

'Yeah, we do, we do,' Jon agreed.

After our success at the White Horse we really didn't believe we could go wrong.

We called the pub the Gallery and for a second time set about refurbishing and redecorating. It needed loads doing to it as it was filthy. We had to have the kitchen industrially cleaned before we could even start decorating it!

To afford the £60,000 for the tenancy and the £50,000 we needed for refurbishments, we had to sell our house in Ellesmere Park. So we moved into the upstairs apartment at the Gallery. We put everything we had into the pub but we were convinced it would be worth it.

We made it fantastic. On the opening night, 26 May 2007, people were queuing down the road and we felt a huge sense of achievement for what we had done, but we knew we would have to keep working at it if we were to recoup our investment.

When you buy a pub tenancy you still have to pay the

brewery rent every month. And then there are wages to pay, plus the cost of beer, wines and spirits. It cost £17,000 just to stock the bar when we opened. We were determined to do really good food and employed some brilliant chefs, but that was a big expense, too.

We needed to be bringing in £14,000 a week at the Gallery just to break even – the rent and rates alone were almost £3,000 a week. From day one it was a struggle.

Upstairs we had a restaurant and piano bar with a white grand piano, and downstairs it was a traditional pub with entertainment like discos, bands and karaoke.

We employed Nick Cochrane as bar manager because he'd worked in the licensing trade before and I knew he was a real grafter and a great man to work with. Then Jon did all the bar and cellar work during the day and acted as maitre d' in the upstairs restaurant every evening – he was doing everything!

Then, about two months after we opened, the smoking ban came into force and that really hit us, as it hit so many pubs. When the ban was introduced in July 2007, thirty pubs a week were closing in Britain. By December of that year it had reached forty-five.

Next, the rent went up. We were also feeling the squeeze from the smoking ban, as well as competition from cheap booze in supermarkets and the beginning of the credit crunch. And while the big pub chains subsidise a lot of their food and use cheap ingredients, we wanted fresh vegetables and the best meat, but it was all costing a lot. Everywhere we turned we seemed to be spending a lot of money. Some weeks we would break even and bring in £14,000, but more often than not we would only get it to £11,000 or £12,000, and some bad weeks it was just £9,000. It wasn't enough and we were still working our arses off.

Weekends could be quite busy; often the footballers would come in and sometimes we had really successful nights. But that wasn't enough to get us through Monday, Tuesday and Wednesday nights when it could be empty and I'd be thinking, 'How on earth are we going to pay the wages this week?'

Nothing we tried seemed to work. We had jazz musicians, a resident house band, a brilliant pianist and we even got singers to come over from Puerto Banus, but still we weren't getting enough customers spending enough money.

For the first seven months, Jon and I lived above the pub but that was very stressful, particularly as I was in some big storylines in *Coronation Street*. By then, as well as my real life pub, I was also landlady of the Rovers because Steve had bought the business and Liz was running it.

Then Liz started her on-off relationship with Vernon Tomlin, whose character was partly based on my Jon. For years I've been great friends with Daran Little, who used to be the *Coronation Street* archivist and is now a hugely talented writer on the show, and when we moved back to Manchester I introduced him to Jon and they got on really well. So when a new character called Charlie Stubbs arrived in *Coronation Street*, Daran made him a builder, just like Jon. But then Charlie's character evolved and he ended up being a horrible bully (not like my Jon!). So when Vernon, another new character, came into the show, Daran tried again and made him a drummer in a band, just like my Jon.

Vernon was played by Ian Reddington and he became a great mate. We had real fun together but we also worked very hard to make Liz and Vernon's relationship believable. For Liz, Vernon was a touch of showbiz. It was like she was thinking, 'There's Deirdre with boring old Ken and here am I with a muso who wears hats and is dead exciting!'

Ian had to work hard to establish himself as Vernon because when he first appeared, what the viewers at home saw was Tricky Dicky from *EastEnders,* which had been a massive role for Ian a few years earlier. His hard work paid off though and it all went really well.

Then of course Jim McDonald returned to Weatherfield and it was high drama again, leading up to the climax when Jim beat up Vernon on Liz's wedding day.

I had tons of lines to learn at that time and would be lying in bed trying to memorise them while the music was still playing in the pub downstairs, until two o'clock in the morning. I'd be trying to concentrate on my scripts then be thinking, 'It doesn't sound very busy down there tonight,' or 'I think the band struck a duff note there.' Then I'd have to be up four hours later to be in work for 7.15am.

Ben, Josh, Jon and Danielle were all working in the pub then and also living in the flat with us. We were starting to get on top of each other and things were getting strained between us all, so Jon and I rented a tiny two-up two-down house across the road to get a bit of our own space. We thought being away from the pub for just those hours when we were asleep might make it a bit less stressful. But we were seeing less and less of each other as Jon was working every hour to try and keep the pub going, because by then we knew we were in serious trouble.

Soon, my *Coronation Street* money was going on paying the wages or the brewery bills. We were taking out loans, buying on credit and we were both thinking, 'Hang on a minute, we're sinking. We are really sinking.'

The only time Jon and I ever spoke to each other was in
the pub in front of customers and staff and we'd be going,
'Hi, how are you? Yeah, I'm great, thanks.' We had to keep up
the pretence that everything was fine even though we knew
it wasn't. The only other time we were together was at six
o'clock in the morning when I got up for work or one o'clock
in the morning when Jon came to bed. By then we didn't
have the energy to think straight, let alone talk. We didn't
row really but we became like two people going through the
motions of our lives, separated by an invisible wall. We never
went out anywhere together or had a laugh like the old days.
All we could focus on was keeping the pub afloat.

When we had taken on the Gallery we had kept the White
Horse and employed a manager to run it but now that was
also losing money. The manager was really good but it just
wasn't attracting the same numbers of customers any more.
In the end we decided to sell our lease on the White Horse to
pay off all the money we owed the brewery. I thought, 'Well at
least now we can just concentrate on the Gallery.'

We tried to cut costs wherever we could. I'd think, 'Well,
instead of loads of fresh flowers on every table, I'll put just
a few in each vase,' but it wasn't enough. Soon we had to
lose staff because we could no longer cover the wages bill.
It was horrible having to sit down with Nick Cochrane and
explain that we couldn't keep him; we'd known each other for
years. But he knew what we were up against and was incredibly understanding.

I would often go straight to the pub from work, have my tea
there then help out with anything that needed doing. And if
I had a Sunday off from *Coronation Street* I would be scrub-
bing the upstairs bar.

Occasionally we would have busy nights that would give us a glimmer of hope. Denise Welch had her fiftieth birthday party there and it was a fantastic night. And the dray men who came to deliver the beer said we were the only pub for miles around that was selling any. But it still wasn't enough to cover our costs.

Each morning when I drove to work I'd pass more pubs closing down, and we knew it was possibly only a matter of time before we joined them. But because we kept getting glimpses of success, we thought if we could weather the credit crunch then everything would be OK.

Our accountant had lots of other pubs on his books and he was saying they were all in the same boat, but Jon and I aren't quitters and we were determined that we could make it work. So we carried on fighting. But we were stuck between a rock and a hard place. We would only get the money back that we had paid for the lease if the brewery found someone to take it over, and that was never going to happen now the country was in the middle of a credit crunch.

On top of that, all our kids apart from Rebecca were working and living in the pub, so what would happen if we gave it up? Then they'd be out of jobs and homes too.

By then we'd ploughed more than £200,000 into the pub but still our debts were mounting and things were getting worse. It was a nightmare.

Our mortgage payment on our little flat in Spain bounced and we had to go back there one weekend to sort it out. And another time the electricity in the Spain flat was cut off.

At that point I had lost track of quite how bad things were and the fact that we were by then about £150,000 in debt. Jon had been doing the books and was trying to protect me from the full reality of it. I think he also didn't want to admit to me or to himself that we had failed – he had never failed at anything in his life before. We were both stressed and barely speaking to each other, our kids were angry with us and our staff were fed up.

I threw myself into *Coronation Street* to escape what was going on at home. Jon felt I was becoming more and more withdrawn and that I must have stopped loving him. I hadn't but I felt very low. I was exhausted from fighting to keep the pub afloat and whenever I wasn't working, all I wanted to do was sleep.

One Thursday evening towards the end of the summer of 2008, we had dinner with our friends Gill and Tony in the restaurant at the Gallery. We sat in a bay window with the pianist playing, drinking the best cocktails and eating fantastic food cooked by amazing chefs. But there was only us and one other couple in there. It was undoubtedly the best restaurant for miles around, but it was deserted. Jon turned to me and said, 'We've got to give this up.'

We went home and talked about it all night. We had found out that the pub had had four owners in the four years before us and we'd made it busier than any of them, but still it wasn't making enough money. We should really have given up at the start of that year but we had carried on, hoping things would improve. This time though we knew it was the end. Jon and I were devastated that we'd been defeated but we were angry, too, that so many things had conspired against us.

Danielle and Jonathan had just returned to Spain, which made the decision a little easier because at least we didn't have to worry about making them unemployed.

The next morning, Jon called a meeting and told everyone we were packing it in. We scraped around to find enough cash to give all twenty of the staff one week's money in hand. By then the brewery had told us we owed them £67,000, and we were £18,000 in debt to the guy who supplied us with spirits. On top of that there were all the other suppliers and the Inland Revenue asking for money, which brought us up to around £150,000 in debt. It seemed everywhere we turned there were people saying, 'Where's our money?'

We had to get all our belongings out of the pub before we handed the keys back to the brewery, otherwise we feared we might have lost everything, so on the quiet that weekend, Jon moved it all into our little rented house. Then on the Monday morning, he went to see the brewery to hand over the keys and to tell them we were quitting.

It wasn't long before the newspapers got hold of the story that we'd had to give up the pub. There was a huge headline in one tabloid saying, 'Bev's Bust!'

Then one weekend when Jon was down visiting his mum, there was a knock on the door and I was confronted by someone from the brewery with a letter saying we had twenty-one days to come up with the £67,000 that we owed or we would be made bankrupt. Initially I was terrified to find this guy at my front door, but it turned out he was a big Corrie fan and we started talking. He told me he had lots of other pubs to visit and issue with statutory demands for money.

We were very, very close to going bankrupt and in hindsight it might have been easier if we had declared ourselves bust, but we didn't want to do that. We owed friends money and if we'd gone bankrupt they would have been the ones who would have lost out and never got their money. As it was, Jon arranged meetings with every single person we

Let's get physical! Here
I am posing after my
No.1 fitness video

Look at the lycra
on that!

Shakira's got
nothing on me!

If I could turn back time… I never would have let them persuade me to dress up as Cher on *Stars in their Eyes*

Look at me, I can't believe my luck! Me with the Chippendales

Me outside the house I shared with Steve in Spain

One of Liz's trademark mini skirts – my goodbye gift from the
cast when I left the Street in 1998

Me and Julie takin[g]
a punt at the Race[s]

Me with Denise
Welch, she's been a
wonderful friend to
me over the years

Kym Marsh and I at an
awards ceremony, she's such
fun to work with

Me with Bonnie Prince Charles, when he came for a
tour of the *Coronation Street* set

Camilla and I got on
like a house on fire
when she visited earlier
this year

With Rebecca and my gorgeous two grandsons, Sonny and George

Josh and Rebecca –
I'm so proud of
them both

With Jon, I've finally found my soulmate

All glammed up for Denise Welch's 50th birthday

Back to work and smiling again at the National TV awards, January 2010

owed money to and arranged terms for repayment. We knew it would take years to achieve but we were determined to pay everyone back.

It was strange really, because in the meetings with our lawyers about the brewery I was determined to fight. But the rest of the time I had no fight left in me whatsoever. I felt exhausted and was increasingly withdrawn. Jon and I hardly ever went out and all I wanted to do was close the doors and stay inside.

After giving up the pub I couldn't face staying in the village any longer and we rented a house about twenty minutes' drive away, in Holmes Chapel. It was cheap to rent but big enough for all our stuff so it seemed perfect. But the journey to work could take up to two hours during the rush hour which meant a round trip of four hours. It was a real slog but I felt it was just something else I had to get on with.

One evening, Jon and I had arranged to meet some friends for a rare night out in The Ox, a pub near Granada Studios. But as Jon was driving us there I suddenly felt myself gasping for breath, shaking and feeling violently ill.

'I'll be fine,' I said to Jon. 'I'm just feeling a bit nervous about going out.' But as we walked into the bar, my legs suddenly went from under me. Jon grabbed me and steered me back to the car and we drove straight home. I guess deep down I knew it was a panic attack but I simply put it out of my mind as a bit of a 'funny turn.' And Jon and I were both so preoccupied with everything else that was going on that we didn't even discuss it.

It was as if I were in the middle of my own personal cyclone and Jon was in the middle of his cyclone. Jon had never failed at anything before and was struggling with that. Jon and I hadn't fallen out particularly but we were just drifting further and further apart, we weren't talking and our sex drive had gone. Then one night we had a massive row about everything that had happened.

'I just don't know what I want any more,' he said. 'My head is so full of questions and the only answer I have is "I don't know."'

I knew our relationship was in serious trouble and months of pent-up frustration and hurt poured out.

It felt as if we had lost all our money, our business and now our relationship was under threat too. We plodded on together although things didn't really improve.

Our legal battle with the brewery dragged on over Christmas 2008 and into the New Year and it was a subdued time. Our legal bill was already up to £10,000 when our lawyer said he wasn't certain that we would win, even though we had a good case. It had all just become too much and it didn't even feel like Jon and I were friends any more.

By January 2009, I was getting up, going to work, coming home, learning my lines and going to sleep. Then doing exactly the same thing all over again the next day.

I'd given up fitness teaching in the evenings to concentrate on the pub and I really missed that too, both physically and mentally. Training had always been my escape from whatever else was going on in my life. At work, I didn't want to mix with anyone and was staying in my dressing room every minute that I wasn't needed for filming. Once I rang Jon saying, 'I can't go down there, I can't face everyone.'

I knew I was getting low again but I thought it was just exhaustion over the battle for the pub. I felt a failure and my self-esteem was at rock bottom. On top of that I was desperately worried about my mum and Josh. Because just at the time I felt I had nothing left to give, they both needed me more than ever.

17
MY LOST BOY

....

There was another reason why we had decided to give up the pub. And it was nothing to do with money or the credit crunch. It was actually one of the saddest episodes in my life.

Because at just eighteen, my son Josh had become an alcoholic. To make matters worse, if they could have been any worse at that time, he was also addicted to smoking dope.

How could we continue to be selling alcohol when I could see at first hand just what damage it could do to people?

Josh had struggled ever since leaving school. He was badly affected by me and his Dad splitting up when we were in Spain and for a long while he was a very sad little boy.

After we moved to Manchester he enrolled at college but he struggled at sticking with anything.

First he studied acting but that didn't work out. Then he began a course in animal care because he has always been mad about animals, but after a short while he gave that up too. Then he decided he wanted to train to be a chef because he loved cooking but again he dropped out.

For a while Jon and I thought he was going to college every morning but he wasn't even turning up.

He didn't seem to have any get up and go or ambition and it was worrying me.

When we opened the Gallery Josh came and worked for us and Jon and I both hoped he would enjoy it there and settle down a bit. But we had to push him all the time – he wasn't really interested in working that hard.

For a while Josh had been getting the shakes in his hands and one of his legs. As the weeks went by, the shaking seemed to be getting worse. It wasn't all the time but when he had an attack it could be quite bad. Neither he nor I could think of anything that was causing it because it wasn't particularly at times when he was stressed or anxious.

But sometimes I'd watch him serving customers in the pub and his shaking would be quite extreme. I wanted him to go to see the doctor but he wouldn't do it.

Josh had a girlfriend, who seemed a nice enough girl, and sometimes he'd go and stay over at hers for a couple of days, but increasingly he seemed to be becoming a loner. It concerned me, especially as we were all living together in the pub.

His moods were very up and down and he was distant and withdrawn. I'd tell him he really ought to see his grandparents but he wasn't interested. In fact he wasn't interested in anything.

He looked permanently exhausted and as if he didn't care about anything. I knew something wasn't right but I couldn't pinpoint what it might be.

There had also been a few incidents where money had been taken from our bedroom. We knew it must have been Josh, but he denied everything. We were really angry and hurt by what he had done, particularly because he was handling money in the pub every day and we had to be able to trust him, but it was really hard to get through to him.

His bedroom was a total disaster. It wasn't just normal teenage messiness, it was complete chaos, as if he had no interest or even awareness of what was going on around him.

Many times I sat down with Josh alone and tried to talk to him about what was going on.

'Oh Josh, you seem so unhappy,' I said to him one day. 'It's like you don't have any direction in your life. Whatever your dream is you must try to go for it. Do you know what your dream is?'

But he just couldn't answer me.

Then we started talking about his shaking and what might be causing it.

'Maybe I should go to the doctors,' he finally agreed.

So I made an appointment with our GP and we went along together.

The doctor examined Josh and asked him lots of questions and at the end of the appointment said he was a little worried that he might have the early stages of Parkinson's disease.

He said he wanted Josh to have a brain scan and tests to see if he really did have the condition or if it was something else.

I was worried sick about him. He was still just a teenager but I knew that if it was Parkinson's he would have it for life and just get sicker and sicker.

I took Josh for the tests and a few weeks later we got the results. Thankfully, it wasn't Parkinson's disease. I was so relieved. But our doctor explained they had detected that Josh had a disorder called essential tremor, which affects thousands of people nationwide, causing them to shake uncontrollably particularly when carrying out simple tasks like pouring a glass of water or writing.

The doctor said there was little that could be done to stop the shaking and although he could try prescribing beta blocker drugs, the shaking didn't yet seem quite serious enough for that.

Afterwards the doctor had a long chat with Josh on his own before calling me back into the room.

'I think Josh might also benefit from counselling,' he said.

I too was worried that there was more wrong with Josh and I hoped that maybe the GP was right and talking to someone about what was going on inside him might be helpful.

So I dug out the telephone number for Win, the lady who counselled me when we had been living in Bolton.

She was still working locally and I made an appointment to take Josh along to meet her.

He was adamant that he didn't need to go and in the end I said we were going to see someone who could help him without actually saying it was a counsellor.

When the appointment was over though he was furious at me all the way home because he felt I'd tricked him into seeing Win.

'I didn't need that. I didn't need that,' he kept saying. We had a huge row and it ended with him storming off.

But a couple of days later he took me to one side and apologised. 'OK Mum,' he said, 'I think I did need that – I'll go back.'

The next time we went to visit Win he talked with her for hours and hours. She then took him in to see a doctor at her clinic, who also had a long conversation with Josh about how he had been feeling.

At the end of the session Win asked to speak to Josh and me together.

'We think Josh has got a problem with alcohol and with dope,' she said. 'We think he ought to go into rehab.'

I was stunned. Totally shocked. I honestly had no idea that was what was wrong with Josh. I know you read things about how moodiness and being withdrawn can be a sign that your child is taking drugs, but it never occurred to me that might be the problem with Josh. I just thought he was feeling a bit down and that maybe that had been caused by his shaking.

Josh had certainly hidden his drinking and drug taking from us extremely well. But we've since learnt that that is exactly what addicts do – they can be very secretive in order to hide the truth from those closest to them.

We've since discovered that Josh was smoking dope with a group of friends he had at the time and whenever we weren't around.

Jon and I enjoy going out and having a drink. But we aren't at all into drugs. I've seen actors who smoke a lot of dope; they lose all interest in everything and can't remember their lines and I really don't like it.

And while we might have thought that Josh had perhaps smoked the occasional joint, we would never have thought he would have done anything more than that.

At first Jon and I weren't even sure whether Win and the doctor were right with what they were saying. We found it hard to believe that Josh really had an addiction. Loads of kids Josh's age go out and drink too much but are they really alcoholics?

We were just totally confused about the whole thing.

When people use the word 'alcoholic' you have visions of people drinking vodka for breakfast or tramps on park benches, but Josh was never like that at all. He had never appeared drunk when he was working in the pub and I'd never smelt anything suspicious on his breath.

Jon and I talked endlessly about what was the best thing to do. I was terrified that if he went into rehab in Britain the story would get into the newspapers, and that was the last thing that Josh needed at that point.

The other problem was that by then Jon and I were so skint we just couldn't afford to send him to the Priory, which certainly wasn't cheap.

We talked to Win about our dilemma and she told us about a rehab clinic in South Africa that she had helped to set up. It was a Christian-based clinic and followed the twelve-step recovery programme.

We researched it on the internet and I telephoned the man who ran the centre, and after a lot of thought we decided it appeared the best place to help Josh. Being thousands of miles away also meant he would be totally anonymous.

But finding the £2,000 a week fees was still going to be a struggle. The centre manager was a guy called Colin and he'd seen *Coronation Street* but I had to explain to him on the telephone that I hadn't got JR Ewing money and we were running a business that might well not survive.

In the weeks that followed Josh was constantly changing his mind about whether he wanted to go or not. To be honest, we didn't even really know ourselves whether it was the right thing or whether Josh even really had an addiction. He certainly had a problem though, but sometimes it just seemed to be a problem with life.

The staff sent us a list of everything that Josh was allowed to take with him. It was all very strict with just a set number of pants, jeans and tops allowed, all of which had to be labelled for mass laundry. His mobile phone and other gadgets would be taken off him on arrival.

In the weeks before he was due to leave I went out and bought a new suitcase, then washed, ironed and packed his clothes. It was just as well because on the morning he was due to fly out, Josh wandered downstairs at the pub with a black bin liner half filled with filthy clothes that he was planning on taking with him.

I found that really upsetting. It was like he had no self-respect left and was just totally out of it.

Jon and I drove him to the airport, where we were meeting a member of staff from the clinic who would escort Josh on the flight to ensure he boarded the plane.

Watching him walk through the departures gate was heart-breaking. That was my son and he was going to the other side of the world and he just seemed totally lost.

I was out of my mind with worry and was terrified he wouldn't get on the flight or would go missing at the other end.

Josh was allowed to call us once a week. He would reverse the charges or we'd call him straight back and he would tell us about all the counselling sessions he had been having and how he was feeling.

I think he had some very, very painful counselling in which he faced some of his own demons and talked about his child-hood and how it had affected him. Josh had been very badly scarred by me and his Dad splitting up, because when he was very young Steve and him had a great relationship. While I was working it would be Steve taking Josh to Toys R Us and buying him loads of expensive toys. As a young boy he never wanted for anything materially.

When I looked back at that time when we had first moved out to Spain, I felt so guilty. Because it was our fault – it was mine and Steve's fault that Josh was hurting so much when we split up. And he carried that hurt with him as he grew up.

But within a few weeks of Josh being in South Africa I could hear a change in his voice and I knew the rehab was really helping him. Dope and alcohol are both depressants and I could tell that kicking them was making him feel so much better. He still didn't tell us exactly how much he had been drinking and smoking but it emerged that he had also had an eating disorder and had been comfort eating. I had been worried about how much weight he'd been putting on and thought he was in danger of becoming obese, but I hadn't realised the reasons behind his overeating.

With Josh in South Africa, every month I would be desperately waiting for my pay cheque to come in from *Coronation Street*, then forwarding it straight out to the rehab clinic. I would even be ringing my agent, asking her to send it to me just as quickly as she could, because we had absolutely no other money to pay the fees.

At one point we were four weeks behind on the fees and I was terrified they were going to send Josh home before he was fully better. He had initially only been expected to stay a few weeks but he ended up being there four months.

But so long as Josh was making progress I was happy for him to stay, no matter how desperately I was missing him.

At the same time as Josh was in rehab in South Africa a close friend of mine was also admitted to a clinic to deal with her alcohol addiction.

One day I returned home from visiting her and I said to Jon: 'What are we doing?' My son is in rehab, now one of my dear friends is in rehab and here we are selling alcohol. This is just madness.'

So that too became a big deciding factor in our leaving the pub.

When Josh arrived home he got off the plane almost like a different person. He really seemed to have turned his life around.

He looked happier and healthier and had regained his get up and go. I had my boy back. Back from South Africa and back to the funny and lovely boy I'd known before.

Sadly though, my mum was now gripped by an illness from which she would never return.

18
SAYING GOODBYE TO MUM

....

I was round at Mum's for Sunday afternoon tea and it was quiche – again! She'd made it the Sunday before and the one before that, too. Stephanie and I sometimes used to giggle about it, how Mum had started making the same meals over and over again. What we didn't realise was that this was an early sign of the most horrific disease, which was to destroy our mother day by day until she was no longer the woman we knew and loved.

It was only when Mum's Alzheimer's disease was diagnosed that we were able to look back and see the first signs of it developing years earlier.

I get very angry when I think about how few times of happiness Mum has had in her life. Her childhood was very pressured and her mum made her very aware of the sacrifices that had been made to give her a life away from the mill. Then she married my dad and had me, and I think she was truly happy for a while. But then she lost her little boy so that was all spoiled. When Stephanie was born, things were better again but soon after that came Grandad's trial and his death and she never got over that. Then, when she was only forty-seven, Dad died and her life really came to an end.

For the next twenty-five years she never looked at another man or went on a single date. Financially she was comfortable but she became very insular. She hated weekends because when she closed the curtains on a Friday night, she might not see another soul until Monday morning. Steph and I would make sure she was with one of us almost every weekend.

When Dad was still alive, he and Mum would socialise a great deal with other couples. They'd go to dinner dances together on a Saturday night or for a drive out into the country. After Dad died though, some friends seemed to stay away, as if her widowhood might be catching.

Mum missed their old friends, but by then, with Dad gone, her whole life had been taken from her anyway.

One friend that did stay in touch was Joan, who was married to a chap called Gerry, and my parents used to socialise with them a great deal. Mum and Joan would take it in turns to ring each other.

Then, in 2003, Joan and Gerry's daughter called to say her mum had cancer and wanted my mum to go up and see her. Mum said of course she would, and started visiting as often as Joan wanted and helped nurse her a bit in the weeks before she sadly died.

After Joan died, Gerry and my mum grew closer. Mum had never got over dad and Gerry was struggling on his own. One day he rang her. 'How the hell have you stood this for all this time?' he asked. 'I'm climbing the walls with loneliness and boredom – how have you coped with this for twenty-five years?

'Gerry, I don't know, I don't know,' Mum replied.

Over time their relationship developed into something more. He would pick her up and they'd go to a garden centre for an afternoon or drive over to Scarborough for the day, things like that.

I don't think they were having a physical relationship, it was just a bit of company for two very lonely people. Mum had had other men chasing her over the years but she was never interested. With Gerry it was easier though, because they'd known each other in the past.

Steph and I were a bit uncomfortable about it though, and his kids can't have been too happy either, because they were still coming to terms with losing their mum.

Then Mum and Gerry went on holiday together and it did seem that she got a new lease of life. We thought that if she had finally managed to find a bit of happiness again, that was good. But by then Steph and I had noticed Mum cooking the same meals whenever we went round, and that she kept telling the same stories from her childhood over and over again. She could tell a story about the day her parents bought her first piano, when she was eleven, in incredible detail. But two hours later she would be telling us exactly the same thing all over again.

We thought something wasn't right but we honestly didn't know what it was. She was on tablets for angina and we thought maybe it might be those having an effect on her.

I don't know whether Mum knew there was something wrong with her and was trying to pretend everything was fine. Certainly on the outside she still appeared perfectly normal. She was still young-looking and had a great figure. She did sit-ups and stretches from my first fitness video in the mornings, every single day.

The first Christmas that Jon and I were living back in Manchester, we had lunch at Steph's house. There were four older ladies there – Jon's mum, Steph's mother-in-law, Rebecca's mother-in-law and my mum – and they were all mucking in preparing the meal apart from my mum, who just sat in a chair.

'Mum, don't you think you should help?' I kept asking.

'Oh no, they're fine,' she said.

I was a bit embarrassed and annoyed with her. Then after lunch, Mum said, 'I'm so proud of my girls,' meaning Steph, Rebecca and me. Well, I absolutely lost it with her then. 'You forget Josh every time,' I said. 'It is bloody outrageous, even when it's his birthday you just give me £20 to get him something because you can't be bothered to shop for him yourself.'

Mum started crying but I was boiling. Now I know that the Alzheimer's was coming on and that was why Mum was struggling with remembering things, and that makes me feel terrible. I'll feel guilty about that until the day I die.

Then, three years ago, Mum and Gerry announced they were getting married. Steph and I weren't happy about the idea, particularly as the plan was for her to sell her bungalow and move in with Gerry.

'But what will happen if Gerry dies before you – you could end up homeless,' I'd say to Mum.

She didn't seem able to think it through and it was impossible to get a straight answer from her on anything. If Steph or I said, 'Do you really want to marry Gerry?' she'd reply, 'I don't know.'

Mum had always been shy but she was very straight and never, ever two-faced. She seemed to be changing but we couldn't understand why. Steph and I were pleased that Gerry had brought happiness back into Mum's life, and he did a brilliant job in looking after her, but we had to ask her frank questions about whether she really wanted to get married because we knew she was becoming confused.

As the weeks and months went by the problem was clearly getting worse. Once, I cooked her and Gerry a big Sunday dinner and two hours later Mum said, 'Are we going to have some dinner?' But Mum was still fiercely proud and refused to accept there was anything wrong with her. 'I've never felt healthier,' she would say. And Gerry, with all the best intentions, might have been covering up for her a bit, too. Maybe he was hiding from the reality of exactly how poorly Mum was becoming, which I completely understand – we all were. Everyone was pretending there was nothing wrong, but eventually Steph and I were forced to confront the fact that Mum had more or less stopped doing anything. Jon and I were running the White Horse pub at the time and whenever I popped round to see Mum she was always at Gerry's house and it would be him that made us a sandwich and a cup of tea.

Finally, Steph and I told Gerry we were taking Mum to the doctor. We knew she'd kick off about the idea and she did. 'I'm fine, I'm fine, I don't need to go to the doctors,' she said. So we left it for a couple of weeks but then we made another appointment – it was clear there was something wrong. The doctor said he had a feeling it was serious and that Mum needed a brain scan. After the brain scan, the doctors sat us in a room and told us the results – Mum had Alzheimer's disease.

Even though I'd guessed that was what it was, to hear the words was still a shock. Steph and I had both heard the horror

251

stories about Alzheimer's but I still don't think either of us then realised just how horrific it would become.

Alzheimer's disease starts at the base of the brain and progresses, gradually causing the cells to stop working. There is no cure and really it is a case of simply waiting for every memory to disappear. Steph and I bought books on the subject and researched it on the internet, but there was nothing to give us any hope. All we could see in the future was our mum losing more and more of her memory, her speech and then her bodily functions.

To assess how advanced her condition was, Mum was sent to a mental health clinic for tests. Some of the tests involved spelling and she'd have to do things like spell the word 'world' and then do it again backwards. It was very hard to resist jumping in and helping her with the answers. We were all trying to pretend to ourselves and to everyone else that Mum was just fine. But sadly by then, deep down we knew she wasn't.

Doctors said that the best drug available for slowing the advance of Alzheimer's was Reminyl so I immediately rang up and got it for her. Then they recommended Aricept so we tried that, but neither of them was able to prevent Mum slipping further and further away from us every week.

Soon she couldn't even remember the basic sequence required to make a cup of tea. She just couldn't work out that she had to turn the tap on to fill the kettle, switch it on and then put a teabag in a cup.

Even after Mum's diagnosis, Gerry still wanted them to get married, but in the end he realised that she wasn't going to get better. Plus, if she went into a home and they were married, Gerry could have been forced to sell his house to pay the fees and none of us wanted that to happen. So, Mum continued to live at Gerry's and he continued to do everything for her.

It was horrible for Steph and me to watch her slowly decline. One day we were talking about Dad and Mum said, 'Oh yeah, Clive, he walked away and left me.'

Steph and I said, 'No Mum, he didn't walk away. He died.'

'Clive Moxon? Yes, he definitely walked away.'

It was devastating.

Mum, who had never been cruel to anyone and always taught us, 'It's nice to be nice', started making catty comments about other people. And she was becoming a bit cantankerous and bad-mannered. Sometimes, if we were round at the bungalow and Gerry went into the kitchen, she'd say, 'I don't like him'. She'd never been nasty like that before and we knew that she didn't mean it. She was changing in front of us and there was nothing we could do to stop it.

One day, Steph and I took Mum out for lunch and we all went to the loo together and Mum was in there trying to pull her trousers up but she hadn't pulled her knickers up first. Steph and I both cried all the way back to Manchester.

There seemed to be so many 'last times', even though Mum was still alive. Things like the last time we went out for a drive on a Sunday or the last time we sat and shared a box of chocolates. Mum had always loved chocolates but she worried about her figure and would say, 'I'm only going to have two'. Soon though, she wouldn't even think to eat unless she was told to do it.

Mum's memories started going back further and further to when she was a very little girl, but everything in between then and the present had disappeared. We'd go through photo albums with her and she would have no recollection of Steph and me in baby pictures, or of my dad in snaps of them together. Sometimes I'd think, 'Why has she blocked us out?' When you have children, they are the most important things in your life and it hurt to think she had forgotten us.

I often felt guilty that I hadn't spent enough time with her before the Alzheimer's disease struck, particularly when I was living in Spain. But then I'd get angry with myself for feeling that way because guilt is really just a form of selfishness.

As the months went by, Gerry was becoming more and more exhausted and everything he was doing for Mum must have been taking its toll on him. We agreed Mum should come and stay with me for a few days. By then we were living in the little house across the road from the Gallery in Hale Barns. It was then that I saw exactly how bad Mum had become. She couldn't work out how to dress herself and didn't even know when she needed to go to the toilet, so I had to keep reminding her. When I gave her something to eat I would have to tell her what to do with it. 'Put it in your mouth, Mum, then chew it,' I would say. 'Just copy what I'm doing.' It was like having to deal with a toddler. In fact, so much of it reminded me of my daughter Rebecca having to look after the two sons she'd had, Sonny and George.

It became obvious that it was too much for any of us to look after Mum on our own – she needed constant supervision and it was becoming too much for just one person. We talked about her coming to live with me and that I'd hire a twenty-four-hour nurse but it seemed even that wasn't going to be enough to cope with her needs. The only option seemed to be for her to go into a home, but Gerry really wanted to avoid that.

So Steph and I waited. We didn't want to break both their

hearts by insisting she went into a home, even though we thought it would probably be best for both of them by then. It all just seemed so cruel. After twenty-five years of loneliness Mum had finally got her inner giggle back again and found happiness with Gerry, and then all too quickly everything had been ruined once more.

I was desperately worried about Mum, and about Josh as well. On top of that our battle with the brewery was continuing and Jon and I were struggling to come to terms with losing the pub. It was all taking a strain on me but my method of coping with it all was, as ever, to throw myself into work. Except that this time I was about to be dealt a blow that even I could not battle through on my own.

19
BREAKDOWN

....

I swerved my Mercedes Jeep onto the hard shoulder of the M6 as a blinding pain ran across my left shoulder. I was convinced I was having a heart attack. I couldn't breathe, I felt boiling hot and the back of my neck was soaked in sweat. I'd had panic attacks before but this was far worse than anything I'd ever experienced.

For a few moments I thought I was dying and I actually hoped that I was. Death would be a release from the feeling of hopelessness that I just couldn't shake off.

Ironically it was Friday 13 February, 2009 – and it was to be one of the worst days of my life.

I sat on the hard shoulder thinking, 'Should I phone Jon to come and get me?'

But after a while I felt a little better and decided not to make a fuss. I started the car again and drove on to work at *Coronation Street*.

Over the last few weeks and months I had been feeling abnormally tired and my energy levels were very low. Inside I had a sense of nothingness. My mood was flat and I felt empty of all emotion. I'd put it down to the problems I was having sleeping. It would take me ages to get off to sleep and then a couple of hours later I'd wake up, terrified that I'd missed my alarm for work. I'd had so much worry with the pub, the brewery battle and my mum that there was plenty to keep me awake at night.

I wondered whether maybe my HRT wasn't working properly any more and was making me weepy all the time and causing my mood swings. I'd also had a bad kidney infection around the time we gave up the pub and I thought perhaps it was recurring or maybe I was still recovering from it.

I'd had depression before but because I was still taking my medication, I didn't think it could be happening again and I really didn't recognise it as that. I even dismissed the increasing number of panic attacks I'd been having as hormonal and connected to my age. 'Maybe this is just what getting old feels like,' I thought to myself. 'But if it is, I certainly don't like it.'

Looking back, I don't think I'd felt normal for about a year, although I can't pinpoint exactly when it started. Ever since we'd returned from Spain, Jon and I had been on the go – first renovating our house, then building up the White Horse then struggling to keep the Gallery afloat. All that on top of six days a week at *Coronation Street*. I think being so busy allowed me to suppress the feelings that were building up inside me and pretend to myself and everyone else that nothing was wrong, everything was just fine.

I couldn't even ring my mum and say, 'What shall I do?' because Mum didn't know how to work a telephone any more! And I hadn't wanted to burden Steph with my problems because she had enough to worry about with Mum. I didn't want to tell friends either, because I didn't want people thinking I was a wimp. I guess I hoped that this horrible sense of hopelessness that I was carrying around would just go away. But by the beginning of 2009, I was just feeling worse. In the past I'd never been able to catnap but now I was falling asleep anywhere, at any time, and I was suffering very bad headaches.

I felt a failure about how things had gone wrong with the pub and I felt a failure too when I looked back at my life. No one in my family had ever been divorced and my God, I'd done it three times! I thought I was a bad partner to Jon, a bad daughter, a bad mum, a bad grandma, useless at my job and utterly unattractive.

Work had also been very busy throughout 2008 and early 2009 and I'd been involved in a lot of storylines and felt exhausted. First, Liz had broken up with Vernon, then she'd had a fling with Harry Mason from the bookies before moving on to Steve's best mate Lloyd, much to her son's disgust. Then I was in virtually every episode in the run-up to Steve's planned wedding to Becky Granger.

Jon knew I'd been feeling low but we hadn't discussed it properly, we were still too caught up in our own problems after the collapse of the pub. But he'd seen the panic attack I'd had the night we were meeting friends in Manchester and a couple of times I'd called him from work in a real state, saying, 'I can't face going down into the green room and seeing people, I can't cope with this job.' I'd known some of those people for twenty years but I couldn't bring myself to speak to them in the studios. I felt I had nothing worthwhile or interesting to say; my self-esteem was through the floor.

After a while though, I'd calm down and tell myself to pull my socks up and get on with it. When I stepped out of my dressing-room door, no one knew there was anything wrong with me at all.

One weekend earlier in the year, Jon and I had to return to Spain because they'd turned the electricity off in our flat because of unpaid bills. We were on the way there when the plane hit really bad turbulence.

'I hope we crash,' I said to Jon.

'What are you talking about?' he said.

'It would be better if we crashed than if I took my own life because then people couldn't say I was being selfish,' I replied quite calmly. 'And everything would be over.'

Jon couldn't believe what I was saying because although the collapse of the pub had hit him hard too, he had never felt suicidal. Yet still both of us thought my low mood was just down to stress from the events of the past year. We had no idea it was far more than that. But we struggled on and were planning a trip to Spain the day after Valentine's Day. I was desperately hoping that a good rest would put me right.

On that fateful Friday the 13th of February when I had the panic attack, I restarted the car, drove off the hard shoulder and continued on to work. When I arrived at Granada Studios I was still feeling strange and again I thought about phoning Jon but eventually decided not to bother him. Instead I sat quietly in my dressing room and gradually felt a little calmer.

It was a really busy day because we were filming the scene where Liz and Becky had a food fight in a Chinese restaurant. It was a really funny scene and in between takes, I was laughing with Kate Kelly who plays Becky. But my laughter was just as much an act as my playing Liz.

I managed the whole scene, word perfect. I was desperate to keep the show on the road and hold it together. But as soon as we finished filming, the floodgates opened and I rushed back to my dressing room, sat down on my own and started crying. I couldn't stop. I felt I couldn't go on any longer. After a while I think someone from the costume department walked in and saw me sobbing. It is all a bit hazy now but she must have been really worried about the state I was in because straight away she called for Corinne, the *Coronation Street* nurse who looks after all the cast.

Corinne arrived in my dressing room and immediately saw I was in a very bad way.

'I'm going to get a doctor to come and see you,' she said.

'No, I'm fine,' I said, desperately trying to pull myself together and not to cause a fuss. 'I'm absolutely fine. I'm going to drive home and I probably just need an early night.'

'I don't think you should drive,' Corinne said. But she couldn't stop me. I was intent on being strong and not appearing to be giving in to anything. But Corinne wasn't convinced and said she was going to ask a private doctor who is available to the *Coronation Street* cast to visit me at home that evening.

I drove the hour and a half home to our rented house in Holmes Chapel feeling totally numb and crying silent tears. It was about seven o'clock when I got home and Jon was out, so I went straight to bed. I lay there, unable to stop crying, my body physically shaking with every sob. People have asked me what was going through my mind to make me feel like that. Was it the pub? Was it work? My mum? But I wasn't thinking about anything by then – my mind and emotions were blank.

When Jon came back he found me curled up in the foetal position and inconsolable. Soon afterwards, Dr Justin Haslam from the Priory Clinic in Altrincham turned up, having been sent by Corinne. Jon admits that when Dr Haslam first arrived he couldn't understand why I needed a doctor at all.

'She's just a bit tired and run down,' Jon told Dr Haslam. 'But we're going to Spain on Sunday so a good rest and some sunshine will sort her out.'

Jon had also booked us a romantic Valentine's night meal, because the following day was 14 February. He'd paid up front for it and cash was still so tight for us that it was a real treat, and he didn't want me to miss it.

But when Dr Haslam came into my bedroom, he could see how ill I was. I can't remember anything at all from this point but apparently I was sitting on the bed in my pyjamas, hugging my knees and rocking backwards and forwards. I was chain-smoking and staring into space. Dr Haslam was with me for almost two hours, and we talked through everything that was worrying me at the time – the money we owed; not letting people down; my mum's failing health. I also told him how chaotic life had become for me – I was working six days a week, helping out in the pub til late, learning lines until 1 or 2am before getting up and starting the whole exhausting routine again at 6am the following day. As an actress I had always taken care with my looks, but by this point I had completely given up caring what I looked like.

I was mortified that I had broken down in public. Although things had been very bad behind closed doors for quite some time, what had happened in the dressing room forced me to confront how bad things had become. I felt my life had spiralled out of control because I was so used to being a driven, capable person, used to solving all life's problems. Life didn't seem worth living any more and I was convinced I was just burden on everyone I loved. I really believed that everyone would be better off without me. Dr Haslam tells me that I spoke in a distinctly unemotional way, like a news reel.

Dr Haslam listened to me and then went downstairs for to talk to Jon.

'I think Beverley needs to be admitted to hospital,' he said.

'What for?' said Jon

'Jon, she is clinically depressed.'

Still, Jon couldn't quite understand how ill I really was and kept insisting a break in Spain would sort me out.

Dr Haslam told him that he wanted me in the Priory as soon as possible because he was worried I was in such a state I might harm myself. I had certainly reached the point where I didn't want to be alive any more. He also said I would need to be in the Priory for a minimum of eight weeks because I was seriously ill. Jon was utterly stunned. After all, I'd gone to work quite normally that morning and twelve hours later he was being told I had severe mental health problems and was at risk of killing myself. Dr Haslam explained that it was a bit of a classic case – people who are very strong and capable can battle on against the odds and under a huge amount of stress up to a point, but then it eventually hits them. He said I needed urgent professional treatment in order to get better, this wasn't going to just go away.

'Jon, you and Beverley can go to Spain,' Dr Haslam said. 'But you'll take the problem with you. And you'll bring it back again, too.'

After Dr Haslam left, Jon came up and sat on our bed.

'Maybe we can get our money back on the flights to Spain,' I said. It was weird because one part of me was still thinking rationally but the rest of me was totally gone.

'Do you want this, Beverley?' Jon asked me. 'Do you want to go into hospital?'

'I can't carry on like this,' I replied. 'I need help.'

I had to wait until the following morning to be admitted, while they sorted out privacy procedures at the clinic to ensure news didn't leak out that a member of the *Coronation Street* cast was in there. The next day, Jon and I got up, put on our tracksuits and drove the twelve miles to the Priory Clinic in Altrincham. It was Valentine's Day and all over the country other couples were setting off on romantic breaks while I was on my way to hospital.

I don't remember anything about that journey at all and Jon says I sat in the passenger seat barely speaking.

When you read about pop stars and film stars going to the Priory you tend to have an image of a glitzy five-star hotel, but people forget that it is a working hospital – and they achieve fantastic results. To protect my privacy, and I desperately didn't want my illness to leak out to the newspaper, I was put in one of the older, smaller rooms on a side corridor. My room was no more than 12ft square, with one window that barely opened, to prevent people escaping, one single bed, a television and plain magnolia walls. There wasn't even a picture on the walls to look at. In an adjoining bathroom there was just a basic shower and a toilet. We had to arrange a payment plan that is still ongoing. Of course I know now that they keep it basic like that on purpose, to stop people using it as a hotel and to help them focus on getting better.

At the end of the corridor was a big nurses' station and all around the hospital there were other patients, clearly suffering pretty bad problems. But I was beyond noticing much of that stuff at the time. In the first few days at the Priory, I've been told that I went from bad to worse, as without the distractions and obligations of my everyday life, I sunk lower. I had shrunk into myself to such an extent that I was almost totally silent and couldn't even engage in the hospital's therapy programme. I, probably fortunately, can't remember much of those dreadful early days, but the doctors say I was in free-fall and they became more and more concerned that I might take my own life.

That first night, they started me on medication as they began the search for a drug that would begin to make me feel better.

By the following day I was still felt very low but a bit calmer. Jon came in to visit and, looking around my room, he said, 'Are you sure you're happy to be here, Beverley?'

'I'm not right,' I said. By then I'd admitted it to myself. 'I've got to get better and this place can help me.'

I'd only been in there a couple of days when a reporter from a newspaper turned up outside our house in Holmes Chapel. At first, when Jon saw another stranger in a suit at our front door he thought it must be more bailiffs. But then the reporter introduced himself and said, 'We were wondering why Beverley had been admitted to the Priory?'

Jon was totally taken aback. The whole thing had been supposed to be top secret because the last thing I needed at that time was for the whole world to know how ill I was. It turned out that another patient's visitor had seen me going outside to have a fag, taken a picture of me on their mobile phone, then kindly sent it to the press! The Priory is incredibly discreet and does everything it can to protect the privacy of its patients, but this person had clearly gone to great lengths to take the photo. Looking back, I'm so relieved the papers didn't print it!

Jon immediately called the *Coronation Street* press office, which swung into action, warning the newspapers it would be against Press Complaints Commission rules to breach my privacy on a medical issue.

Meanwhile, Jon dealt with the reporter in his own style, 'You're trespassing and if you don't leave I'll set the dog on you,' he said. And if you've seen our big American Akita dog, Zen, that's not a threat you would take lightly!

Unknown to me, Jon then had to have meetings with the managers at the Priory to ensure my privacy was maintained. A nurse was placed on the doorway to the wing where I was staying and everyone who passed through had to be signed in and out and had to give up their mobile phone. I can't remember this time at all but apparently I couldn't understand why whenever I asked Jon to take me out for a fag he'd make me go down a corridor and out the back exit. 'Why can't we go out the front?' I'd say. Jon would make up excuses; he didn't want me to have even more to worry about.

With clinical depression, finding the right levels and combinations of drugs for someone is very difficult and can take a while. After about three days the drugs I was being given really kicked in and the next few weeks become a total blur. I only know what happened next from what Jon and the doctors told me afterwards.

By the fourth day I was a zombie. I lay on my bed in the foetal position staring into space, day after day. It was a total and utter breakdown. I didn't wash, didn't do my hair, didn't watch television and barely spoke. I was practically in a vegetative state, totally separated from the rest of the world.

The first time Jon saw me like that, he was horrified. He couldn't believe how far I had fallen. I was in the same pyjamas I'd been wearing since I arrived in the Priory and my hair, which is usually straightened and tidy, had gone frizzy and was matted all over my face. He says I looked like something out of *One Flew Over The Cuckoo's Nest*.

I couldn't speak properly but was making slurring noises that no one could really understand. I had no idea who anyone was around me and Jon could have been anybody at all as far as I was concerned.

When I needed the toilet, Jon or one of the nurses had to lift me out of bed then support me as I shuffled across the room. I was like a hundred-year-old woman, hunched over and only able to drag my feet along in steps no longer than six inches.

Jon was terrified that the treatment was making me worse, not better. He feared that there was no way I could come back from something as severe as this and thought he was losing me for ever. As for me, I didn't have the slightest clue what was going on. It was like being in a coma and I remember nothing about it.

For ten days I was like that, lying curled up on my bed, totally motionless. I couldn't bear the lights being on because they seemed too bright, so most of the time I lay there in darkness or gloom. When Jon visited he would sit in an armchair next to me in semi-darkness while I lay in silence on the bed. My meals were brought to me but I barely ate.

Few people knew how poorly I was. Jon told Rebecca and Josh but he kept the truth from a lot of my friends.

One day, Alison Sinclair and Janice Troup from the Granada press office came to visit me. It must be quite telling as to my insecurities about work because apparently, when I was told they were coming I dragged myself up in bed, tidied my hair and even put on some makeup. Even in the middle of the worst imaginable breakdown I couldn't bear people from work thinking I wasn't coping or was unprofessional. But Alison and Janice had only been there a short while when they saw the shocking reality of my situation, as I broke down again and started crying uncontrollably.

I can't remember them coming to see me at all and have only been told about it since. I have no memory of my close friend and hairdresser Adrian Wilde visiting either. Recently he told me he left the hospital crying because he was convinced I was going to die.

Our friends Tony and Gill were amazing. Gill would pop in every week and bring me a latte and a muffin even though I had no idea she was there. She'd talk to me even when I couldn't respond and an hour or so later she'd leave, with the latte and muffin still untouched by the side of my bed. A couple of my mates from the cast also came in to see me, although I can't remember anything about it. Then the doctors said it would be best for me not to have visitors other than close family, I was just too ill.

One day when Jon came in, I turned over in bed and looked at him. 'I want to die,' I said. Then I unfurled my fingers and showed him a handful of pills that I'd been given but managed to hide away. It wasn't a cry for help – I really meant it.

I felt unlovable, worthless, ugly and unattractive both physically and as a person and I saw no point in being alive any more. Nothing could ever be any better, nothing could ever be any worse. I just wanted it all to stop.

Jon was obviously terrified when he saw the tablets but he kept calm. 'Well Beverley,' he said. 'I think you should give it another day before you think about doing that. Let's just see how it goes.'

Then he left me, but what I didn't know was he went

straight to the nurses' station and told them about my stash of pills and that they had to stop me harming myself. The pills were taken away and I was put on 24-hour suicide watch, which meant the nurses had to keep checking on me, day and night.

When I found out my plan had been ruined, I was furious with Jon. 'You bastard, you f****** bastard,' I yelled at him during his next visit. 'You obviously don't love me. If you really loved me you wouldn't be stopping me from doing what I want to do.'

Jon just stood there and took it. I suppose by that point he really didn't know what else to do. He's told me since that he used to leave me at the end of his visits then go back to the car and cry his heart out.

But I hadn't given up on trying to kill myself. A couple of days later Jon was visiting me when I said, 'I'm still going to do it. I'm going to slit my wrists. I've worked out they come and check on me every hour, so I'm going to wait until they have just been and then I'm going to smash that lightbulb up there and slit my wrists. No one will be able to stop me.'

Jon believes that at that point I was saying out loud what I was thinking in my head without realising it. Thankfully though, he heard what I was thinking and the lightbulbs were removed from the room. It meant I was in darkness all the time but that suited me.

At the same time as all this was going on, our battle with the brewery over the Gallery was on the point of reaching court. Then, ten days after I went into the Priory, the brewery offered to drop any demand against us if we both agreed to pay our own costs. With me being so ill Jon just wanted it to be over, so he agreed. Although of course Jon then had to work out with our lawyer how we would pay the £12,000 we now owed him.

I'd been in the Priory for about twelve days when Jon arrived one afternoon to see me. 'Beverley has had a better day today,' someone said.

Jon rushed to my room, expecting to see me up and about like my old self. Instead, I was still lying on the bed, barely conscious. Jon totally lost it and stormed back. 'Do you think I'm a f****** idiot?' he raged. 'She is *not* having a good day, she can barely move, she's lying on the bed curled up in a ball like an old person. No, Beverley is a vibrant, intelligent, sexy woman and in that room she is a zombie.'

Poor Jon. You see the staff could see the medication having a slight impact on me but to Jon I was still totally lost and he was terrified that I was never coming back.

Jon knew that my friend Denise Welch had also suffered from depression, and one day he left a message on her answering machine saying, 'Hi Denise, Beverley really needs you right now. And I could do with some support, too!' Within an hour, Denise was on a train to see me. Her husband, Tim Healy, was brilliant with Jon as he knew just what it was like to have a partner with depression. Tim and Jon both ride motorbikes so they would go out on a ride together to get away from everything.

Jon's son Jonathan, who was then nineteen, was also a massive support to him. Jonathan was about to go into the Grenadier Guards and had been staying with us. Every evening when Jon came home from visiting me, his dinner was cooked, the house was spotless and the dogs had been walked. At least that was something Jon didn't have to worry about.

He certainly had enough to worry about with me though,

because after weeks of being in the Priory, I still wasn't responding to any of the different medications that the doctors had tried on me. I kept saying I didn't want to carry on, that I had nothing to offer any more, and I just wanted to be dead. We were desperate to find something that would make me feel better and they tried everything but I wasn't getting better, if anything, I was getting worse. I was so severely unwell, and the nature of my symptoms meant I couldn't engage in any form of talking therapy. The doctors said that in the most serious cases there was one last resort that might help – electric shock therapy.

20
THE CLIMB BACK UP

....

'No way, no way,' Jon seethed down the phone. 'You've been drugged up to the nines and now they want to electrocute you!'

I'd rung Jon and slurred down the phone to him that the doctors were now suggesting ECT – Electroconvulsive Therapy – or electric shock treatment as it is more commonly known.

Dr Haslam said it was only used in extreme circumstances and he was worried about the side effects of the treatment as it can affect memory and obviously I have to remember my lines for work. But we were all desperate to find something that could make me feel better as the drugs didn't seem to be working. They had tried other medications for about ten days, trying to kick-start my recovery, but I still hadn't improved. If anything, things were getting worse. Dr Haslam explained that it might take between four and six sessions of ECT before there was any improvement and it can take over three months to recover. But it became apparent, it was the only option. I would have tried anything.

Fifteen minutes after my phone call, Jon was back at the Priory and we were discussing what to do next.

In ECT an electric current is pumped through the brain to create seizures that jumpstart the production of the chemicals that the person suffering from depression is lacking. Some people see ECT as a controversial treatment and it is not a treatment to be undertaken lightly – it is only used in the most extreme forms of depression where drugs have failed to help. That was where I was and when you're that low, nothing scares you because nothing can be as bad as where you are at that very moment.

I was in no fit state to make any decisions for myself and don't even remember the conversations taking place so it was up to Jon, who was listed as my next of kin, to give the doctors the go-ahead, or not. To him, what the doctors were proposing really was like something out of *One Flew Over the Cuckoo's Nest* and I can understand now that it must have been a really tough decision. At the time I was raging at him. 'This will make me better and you're not letting me have it,' I yelled. 'You are stopping me from getting better.' In the end I think he accepted the doctor's expert advice and gave in to the idea, but he was still terrified it might have some awful effect on me.

My memories of this period are very hazy but I remember being taken in a car twice a week in my pyjamas, with two or three other patients from the Priory, to an ECT unit in the grounds of a neighbouring hospital.

The first time I went was very scary. The thought of being electrocuted conjures up images of Frankenstein's monster and horror movies. And even though it is nothing like that nowadays, you can't help thinking that it might be.

A nurse helped me as I shuffled from the car, hunched up and barely speaking, into a waiting room where the group of us from the Priory sat until we were called in. I think we must have been in alphabetical order because I was the first one to be summoned.

From the corridor I was taken into a little room and as soon as I went in the door I was struck by a really weird smell. Even now I can smell it when I think about it and I'm convinced it was the stench of burning flesh. That may just have been my vivid imagination but that was what it smelt like to me. At that point part of me was really frightened, but another part of me was so lost that I really didn't care what they did to me.

In that room I was helped into a chair by a nurse who then wiped down all the areas of my head and body where the electrodes and monitors would be placed, before sticking the heart monitor on to my chest and the electrodes on to my head. Then she showed me through a sliding door into the room where they actually did the treatment. In the middle of that room was a narrow bed and next to it was the small ECT machine, which would send bursts of electric current surging through my brain.

I was told to lie on the bed and then a needle was put into the back of my hand to give me a general anaesthetic, which knocked me out for the entire procedure. When I was totally out of it, the ECT machine was switched on.

Within minutes it was all over. I came round from the general anaesthetic feeling a little woozy but otherwise no different to before. The fog that I felt I'd been stuck in for weeks was still there.

I was also still taking lots of different drugs. I was on a massive dose of amitriptyline every day as well as diazepam. Dr Haslam said to me one day when he was checking on my progress, 'Beverley, your medication would literally put a horse to sleep. You are one of the most ill people I have ever seen.'

At first it was disheartening that the ECT didn't seem to be having any effect, but Dr Haslam was hopeful that with a few more sessions there would be a breakthrough.

In the end it took twelve treatments. I was taken to the ECT unit twice a week for six weeks. The experience never really got any better and each time I would lie there horrified by the fact that I was about to be electrocuted. The burning flesh smell made me feel sick.

My greatest fear was that the anaesthetic might not work and I'd be conscious when the electric current was going through my brain. One day I went for the treatment and a nurse injected my hand and said, 'OK Beverley, you'll start to feel drowsy in a moment,' but nothing happened. 'I'm not drowsy, the anaesthetic isn't working,' I said, panicking that they were about to start the treatment while I was still conscious. The needle had missed my vein and within minutes the back of my hand had swollen up like an egg, so they had to start again.

After about four sessions, very, very gradually Jon and the doctors could see me lifting out of the almost catatonic state I'd been in. And slowly I began to feel better too. The numbness was lifting.

I think a mixture of ECT and the prescription drugs I was on finally triggered the last bit of life that was still in me and I was able to use it to start pulling myself back up. But I was still very far from normal and to anyone who saw me, I was a slurring, stumbling wreck of a woman. A side effect of ECT is memory loss which is usually temporary, but during the treatment I was struggling with that.

One day when Jon came in to visit, I was feeling a lot brighter and I said to him, 'I think what really might make me better is some retail therapy!'

So Jon agreed to take me shopping. The doctors were encouraging me to get out, so it seemed like a good idea. There was a factory warehouse nearby that I used to go to quite a bit with my friend Gill so we drove over there. When we got there I was stumbling around, forgetting where to go and slurring so badly that the staff asked Jon if he wanted to take me out the back for a sit down and a cup of tea. They must have thought I was drunk.

On another shopping expedition I dragged Jon into a shoe shop and started trying on different pairs. We couldn't afford to be spending money on things like that but I think Jon thought if I was happy and feeling better then I could do whatever I wanted.

Recently Jon said to me, 'Have you ever worn those Ugg boots you bought when you were in hospital?'

'What Ugg boots?' I replied.

'The Ugg boots you bought when you dragged me into that shop insisting on some retail therapy!' Jon laughed.

I had absolutely no memory of buying them whatsoever because I was still so ill. It took me ages to find them at the back of my wardrobe!

Another time we had to go to an emergency 24-hour dentist because the ECT had cracked my teeth and the only one open was inside a 24-hour Tesco store. After the appointment I decided I wanted to whiz round the shop to get some bits that I needed. Jon thought it was a really bad idea because normally I can't go round a supermarket without people staring or saying, 'Hiya Liz', but I was determined. Not a single person recognised me that day. A few people looked at me oddly as if they vaguely knew me, but my hair was curly and my face was pale, drawn and tired and I suppose I looked like a totally different person to the Beverley Callard they had seen on television.

There are entire weeks of my life that are lost for ever. I can't remember them, because of the illness and the effects of ECT. While I was in the Priory, for example, Rebecca, Gideon and the boys were staying in Manchester because she was in a production of *Macbeth* at the Royal Exchange. I went one day to see her in it but I have no recollection of it at all. Josh and Rebecca came to see me in hospital when I was poorly and it must have been horribly upsetting for them, but I can't remember anything about their visits.

Although I was very gradually getting better I would have many days where I went backwards and slipped back to the state I'd been in before. On Mother's Day we all went out for lunch and I collapsed in tears twice at the table. I just couldn't cope with being somewhere with so many people around.

The doctors were reassuring and told us that there would be setbacks to my recovery but so long as each setback wasn't as bad as the last, then I was making progress.

As I started to feel better, Jon would bring the dogs in to the Priory and we'd take them for walks, which I loved.

I started going to therapy sessions in the mornings and gradually I began to recognise other patients around me. Many of them had been there for weeks, like me, but before then I hadn't really noticed anyone.

One day I was in the communal kitchen area and this other patient came up to me and said, 'Hi, I know who you are.'

'Oh,' I replied, not quite sure what to say.

'So, are you a glumaglugorastick then?'

'A what?' I replied, not having a clue what he was talking about. He was talking quite fast and it sounded like a nonsense word.

He repeated himself slowly. 'Are you a glum – in here for depression, a glug – an alcoholic, or a stick – an eating disorder?'

'Oh, in that case I'm a glum,' I said.

Then he just wandered off. It was so funny and gradually I was learning to laugh again.

I found the group counselling sessions quite difficult. Maybe it was because I knew that the others there would recognise me from *Coronation Street*, so I couldn't have the same sense of anonymity that they did. I really do find those sorts of situations very difficult anyway. People think because of my job I must be really confident but I'm really not. I'd sit in the groups thinking, 'I'm here with six other people and a counsellor and I can't say a word. I've got to try, I must try.' But most of the time I couldn't do it.

I also had one-on-one counselling and spent time talking about my low self-esteem and lack of confidence. The sessions made me see that I've spent a lot of my life people-pleasing and that I have to learn how to say no and how to start feeling better about myself.

Eight weeks to the day that I went into the Priory, Jon and I had a meeting with the doctors, who said I was making such a good recovery that I would be home soon. As I packed my bags one week later and Jon drove me home, it was an incredible relief to be returning to the outside world, but I was still quite poorly and very tired. I'd had twelve general anaesthetics in six weeks while having the ECT, and that alone took a toll on my body. Though I had been warned before receiving the treatment that one of the major side-effects of having ECT was memory loss, I was still struggling to remember the simplest things.

Jon had talked to the doctor, who agreed that he could book flights and take me straight out to Spain to stay at our apartment. We stayed in Spain for six weeks and it was a real time of healing for both of us. We'd been through so much over the past year and it was the first time in ages that we had spent together on our own.

While I was in the Priory, Jon had enrolled on a course to study counselling. He had become interested in the issue after I became ill, and had watched a television programme in which the Falklands veteran Simon Weston talked about the desperate need for ex-army staff to help counsel servicemen and women suffering from psychological problems. Jon decided that was what he wanted to do and set about trying to achieve it.

Every week, Jon flew back from Spain to attend his counselling night classes and to meet with our creditors. While I was in the Priory, he had worked out a schedule of monthly repayments to everyone to whom we owed money.

It felt as if things were slowly getting better, although the setbacks continued and I still suffered panic attacks and had some very bad days where I felt utterly flat and really saw very little point in being alive. Some days I couldn't face getting out of bed at all and Jon would be on the phone to Dr Haslam, worried that I was relapsing. The doctor always reassured us that this was normal and reminded us that there would be blips along the way but they would occur less frequently and be less severe each time.

One day we were in a restaurant in Spain when someone

just started taking pictures of me. I couldn't cope with it at all and started crying so badly at the table that Jon had to help me out and take me back to the apartment. I was still at a point where if I could have done, I would have closed the door of the apartment and stayed inside and watched television for six weeks. But Jon encouraged me to go out, and we got into a little routine of walking down to the beach every day then stopping for a drink in a beach bar on the way home. But even just going for a short walk exhausted me. All the drugs I had been given in the Priory, and the ECT, had taken a terrible toll on my body.

But despite still feeling very tired and fragile, I think Jon and I fell in love again that late spring in Spain. One afternoon we had a few drinks in a beach bar and we giggled all the way home. It was like we were best mates again, the way we always had been before the pub and the debts and the brewery battle and work and then my illness ripped us apart.

As the weeks went by, I was anxious to get back to work. Steve and Becky's second attempt at getting married was coming up and I knew *Coronation Street* would want me back for that. I wanted to get back, too. I've always hated the thought that people might think me unprofessional or unable to cope and I was desperate to prove that wasn't the case. On top of that, we couldn't possibly afford for me not to go back to work if we were ever going to get out of debt. I was just grateful that *Coronation Street* still wanted me after everything that had happened. I was desperate not to let anyone down.

I was also very worried about my poor memory and was panicking about whether I'd be able to learn my lines. While we were in Spain I could watch a DVD and not be able to remember a single thing about it by the following day. And I would read the same paragraph of a book over and over again because each time I put it down I couldn't remember where I had got to. So how on earth was I going to remember all my lines for Corrie? I wasn't going to let that stop me though and in June 2009 we returned to Manchester ready for me to go back to work.

Dr Haslam was concerned that I was going to put myself under pressure by returning to work so soon – most people take two years off after ECT. But working was my passion and it might actually make me feel better and more secure to be back on the Street. Most actors worry about where the next job is coming from and I am just the same. In reality I've rarely been out of work in my entire career but that doesn't stop the feelings of insecurity.

Jon was convinced I was going back too soon. He'd seen me at my very worst and knew how seriously ill I had been, but I persuaded him I was fine and that I really would try to take it easy.

While I'd been in the Priory the owners of the house we'd been renting in Holmes Chapel had decided to sell it so we had to get out. It was probably for the best as it hadn't been a happy time for us there. Jon found a small townhouse in Salford Quays to rent and on one of his trips back from Spain he decorated it from top to bottom and moved in all our belongings. He even took a photograph of my dressing table in Holmes Chapel and recreated it exactly in the new house so that when I arrived, at least one thing felt a bit familiar.

I returned to work on 15 June but the minute I stepped back on the cobbles the pressure was on, because Steve's wedding to Becky Granger was of course a massive storyline for his mum.

Liz's sudden disappearance had been explained away by saying she had gone to Spain to look after her son Andy, who had injured himself. A couple of weeks before I was due back, Lance Milligan, who is in charge of the costume department, rang me up and we were talking about what Liz should be wearing for the big wedding. Liz was only arriving back in Weatherfield the night before Steve's wedding, then staying over at Deirdre's to avoid Lloyd, so it had to be an outfit that she had bought in Spain. We thought it would be hilarious if she turned up in a flamenco-style dress – only Liz could do that!

The week before I started filming again, I had popped in to say hello to everybody but I was still nervous about returning. Even after just a fortnight's holiday from *Coronation Street* it feels like the first day of a new school term when I go back, and I can never sleep the night before. This was a much bigger deal than just a fortnight off. I was proud of myself for getting back to work after just four months but I was also terrified that I wouldn't be able to live up to my own high standards of work.

Thankfully, because my dress for that first scene was so funny and over the top it made returning much easier. And of course the only time most people at work see me is when I 'am' Liz, in my costume and with loads of makeup on, so they don't ever see me as Beverley. That kind of helped, too.

On my first day back, Kim Crowther, who was the producer, and Kieran Roberts, the executive producer, were saying I looked fantastic but they were worried that because I appeared so well, people might forget that I was actually still quite fragile. They were brilliant at looking after me. Corinne, the nurse, who has now become a good friend, kept a close eye on me all the time and ensured I worked no more than thirty-seven hours a week, which is all Dr Haslam said I was allowed to do. In most jobs thirty-seven hours is a working week, but *Coronation Street* can be anything up to seventy-two hours a week. And that doesn't include the time spent learning your lines!

It is a wonderful job but it is very pressured. You have to be word perfect every single time and if you forget the lines you can't just ad lib and hope for the best because scriptwriters have laboured over those words and what they do is an art.

In the first few weeks after my return I really struggled to learn my lines. I was often up until half past two in the morning reading the script over and over again, hoping it would stick in my mind. Four hours later the alarm would go to wake me up and the lines would have totally disappeared from my brain. I wouldn't be able to remember a thing. It was terrifying. I'd spend the next few hours before filming started going over the lines again and again and, thank God, I never had a single time on set where I forgot what I had to say. I can't understand how that happened though because whenever I wasn't in front of the camera, I would be totally blank.

I was also existing on hardly any sleep because I had to get up so early in the morning to take my medication. I was still on very heavy dosages of prescription drugs and for the first couple of hours after I'd taken them I would slur my words so that it sounded as if I were drunk. I had to make sure I had long enough after I'd taken the tablets to start sounding normal before I arrived at work. I felt utterly exhausted because not only was I having to act the role of Liz, I was also having to act being better than I really was. And inside I had this rising sense of panic.

For the first two weeks I was working every day as we

filmed the wedding (which this time did go ahead) and the aftermath, when Becky was arrested by the drugs squad.

I was feeling tired and one morning when I got up for work I was very tearful. I don't think I was relapsing, it was just a bit too much too soon.

Jon said I should call in sick but I wouldn't do it.

'I've got to go in, I've got to go in,' I kept saying. In *Coronation Street*, if someone isn't there it upsets all the filming schedules and can impact on loads of people. I didn't want them thinking I was being unprofessional. And I certainly didn't want them thinking I couldn't do my job any more.

In the end Jon took the decision out of my hands, rang Corinne and said, 'Beverley won't be in today.'

'No problem, that's fine,' she replied.

Coronation Street wasn't putting any pressure on me at all. The only person doing that was me.

At this point I still couldn't even sign my own name. I would start forming the letter 'B' and I knew that it was an 'e' that came next but I just couldn't work out how I joined them all together. It was eight weeks after I returned to work that I managed to relearn my signature.

After a few weeks back on set when I was still struggling with my lines, I thought, 'This is it Beverley, you are going to have to leave. You just can't do your job properly any more.' But another part of me refused to give in and so I hung on.

Jon was terrified that I was pushing myself too hard and that I'd make myself ill again but I was determined not to let anyone down at work. I just couldn't shake off that old thought pattern, despite everything that had happened.

Eventually I could no longer deny to myself the fact that although I was back at work, I was still not back to my old self. I'd been in the studio all day, every day, for quite a few weeks and was feeling tired when we finally finished filming my last scene of the day at about half past seven. We were on stage two on the far side of the set and suddenly I realised I couldn't remember my way back to my dressing room. I'd worked at *Coronation Street* for most of the past twenty years but I had absolutely no idea of how to get around the set. I think I'd used up so much effort over the previous few days that I was wiped out. It was a terrifying feeling and I just stood sobbing, all on my own because everyone else had gone back. 'I am never, ever going to be normal again,' I thought.

After a while Sally, one of our Organising Stage Managers, found me. I was still crying as I said to her, 'Please don't tell anyone, Sally but I don't know where I'm going.' Sally walked me back to my dressing room, where I calmed down and waited for Jon to pick me up, as I still wasn't allowed to drive.

On one occasion my doctor was so worried that I was overdoing things that he pulled me out of filming for a day but I hated that. I was still obsessed with not wanting other members of the cast and crew to think I was a failure. At home I also wanted to show Jon I wasn't a failure. Then there were all our kids to think about too. They may all be grown up now, so there is less everyday responsibility, but I didn't want them to think I'd failed either. I was putting myself under way too much pressure, as usual, but I couldn't stop it. It was the way I had always been but I at least knew, for the first time in my life, that it was going to have to change and I was going to have to learn to be easier on myself in future if I was going to stay well.

After Becky and Steve's wedding, work became a bit quieter, which gave me a bit of breathing space. Each week, learning my lines became a little bit easier and every day I felt I had more energy. Soon I was keen for bigger storylines and to get back into fitness training. I was happier, more optimistic and after a very long time when I couldn't face the future at all, I was finally looking forward to it again. The relief was almost overwhelming and I know that my family were all overjoyed to have me back. We had been close to the brink, but somehow, we had made it.

21
THE BEST IS YET TO COME

....

As I look back over the past couple of years I think, 'Phew! I survived it!'

There were times when it was touch and go and Jon feared that I was in such a deep depression that I might never pull through.

All the doctors told me that what I'd experienced would be life-changing, and it has been. Being so poorly makes you realise how incredibly precious life is and how important it is to ensure that we make the very most of it, doing the things we want to do and cherishing every moment.

Mum's illness had already begun to make me very aware of that, even before my breakdown. I would look at my daughter Rebecca having to feed her babies, change their nappies and bath them and then look at Mum, who needs the same things done for her. It has made me realise how vital it is that we make the most of the short time that lies in between those two ends of life.

When I was ill there were a few months when I wasn't able to visit Mum and I feel guilty about that. When I was well enough to see her again she had slid further downhill. One day during the late summer of 2009, Gerry rang and said he didn't think he could care for Mum on his own any longer and maybe it was time to consider finding her a residential home.

Steph and I had known he was exhausted for ages and had thought about finding a home for Mum before, but every time we mentioned it he'd say, 'We're fine as we are, aren't we Mavis?' We didn't want to break their hearts by separating them. Once Gerry admitted he couldn't cope any longer, though, we quickly set about finding a home for her. That proved really difficult because Gerry wanted Mum near him in Leeds, while Steph and I needed her to be close to us in Manchester because we would be the ones called if there were an emergency.

We looked at lots of residential homes all over the place and boy, does that open your eyes. We were just parking the car outside one place when Steph said, 'Oh my God. Look at that woman on the steps, she must be escaping.'

We got out of the car and came face to face with this hunched-up old lady wearing an overall covered in boiled-egg and gravy stains.

'Oh, Beverley Callard!' she said. 'I thought it might be you when I heard your name. Now would your mother be wanting to share a room or have one of her own?'

It turned out the woman wasn't escaping, she was the manager! We quickly said it wasn't quite what we were looking for and got away.

The home we did find for Mum is lovely. In the corridors there are photographs of all the residents and movie stars from their heyday, people like Clark Gable, Cary Grant and Tyrone Power, who Mum had adored. Before she moved in, we decorated her room and lined the walls with her old photographs, which we got blown up bigger. Then Jon put up some shelves for all the ornaments she had been collecting since she was a little girl.

One Thursday morning, Steph and I went to collect Mum from Gerry's to take her to the home. We were all being cheerful so she didn't get worried, and when we got there I said, 'Come on Mum, us three girls are going out now.'

As we walked out of the door, I could tell that Gerry's heart was broken. It was horrific.

When we arrived, we all had tea and I said, 'Mum, this is where you are going to be staying now but Steph and I will be back tomorrow.'

'Oh,' she said, looking around the room. She didn't get upset or even seem to mind, she was beyond that.

For the first month Mum was in the home she seemed better when Steph and I went in to visit her. Sometimes I'd walk in the door and she would say: 'Look, it's our Beverley,' and other days she would say: 'Oh, here is Stephanie.' But then Mum started to regress again. Now, some days Mum will recognise Steph and me and other days she won't. They show *Coronation Street* on the telly in the lounge but Mum doesn't know that it's me on the screen any more. Up until recently I could remind her of the time I took her to Spain and we jumped over the waves and she would laugh and laugh. That was one of the last memories that hung on, but even that has gone now.

Another thing that has come with her Alzheimer's is a phobia of water and now she hates being bathed and having her hair washed. One morning Steph and I tried to bath her but she was fighting us all the time. Finally we were able to lower her into the bath and I was holding her arms, saying, 'Look into my eyes, don't worry, we are not going to hurt you,' when suddenly she turned to Steph and was screaming at her, 'Get out. Who are you? Who are you?' Stephanie was sobbing and yes, she is a grown woman, but she is still my baby sister and it was just horrible. Other times she has been really loving to Steph and nasty to me. It is all just so confusing and upsetting.

Mum's name at the home is 'Dancing Queen' because before Christmas they had a party and she danced non-stop for two hours. There was a DJ playing all the old music from the films with Doris Day, Fred Astaire and Gene Kelly that we used to watch together when I was a child and that Mum had always loved. Steph, Gerry and I went along and she danced with all of us. That evening I felt the inner giggle she'd once had was back.

Some days now she is really nasty and aggressive. She'll wipe her nose on her skirt or make awful noises like an animal and it is devastating because our mum was always so lady-like. Other times she looks so hunched up and weak that I can't imagine she will make it to the weekend. Steph and I feel like our emotions are on a big dipper because she changes so much from day to day.

Last Christmas Day she was in a bad way. She usually sits with a lady called Annie but she wouldn't sit with her that day, so when Josh, Steph and her husband Stephen and I arrived on Christmas morning, she was all on her own. We handed her our presents and she looked at them but she didn't know what to do with them. It was heartbreaking because she couldn't work out how to undo the wrapping paper and I was saying, 'Come on Mum, these are presents, for you.' I read out my gift tag, which said, 'To my mum, Merry Christmas, lots of love, Beverley.' And she just sat there and cried. So sometimes I do wonder if there is a little speck in her mind where she knows what is happening to her. But by the time we got to the third present, she was getting angry. We said, 'Come on, pull the paper off,' but she snarled 'No' and started making growling noises at us.

Afterwards we all stood outside the home and cried. Josh is 6 feet 3 inches and a grown man now but he was so upset. I looked at Steph, my baby sister, in her beautiful red, woollen Christmas dress and it killed me. 'You shouldn't have to go through this,' I thought.

Now Mum sometimes has to be sedated quite often for bath time because she gets so aggressive. She is refusing to eat and has lost three and a half stone. She sips meal replacement drinks but not really enough of them, so we don't think she can survive much longer. I do think now it would be better for her to die because Alzheimer's has already taken all her dignity away. Steph and I are grieving for her even though she is still alive, because the Mum we knew has already gone.

My mum's illness is a huge ongoing source of pain for me but in other aspects of my life, I feel blessed. There is so much to be grateful for, and in the wake of my breakdown, I really am so conscious of all that is good. A lot of my happiness is to do with my relationships, as it always has been.

Steph and I have always been close but since Mum's illness that bond has only strengthened because, from the family we had when we were kids, it's only us left now.

My sister is the beautiful one and the academic in the family. While I left school without even doing my O-levels,

Steph studied hard and now works as a teacher in Leeds. She loves English and writes for pleasure in her spare time. Steph looks like my dad, while I'm more like Mum, but our voices are very similar. I'm sure people think she's the sensible one, but she has her moments!

One of my greatest pleasures now is being a grandma to Sonny, who's now four, and George who is two. I feel guilty about not seeing them more frequently because they live in London and we're in Manchester, but when I do seem them it is fantastic.

As a grandma you can be a bit naughty and spoil them. At Christmas, my kids, Jon's kids and the two grandsons were here and we had a wonderful time. When they went I had a mega clean up, then sat down to enjoy the peace and quiet, but after a couple of days I was thinking, 'Oh, it's a bit too quiet now. I want them all back.'

When Rebecca was little she loved watching films, just as I had as a girl, and she knew all the songs and all the dialogue in *West Side Story*. Now her little boy, Sonny, is the same. He is clearly already mesmerised by show business.

Rebecca's husband, Gideon, is a great son-in-law. People used to say to me I'd never think any man was good enough for my baby daughter but he really is. When I look at them I can see they love each other so much.

Rebecca hasn't had any contact with Paul, her dad, for years. She was about eighteen and a half and working at the West Yorkshire Playhouse in Leeds when one day she received a phone call at the stage door.

'Hi, it's your dad,' the voice on the phone said.

Rebecca hadn't heard from him since she was a toddler and she was so shocked that her knees gave way beneath her.

She had recently been in *The Borrowers*, which had won a Bafta.

'Why now? Why now?' she kept asking.

She asked me to go along with her to meet Paul, and though we had a nice time together, I think there was just too much water under the bridge and that was the last time they saw each other.

Rebecca does keep in touch with my ex-husband, David, who was always wonderful with her. He lives in Singapore now and writes educational books but whenever he is in England he visits her.

Josh has done brilliantly well too and I am so proud of what he has achieved. He has completely turned his life around and has started another college course but this time he is sticking at it. He is studying counselling and has two part-time jobs to support himself. He also has a lovely girlfriend who he moved in with at the end of last year.

He has also been building a relationship with his grandparents, Steve's mum and dad, and with Steve too. It hasn't been easy but Josh has worked very hard at that.

He goes to both Alcoholics Anonymous and Narcotics Anonymous meetings regularly and hasn't had a drink for eighteen months. He has even encouraged me to write about his experiences in this book in the hope that it might help others with an addiction to believe that they can come through it and life can get better.

From the moment you discover you are pregnant you worry about your children, and I'll never stop worrying about Josh or Rebecca, but fingers crossed they are now both happy and healthy.

Financially, Jon and I may have a long way to go but I know we will get there.

I still absolutely love my job and consider it a privilege to have been part of Corrie for so long. I'm also trying to find more balance in the way I approach it than I have in the past.

Work was tough for the first few months after I went back but as my memory improved I found it easier to learn my lines. Now I'm excited that Liz is going to be at the centre of some great storylines in the run-up to *Coronation Street's* fiftieth anniversary at the end of 2010.

As I look back over more than twenty years, on and off, of playing Liz, I see how she has developed and matured. She is a grandma herself now, just like me, and while her character used to be entirely high drama she has become far funnier over the years. I love Liz, but I fear she will never get her happy ending. She needs a man and is no good on her own but she is no good with a man either. That's brilliant for me though because it means she gets great storylines.

I feel very lucky because Liz is such a popular character with viewers. I get loads of fan mail every week, which I always reply to because I'm proud that people are so fond of Liz. I think maybe her popularity comes from the fact that men fancy her and women like her because she's fun, feisty and has that ability to bounce back.

At the end of 2009 there was a storyline where Liz's enemy Teresa organised a Vicars and Tarts party but called it a Vicars and Lizs party and everyone turned up in the Rovers dressed in tight tops and miniskirts. At first, Liz was complimenting Fiz on how good her new look was but then she realised what was happening and started to cry. Within two days I was inundated with letters from viewers feeling sorry for Liz. It is amazing how much sympathy people have for her.

And then there is the fascination with her dress sense! Her miniskirts and plunging necklines have become a national talking point over the past two decades. I think Liz's worst article of clothing has to be the red Lycra top with long sleeves and two cut-outs over the shoulders. It is just so ugly. Another of the most awful costumes I've had to wear was the outfit Liz turned up in when she took up Brazilian Crunch classes: red high heels and a fishnet body stocking with a red mesh top and ra-ra skirt!

Liz always seems to get big storylines in the middle of winter so I'm stood outside in the freezing cold wearing a Lycra mini skirt and stilettos that make your toes so cold they go numb. At least Emily Bishop gets to weary furry boots and a big coat!

Liz also has the gold L she always wears around her neck and her distinctive zigzag necklace, which we've had literally hundreds of letters about from viewers trying to find one the same. It has broken twice but the costume department have to keep repairing it because we can't find another one anywhere.

Since I've been ill I've put on a bit of weight because of my medication and not being able to exercise. That has just made wearing Liz's clothes even harder as they are unforgiving to say the least. My tummy is still quite bloated from the drugs, so sometimes I look at myself in Liz's tiny size eight skirts and think I look like an egg on legs!

ECT can be tough on your skin too and some days I look at myself and I see bunny rabbit crinkles at the side of my mouth, a turkey neck and hands that look like chicken feet and I think, 'I've turned into a bloody pet shop!'

Looking back on my time as Liz, I find it hard to believe that more than twenty years has gone by. Sometimes I look at the McDonald boys, Simon and Nick, and think, 'But you are so grown up. How did that happen so quickly?'

When it was Steve and Becky's wedding the four of us McDonalds were back together on screen and we loved it. We've said to the writers and producers that we'd all really like to be reunited and who knows, maybe one day it will happen.

As long as the storylines are there for Liz, it will always be too tempting to stay in the show. We get our scripts on a Tuesday and when mine comes it always feels a bit like receiving a present because I don't know what is inside, but then I open it and there will be a great storyline and I feel all giddy and excited.

I love working with my friends who have been in the show for years, but I also love being on set with Kate Kelly who plays Becky and Kym Marsh, who plays Michelle. Kym and I get on brilliantly and we have a real giggle together.

I am massively loyal to *Coronation Street*, it is a national institution and I hope it is around for another fifty years after this. But being so ill was a life-changing experience and it has made me feel that if there are other things I want to do, I've got to get on and do them. Recently, Jon and I took part in a *Celebrity Mr & Mrs* show on television, which I would never have done before but now I think, 'Why not? It'll be a laugh.'

Since I've been ill I haven't been able to teach fitness classes and it does feel as if there is a part of my life missing. I hope to return to teaching again soon though and that will be a big step forward for me. I love doing it and it's good for me mentally and physically.

I'm not a hundred per cent better yet, but I'm well on my way. Dr Haslam says it is completely remarkable that I have bounced back so quickly. I'm very grateful to him and all the staff at the hospital for helping me get better. Recovery from depression is not a straight line though and I've had many dips and am sure there will be more to come. For a few days at the start of 2010 I felt very low again. It started with a metallic taste in my mouth, which other sufferers of depression have told me that they get too, and then my mood became very flat. I went back to my doctor, who prescribed a new drug and by the following teatime I was feeling much better.

I think I'd been feeling disappointed that I hadn't come as far in my recovery as I had hoped I would – but that is part of my problem, always pushing myself too hard.

I'm convinced my depression is caused by a chemical imbalance and is somehow hormonal too. Looking back, I think Mum may have suffered with depression and that our illnesses are somehow related. After her little boy died she was prescribed the tranquiliser librium and later, some days Steph and I would come home from school and Mum would be having a lie down on the green leather sofa. We'd say 'Oh, she's fed up again,' but we had no idea then what I now suspect she was really feeling.

I don't really want to admit this but if I'm brutally honest I sometimes do wonder if I also have a slight tendency towards manic depression because I can have touches of manic behaviour. If I start something I have got to finish it, no matter what it is. I can never leave dirty washing in the laundry basket; it has to be done, it has to be. And I wash blacks then coloureds then whites all separately and all my whites have to be soaked first.

I'm the same at work. I won't be happy until I know my lines inside out. I push myself very hard as if I'm trying to prove myself all the time.

When my marriages were failing, when I had cancer and when the pub was going under, my way of dealing with these things was always the same – to throw myself into work and push myself as hard as I could. I felt it would be wrong to show I couldn't cope so I kept on fighting, proving I was strong. No matter what was going on in my life, I carried on getting up each morning, putting my makeup on, turning up for work and doing whatever was required without letting anyone know how I was really feeling.

I think that fighting to repress my feelings for so long is what made my breakdown so severe when it came.

I've since learnt that depression is called, 'the curse of the strong'. Now I have to learn that it is also strong to admit when you are feeling low and to say, 'I need help'. Through counselling I am also trying to work on my self-esteem. It sounds terribly American to talk about having therapy but again I've had to accept that I need help if I am to overcome these feelings of worthlessness that sometimes overwhelm me.

My counsellor recommended a book called *Overcoming Low Self-Esteem* by Dr Melanie Fennel and when I started reading it I thought the author must have bugged my house. I couldn't believe that she knew exactly how I was feeling and how I would criticise myself. It's things like, if I'm going out I'll try on twenty outfits but think I look horrific in all of them and all I really want to do is wear something baggy that will hide me away from everyone.

A couple of weeks ago I received a call asking me to attend the National TV Awards. I said I'd love to go but the minute I put the phone down I thought, 'Why did I do that? I'm going to look old and ugly and the papers will do that thing where they say 'what not to wear' with a picture of me and I'll be feeling really insecure all night and then I won't want to go back to work because I won't feel good at anything.'

I'm really not sure where these feelings of low self-esteem come from. I had the most loving and fortunate childhood anyone could hope for and my parents never made me doubt myself. But I think perhaps I always lacked confidence and by acting the clown, I was able to cover up the real me. Then my marriage to Steve only chipped away at my self-esteem further. Even now I'm sure most people who met me would have no idea how shy and uncomfortable I can feel in certain situations, because I tend to overcompensate to hide how I'm feeling.

I've reduced the amount of drugs I take since leaving the Priory but I still take three different medicines every day. I don't know how long I will be on the drugs and although I will obviously keep taking them as long as I have to, they are a nuisance. If I go out somewhere I can't take them until I get home because they make me so tired and a bit like a drunk. But I can't take them too late either because then I'm like a drunk the next morning. I need a couple of hours in the mornings for the effects of the drugs to wear off, so if I'm on set at 7.15am I get up at quarter to five to make sure I'm OK in time for work. Sometimes I will be at work until eight o'clock at night so it is tiring.

Every night when I get my tablets out it does feel a bit like *Valley of the Dolls*, but they are making me better so I have to stick with them. I just pray to God that they continue to work because sometimes I do get frightened that the depression may come back and get me.

For a while I found it hard knowing there were whole weeks of my life when I was in hospital that I couldn't remember. Now I've just accepted I have to live with it and if anyone asks me something about the missing period, I just say, 'I'm really sorry but I don't remember that because I was completely off my trolley.'

For years I never spoke about having suffered from depression. I admired people like Denise Welch and Stephen Fry who were able to talk publicly about it but I just couldn't. Perhaps I thought it was a guilty secret I shouldn't admit to. But when I became very ill I found it hugely comforting to speak to other people who had suffered in the same way. When you have depression you can feel totally isolated, when really there are thousands of people who have been through it. As I said, being so ill was a huge and shattering experience for me, and it is what made me decide to write this book. It made me want to tell people that I'd had depression and to let them know if they are in the middle of it, that they are not alone. If it helps just one person going through what I have experienced, then it will have been worthwhile.

Not only has my illness been life-changing for me, it has also had a massive impact on Jon. He is now doing the three-year course that will make him a British Association Registered Counsellor. He has gone from having no experience of depression and mental health issues to being incredibly knowledgeable and very understanding. He is also back drumming in a band again, which he loves.

We are still living in our small rented house in Salford and it will probably be a while until we can buy somewhere again because we have such a bad credit rating now that we wouldn't be able to get a mortgage. But we're happy where we are with our dogs, the Japanese Akita, Zen, and Tilly, the stray that we found in Spain.

For a while, when we were losing the pub, battling the brewery and I was becoming ill, Jon and I drifted apart as we both got caught up fighting our own personal battles for survival. But now we're closer than ever and we are fighting all our battles together.

After struggling for so long in relationships that didn't work, sometimes it scares me that things are so good with Jon. He is romantic, sexy and kind, but most importantly he is my best mate. We can talk about anything, we're both into fitness, we both love reading and good food and we both enjoy partying but then we both enjoy quiet nights in, too. We just sort of fit. Sometimes we will go out for dinner at a nearby restaurant, or we'll just stay in and watch a film together. It is simple stuff but it is good. We've got our relationship back.

Living with depression is a constant struggle though and I'm sure it will probably always be with me now. I've had plenty of setbacks and I'm certainly not entirely over it. But I'm beginning to win the battle.

Before I had depression, I was an optimist. I used to believe that the best was always yet to come. When I became ill I didn't imagine I would ever get that feeling back again. But I have.

I've had some amazing times in my life but now I can again believe that the best is still to come. I'm here, I've got Jon, two wonderful children and two gorgeous grandchildren and I've survived some of the worst that life could throw at me. After all, I'm unbroken. I hope.

22
HAPPY ENDING

....

Oh my goodness, the best was definitely yet to come when I wrote that last chapter! Just over a fortnight after the hardback version of this book came out Jon and I disappeared off to our apartment in Spain for four days. I'd been so busy at *Coronation Street* and doing newspaper and television interviews about the book that we'd hardly had a chance to talk properly in weeks. We were desperate to spend a few days of uninterrupted 'Jon and Bev' time together.

Jon and I got off the plane, whizzed to our apartment, threw on some beach clothes and went down to our favourite beach bar. It was a boiling hot day but it is a fantastic, authentic Spanish bar with straw umbrellas and a beautiful breeze blowing through it and once we had sat down with a jug of Sangria we instantly felt the stress lift off us. We sat there for a couple of hours talking about anything and everything.

'I can't believe it's only just over a year since you were in the Priory,' Jon said. 'I never thought you'd be this well ever again.'

'Me neither,' I laughed. I felt so much stronger than I'd done in months and thankfully we had reached the right balance in my medication so I was feeling really good.

Then Jon and I talked about each of the kids: what they were doing and all those concerns and worries that all parents have.

'Now, there is one other serious thing I'd like to talk to you about,' Jon said.

'Oh yes?' I replied. It sounded a bit ominous!

'Yes,' he went on. 'We've been through a hell of a lot together over the past couple of years.'

'I know, I know,' I said. But Jon was still talking.

'And that's why, Beverley,' he said, pausing slightly, 'I really think we should be married. We've been together nearly eight years and I just want you and me to be husband and wife.'

I just looked at him for a couple of seconds, not quite believing what I was hearing. Then I started crying.

'I can't believe you actually want to be married to me,' I finally managed to say. 'I can't believe it, after the Priory and ECT and everything else.'

And I really meant that, it wasn't false modesty at all. It is incredibly hard for someone whose partner has depression. Not only does the person with depression feel completely unlovable, they also find it very hard to show love. But Jon had supported me through all that and still wanted to marry me! I like to think I'd move heaven and earth for Jon but I do wonder whether I'd have been strong enough to support him in the way he supported me. And I couldn't believe he'd proposed to me there, at that moment. I was sitting there looking like death because I was so pale and pasty after a Manchester winter. I was wearing an old bikini, a sarong, a baggy t-shirt, flip-flops and a huge sun hat. It was hardly high glamour!

The whole thing had hit me totally out of the blue. I really hadn't had the first clue that this had been brewing in Jon's mind. When I finally stopped crying I became really giddy and excited about the whole thing. Then after a while I went back to being really emotional again. It was about half an hour later that Jon said: 'Er, Beverley, you still haven't given me an answer yet.'

'Oh, it's yes,' I said. 'Definitely yes.' And then we both started crying!

We spent the rest of the evening on the phone to the children, my sister Steph and Jon's family, telling them the news. We rang the girls first. Rebecca instantly started screaming, then said: 'What are you going to wear?' Then we rang Danielle, who also started screaming and only stopped to ask: 'What are you going to wear?' That's girls for you!

Then I rang Josh. 'About time too,' he laughed.

Next Jon called his brother Andy. 'About bloody time,' he said.

'Well we thought we'd better do it quickly because Beverley will be showing soon,' Jon said, totally deadpan. There was an agonising pause on the other end of the line.

'You're joking!' Andy said.

'Yes, of course I'm joking, you fool,' laughed Jon.

My next call was to Denise Welch, who had just arrived at Los Angeles airport. She's had so many desperate phone calls from me over the years that I think she thought it must be another crisis.

'What is it, darling?' she said when she heard my voice.

'It's good news this time, Den,' I said. 'Me and Jon are getting married.' I think they must have been able to hear her squealing all over LA!

At first we thought about running away and getting married as quickly as we could, just the two of us. But I wanted my mum to be there and all the children. And we also wanted to invite all the family and friends who'd supported us so well during the tough times of the past few years. So, quite quickly, we went from the idea of it being just the two of us, to having a guest list that stretched to well over 100 people.

We knew we didn't want a long engagement. We were both desperate to be married, so what was the point of waiting? But, not ever being one to do things by halves, planning the wedding was going to be a big job. I'd begun drawing up lists and plans before we'd even returned home from Spain.

Three hours after our plane touched down at Manchester Airport we were at Hazlewood Castle between Leeds and York, which I'd always thought would be the perfect place for a wedding. My friend Coleen Nolan and her husband Ray had married there and I'd seen the pictures and thought how wonderful it looked. It was my dream location, a huge Norman castle with a romantic little chapel in the grounds for the marriage service.

As we walked around its beautiful grounds, I said to Jon: 'Oh, this is just perfect. This is where I want to marry.'

We spoke to the manager of the castle about available Saturdays and the only date he could offer us in 2010 was 30 October. So that was it – the date was set.

First though, I wanted to check that it was OK with Kym Marsh. She was due to marry her fiancé, the former *Hollyoaks* actor Jamie Lomas, a few weeks later, and I didn't want her to think that I was trying to overshadow her big day.

'Don't worry at all,' Kym said, when I called her to explain. 'Me and Jamie have already decided to postpone our wedding until next year so it will be absolutely fine.'

I was delighted and immediately threw myself into sorting the wedding in just five months.

At first I was only planning on having a couple of bridesmaids but the more I thought about it, the more I wanted to include all the women who'd helped me and Jon through the past few years. And so I ended up with 23 bridesmaids! And they were 23 of the strongest, feistiest women you could ever meet. They've all been through their fair share of troubles over the years but they've come through their problems with humour and warmth and that is why I love them so much.

The thought of walking down that aisle on my own was utterly terrifying, which was another reason why I went for so many bridesmaids. I reckoned that maybe people would be staring at them rather than me.

The final line-up included Danielle and Rebecca, my sister Steph and Jon's sister Lorraine and then Kym Marsh and Kate Kelly from Corrie and my mates Denise Welsh and Coleen Nolan. But, as you can imagine, with so many bridesmaids, it was one hell of a hen do! We totally packed out a nightclub in Manchester, drinking and dancing until the early hours. Shobna Gulati who plays Sunita and Debbie Rush who plays Anna Windass in Corrie also came along and we didn't stop laughing all evening.

At first I thought we were going to be able to get Mum out of the home and bring her along to the wedding but as the weeks went by I became unsure about whether we'd be able to manage. Mum is incontinent now and can barely eat either.

'What do you think I should do?' I asked one of the doctors when I was visiting Mum one day. 'Do you think she could make it to my wedding?'

'I'm sorry, Beverley,' he said quietly, 'but I think it would be totally unrealistic for you to take your mother out for the wedding. It would be stressful for her to be in unfamiliar surroundings and she really wouldn't know what was going on.'

I knew he was right but it still hurt. And as the wedding day grew closer I often got waves of sadness when I thought about how Mum wasn't able to be part of the preparations.

One weekend, Jon and I went back to the castle to decide on the menu for the reception and to meet the vicar who would be marrying us. I think I must have been a bit nervous because I went barrelling up to him and said: 'Hi, I'm Beverley and I do believe in God.' Then I turned to Jon standing next to me. 'And this is Jon,' I said. 'He doesn't.' Jon just stared at me as if he wanted to kill me!

Planning the wedding was so exciting but very full-on, making sure everything was going to be just perfect.

Thankfully *Coronation Street* said I could take a few weeks off before my wedding to get all the last-minute arrangements sorted out. I wanted everything to be absolutely perfect this time and with Corrie being such long hours, six days a week, it is very hard to concentrate on anything else but work when you are filming.

So I decided to put my feet up and spend a few weeks choosing table decorations! But that didn't last very long. Soon my agent Neil was on the phone asking whether I fancied making a new fitness DVD. It had been nearly a decade since I had made my last one. That had sold more than a million copies but so much had happened since then. Still, I thought about it for a nanosecond then replied.

'OK,' I said. 'But you know the rules. I'll only do it if it can involve real women and be really useful to real women too.' So that's what we did.

I'd been back teaching fitness classes in Manchester for a few months and I was loving it. The medication that I'd been taking after my breakdown in 2009 had made me put on weight, which I hated, so I was glad to be back working-out and getting into shape again. I felt fit and strong enough to do it and when I saw how I was able to really make a difference to the lives of some of the women in my class it reminded me how much I loved doing it.

So making the fitness DVD was just the next step on from there. I love working with real women because it allows people using the DVD at home to feel that if someone like them can do all these exercises, then they can too. The group of women were fabulous and they were able to see real results in their bodies very quickly. We called the DVD *Beverley's Boot Camp* and I devised all the routines myself. It was exhausting doing all the training sessions and filming but I was determined to get it right. When I saw the finished cut I felt so proud. It was only 18 months earlier that I'd thought I'd never be able to do fitness work ever again and here I was having made my own workout DVD.

Then I got a call inviting me to appear as a panellist on *Loose Women*. At first it was only for couple of days a week while Coleen Nolan was off sick, having fractured her fingers in an accident at a riding stables, but it was too good an opportunity to turn down. I've always loved watching the show but never thought I'd go on it because I used to hate talking publicly about my life. But then, after being ill and deciding to write this book, I thought: 'Why not? I've already told the world everything there is to know, so what's the problem?'

I used to want to keep so much of my life private but, strangely, writing this book and telling the world that I was a teenage mum, a victim of domestic violence, that I've been married three times and that I've been in the Priory, has been incredibly liberating. Everyone knows everything about me now and if they don't like it then that's too bad; I no longer feel I have to hide anything about my past.

I finally felt happy to go on *Loose Women* and talk about anything at all. In fact, my biggest fear that first day on the show was saying too much! As soon as the cameras went on all I could think was: 'I mustn't swear, I mustn't swear, I mustn't swear . . .' But of course the more you think about it, the more you think you're about to do it. It's not as though I swear all the time normally but because *Loose Women* is just like a few mates having a chat it is so easy to just slip into your everyday speaking habits.

I absolutely loved doing the show and it must have gone OK because after that I was invited back on twice a week. I was thrilled.

What with appearing on *Loose Women* and filming the DVD, the weeks before the wedding just raced by.

The only sadness was that Mum wasn't going to be able to be there with us for our big day. The doctors had told me and Steph several times that the end was drawing near. Then, one day when we were visiting, they called us to one side and said they were considering withdrawing her medication, but to do that they would need our consent. Their concern was that the drugs she was on were prolonging her life but not improving it in any way.

Steph, her husband Steve, me and Jon sat down and talked about it for hours. We knew that the doctors felt removing the medication was the best thing to do, so after much consideration we decided to follow their advice. But it was still devastating for us because it meant without any doubt that our mum was now dying. She had lost so much weight because she was surviving on just protein shakes as her brain had even forgotten how to chew food. Strangely though, she still loved a coffee with two sugars, just as she had always done.

When the doctors first did away with the medication Mum became very withdrawn for a few days, but then we noticed slight changes in her behaviour. She still didn't know who we were, but when we went to visit she'd look at us and smile and say, 'Oh,' as if there was a slight flicker of recognition there somewhere. She hadn't done that in months. And then she started eating just the smallest bits of sandwich too, which meant she put a little weight back on.

It was her eightieth birthday on 13 September and so me, Jon, Steph, Steve and my Auntie Jean and Uncle Frank all went to visit with presents and a birthday cake. She didn't know what was going on of course but I'm sure she realised she was the centre of attention that day and she had a great time.

But we knew Mum was really very weak. Three times we were called by the home to say that the end was very close. There was certainly no way she'd be able to travel for my wedding.

On the night before the wedding, Jon and I travelled to the castle together – but then we checked in to separate bedrooms well away from each other. This might have been my fourth wedding but I was still going to do things properly!

I woke up the following morning feeling a mixture of excitement and outright terror! Of course I wanted to be married to Jon but the thought of walking down that aisle with everyone looking at me was so frightening. I could go on any stage and play any role with any accent and it wouldn't bother me at all. But to appear as Beverley felt so scary.

Before the big ceremony in the castle chapel we had to have a small civil ceremony in a room inside the main building which was licensed for weddings. Jon and I turned up in normal clothes with Kym Marsh and Jamie Lomas as witnesses. We hadn't invited anyone from our family to be a witness because we felt that whoever we chose, it would mean we were missing out someone else. When I asked Kym and Jamie if they would do it, they were overwhelmed.

It was a very quick ceremony and we had deliberately decided to keep it low-key because our main wedding service was to be in front of all the guests later on. But when the registrar pronounced us man and wife it was still incredibly emotional and I was blubbing all over again.

Then it was back to my hotel room where my bridesmaids were waiting to help me change into the frock I would be wearing for the big service. I'd had a beautiful ivory dress made by Suzanne Neville, who has designed wedding gowns for loads of celebrities and always creates very classic, elegant styles. My dress was sleeveless with a sweetheart neckline and was cut on the bias and quite fitted with a long train. It was just perfect.

Then all my bridesmaids were in little black dresses with hot pink accessories. I thought a sexy LBD was the perfect outfit for my feisty girlfriends.

My gorgeous Josh gave me away and I felt so proud of him as he took my arm outside the church. He too has been through the mill over the past few years but he has come out of all that an incredible, strong young man.

I was hanging on to him for dear life as we walked down the

aisle and I saw all our closest friends sitting in the congregation. These were the people who'd helped us through the hard times and I was so glad they were there to share our happy ending too.

And then, of course, at the front of the chapel was Jon, standing next to his three best men, his sons Ben and Jonathan, and his best friend Tony.

Oh my God, he looked gorgeous. And never have I been so sure that I was doing something so right. Jon had stood by me through everything. So when we said those vows – in sickness and in health and for richer and for poorer – I knew that we both utterly meant them. We already knew how tough those things could be, but we'd come through them together. The service was beautiful and so emotional. It really did feel like our reward for surviving the hard times.

In the evening even more guests arrived and goodness only knows what time the last of them rolled into bed. What a night!

Like I've said before, I'm now strong enough to believe that the best is yet to come again. But whatever the future holds, it would have to be pretty damn good to be better than being Mrs Beverley McEwan!

Special Thanks

....

To Anthony and Gillian Akaraonye, THANK YOU. Forever friends.

To Corinne McParland, a dear friend and a wonderful person. Thank you for never letting go.

To Adrian Wilde, our friend who is always there.

Denise Welch and Tim Healy – a massive thank you for keeping Jon and I on life support.

To Steve and Sue Ratcliffe for coming back into our lives.

To Neil Howarth and Amanda Beckman, thank you so much for your love and support and for helping me climb back up.

To everyone at *Coronation Street*, both in front and behind the camera.

The Priory, thank you to all.

To anyone suffering with clinical depression, please be strong enough to ask for help.

Contact Mindinfoline:
0845 766 0163
info@mind.org.uk

Mindinfoline
PO Box 277
Manchester
M60 3XN

Picture Acknowledgements

....

Author's collection: 1, 2 (top), 3 (top), 4, 5 (bottom), 6, 14 (bottom), 15 (top). © Alamy: 8, 9 (top), 10 (bottom)/ photos Mirrorpix. © Terry Berry Photography, York: 5 (top). © Getty Images: 12 (bottom), 13. © Nicky Johnston: 9 (bottom), 14 (top). © Press Association Images: 10 (middle), 11, 15 (bottom). © Retna UK: 16. © Rex Features: 2 (bottom)/ photo News Group, 3 (bottom)/ photo The Sun, 7, 10 (top), 12 (top & middle)/ photos ITV. © Scope Features: 9 (middle)/ photo John Paul Brooke.

Every reasonable effort has been made to contact any copyright holders of material reproduced in this book. But if there are any errors or omissions, Hodder & Stoughton will be pleased to insert the appropriate acknowledgement in any subsequent printing of this publication.